YOUNG STUDENTS
ENCYCLOPEDIA

Specially prepared with the Staff of

MY WEEKLY READER

8
Indochina
Liszt, Franz

American Education Publications/A Xerox Company

Middletown, Connecticut

Acknowledgements

All photographs supplied by Armando Curcio Editore, SpA, except the following:

Action/Peace Corps—page 1294.

AF of L-CIO—page 1317 top.

American Museum of Photography—page 1355.

American National Red Cross—pages 1366 top, 1366 bottom, 1367 top.

Joy Anderson—page 1314 top.

Armstrong Cork Company—page 1227.

Bell Telephone Laboratories—page 1234 top.

Black Star—page 1336 center right.

Jean F. Blashfield—pages 1306 bottom, 1363 top.

British Information Services—page 1302 top.

Kristi Brown—page 1250 bottom.

Bureau of Reclamation—page 1243 top.

Chicago Historical Society—page 1329 bottom.

Columbia Records—pages 1255 top, 1262 top right.

Department of Public Information, Kentucky—pages 1295 top, 1296 left, 1296 right.

DICTIONARY OF AMERICAN PORTRAITS BY CIRKER AND CIRKER, Dover Publications, Inc., New York, Reprinted through permission of the publisher—page 1373 bottom.

Walt Disney Productions—page 1215 bottom.

Dow Chemical Company—page 1211 bottom.

Ford Foundation—page 1342 top.

Clinton E. Frank for Trifari—page 1270 top.

Girl Scouts of America, Inc.—page 1342 bottom.

The Gorham Company—page 1309 top, 1309 bottom.

Philip Grushkin—page 1273 top, 1318.

Hallmark, Inc.—page 1306 top.

Hawaii Visitors Bureau Photo—page 1288 top left.

Russell F. Hogeland—pages 1337, 1359 top left, 1359 top right, 1359 bottom left, 1359 bottom right, 1360 bottom, 1369 top, 1369 bottom.

Icelandic Airlines—frontispiece.

Illinois Department of Business and Economic Development—page 1331 bottom.

International Business Machines Corporation—page 1342 center.

Iowa Development Commission—pages 1235 top, 1236 top, 1236 bottom, 1245 bottom right.

Israel Information Service—pages 1247 top, 1266 top.

Jamestown Festival Park—page 1256 bottom.

Japan Information Service—page 1304 top.

Japan National Tourist Organization—page 1260 bottom.

Library of Congress—pages 1233 top, 1243 top left, 1276 bottom, 1304 bottom, 1317 bottom, 1320, 1322, 1347, 1354 bottom.

Patricia Maloney Markun—page 1286 top.

National Film Board of Canada—page 1333 bottom.

National Gallery of Art, Washington, D.C.—page 1266 bottom.

National Institute of Drycleaners—page 1333 center.

NBC Photo—pages 1280 top, 1292.

New York City Art Commission—page 1335.

New York State Department of Commerce—page 1370 left.

The New York Times—page 1279 top.

Daniel Ocko—pages 1239, 1246.

Pennsylvania Department of Commerce—page 1357 top.

Qantas—page 1312.

Rohm & Haas—page 1343.

Salvation Army—page 1336 bottom.

Sikorsky Aircraft—page 1314 bottom.

W. & J. Sloane—pages 1225, 1226, 1372.

Smithsonian Institution—page 1278 bottom, 1305 left.

State of Kansas Department of Economic Development—pages 1290 top, 1291.

Bruce F. Tourville—page 1212 bottom.

UNESCO—page 1341.

United Austrian Iron & Steel Works—page 1241 bottom.

United Nations—pages 1212 top, 1228, 1230 top, 1231, 1238, 1242 bottom, 1251, 1328, 1356 bottom, 1361 bottom.

United Press International Photo—pages 1261 top right, 1279 bottom, 1281 center, 1300, 1315, 1336 top, 1339, 1365.

United States Atomic Energy Commission—page 1222 top.

United States Coast Guard Official Photograph—page 1370 right.

United States Department of Agriculture Photo—pages 1216 (mayfly), 1217 (dragonfly), 1219 top left, 1219 bottom, 1220 top, 1220 center, 1221 top, 1221 center, 1221 bottom, 1257 bottom left, 1257 bottom center, 1257 bottom right, 1305 right.

United States Department of the Interior, Indian Arts and Crafts Board—page 1242 top.

United States Department of State—pages 1230 center, 1230 bottom.

University of Maryland—page 1319 top.

Verve Records—page 1262 bottom right.

Vidyavrata—page 1269 top left.

Washington Convention and Visitors Bureau—page 1376 bottom right.

Westinghouse—pages 1371 top, 1371 bottom left, 1371 bottom right.

WHO/Photo by K. Brodie—page 1286 bottom.

World Bank Staff—page 1237.

Wright Aeronaut Corporation—page 1377.

Xerox, Inc.—page 1360 top left.

Zionist Archives and Library—page 1272.

State seals courtesy of the Council of State Governments

Maps from the Pictograph Corporation

▲ *A spectacular volcanic eruption from an underwater volcano occurred in 1963 off the coast of Iceland. A huge cloud of steam, and other gases, was cast into the air. The eruption led to the formation of a new island called Surtsey. (See* ISLAND.*)*

INDOCHINA Indochina is the eastern portion of a long, somewhat rounded peninsula in Southeast Asia. The present-day countries of Laos, Cambodia, and North and South Vietnam are found there. The South China Sea lies to the east, while the Gulf of Thailand is located in the southwest. Thailand and Burma lie to the west of Indochina. China forms the northern boundary. (See the map with the article on ASIA.)

Much of Indochina is mountainous and has a tropical climate. Most of the people farm for a living.

Many live in the rich, rice-growing valleys and deltas of two important rivers, the Mekong and the Red. Besides rice, the people grow corn, rubber, sugar cane, and tea. The main languages spoken in Indochina are Vietnamese, Lao, Khmer (Cambodian), and French. Many people, especially those living in the mountains, speak local dialects. While most people in Indochina practice the Buddhist religion, there are many Catholics, especially in Vietnam. The hill peoples are mainly spirit worshipers. Most of the peoples of Indochina are descen-

▲Sugar cane is important to agriculture in Indochina. The cane is sent to factories to be refined.

▲*The temple of Angkor Wat is one of many fine old buildings located at Angkor Thom, the ancient capital of Cambodia. Five pineapple-shaped towers stand atop the temple.*

dants of tribesmen who came to the area from southern China.

Gradually, Europeans became interested in the area as they searched for spices. The French arrived in the 1600s, and they completely controlled Indochina by 1893. They divided the land into five states called Laos, Cambodia, Cochin China, Annam, and Tonkin. These countries together were known as French Indochina. Cochin China, Annam, and Tonkin were joined as Vietnam in 1945. The French lost control in a bloody seven-year war that ended in 1954.

ALSO READ: ASIA, BUDDHISM, CAMBODIA, LAOS, VIETNAM.

INDONESIA More than 3,000 islands lying southeast of the Asian mainland form the Republic of Indonesia. They make up the world's largest island group and fifth largest

country. Java, Sumatra, Celebes, Borneo, and West Irian are the largest islands. About two-thirds of the people live on the island of Java. (See the map with the article on ASIA.)

The high, mountainous islands of Indonesia have a humid, tropical climate. The rain and warmth make it a colorful country. Beautiful flowers, wild orchids, and ferns are plentiful. Monkeys, tigers, lizards called Komodo dragons, and a rare species of rhinoceros live in Indonesia.

Indonesian families usually live in small villages and grow crops for a living, including rice, sweet potatoes, corn, cassava, soybeans, and coconuts. Rubber, palm oil, sugar cane, tea, coffee, and tobacco are raised on plantations and are often exported. Spices, including pepper, nutmeg, cloves, and mace, are also grown for export. Forests produce rattan, teakwood, and kapok (used for life preservers and padding).

Indonesia has vast mineral resources that are largely untapped. Petroleum is Indonesia's most important mineral product. It is one of the world's largest suppliers of tin. Bauxite, coal, sulfur, nickel, and manganese are mined.

Indonesian dancing is famous throughout the world. Dancers from Bali are especially famous for their graceful temple dances.

The Indonesians speak over 250 languages. Their country's official

INDONESIA

Capital City: Djakarta (2,907,000 people).
Area: 735,268 square miles.
Population: 116,918,000 people.
Languages: Indonesian and English.
Export Products: Rubber, petroleum, and iron ore.
Unit of Money: Rupiah.

language is Indonesian, the most widely spoken tongue. About 90 per cent of the population are Muslims. But many people living on Bali are Hindus. About five per cent of the Indonesians are Christians.

Early explorers called Indonesia the Spice Islands. The first Dutch trading ships arrived in the late 1500s. For more than 300 years, the Dutch controlled the islands, known then as the Netherlands East Indies. The Japanese occupied the islands during World War II. Indonesians fought for their independence from the Dutch after the war. Independence was declared in 1949, and Achmed Sukarno became his country's first president. He remained his country's leader until 1967 when General Suharto became president.

ALSO READ: BORNEO.

INDUSTRIAL ARTS When your baby brother or sister builds with blocks or bangs with his toy hammer, he is not just playing—he is learning to handle materials and to use tools. Later, in elementary school, he may put together models of planes or cars, make scenery for a school play, or make clay figures.

In junior and senior high school, students can learn more about making and building things by taking courses in *industrial arts*. These courses teach the manual skills (the ability to work expertly with the hands) used in industry to make nearly all the products we use.

A course in *industrial drawing and design* teaches the student how to design (plan) the appearance and structure of anything from an engine to a house. He learns how the object's parts fit together to make it work and what materials and tools are needed for its construction. He also learns how to read and to make detailed drawings, called *blueprints*, of the plan.

The student of *woodworking* learns how to design products (such as chairs or bookcases) that will best

▲*A village in Java, one of the islands that make up Indonesia. The houses are made of decorated wood.*

show the beauty of a piece of wood. He then learns how to join pieces of wood and other materials to make his creation strong and attractive. The student also learns different ways to finish wood, to give smoothness and shine to the product.

In *metalworking*, the student learns how metals are made, including those that combine to make alloys. He also learns how to work with the tools used to bend metals into the desired shape. The student often learns welding (joining pieces of metal, usually with heat) and other machine-shop methods.

A course in *electricity and electronics* presents information on how electricity is *generated* (produced) and *transformed* (changed into power) for such things as heat and light. Students also learn how electronics is used for radio, TV, and radar. In this kind of class, students learn to make electric lights and bells themselves. They often learn to repair radios and television sets.

A course in *auto mechanics* teaches a student all the parts of an engine and the way these parts work together. In this course, a student learns to repair engines and to care for them properly. Some schools offer a course in *power mechanics*, in which students learn to use machines and engines that operate on electric power.

▼*Plywood is a very handy material for use in a home or industrial arts workshop because it is strong and may be cut and drilled without splitting.*

▲*Electric welding is the most effective method of joining metals because it creates high temperatures quickly.*

Graphic arts includes a study of all kinds of printing and photographic methods. Students learn to take and develop pictures and to set (arrange) the type used in printing written material.

Students who take courses in *plastics* and *ceramics* learn how to make things out of plastic, clay, concrete, stone, and glass. A student may make something as simple as a bowl or as complicated as a statue. He also learns to fire clay objects in a *kiln* (a kind of oven) to make them harder and stronger.

A knowledge of the industrial arts can save a consumer (buyer) money. Men and women who know something about automobile engines and the workings of household appliances, such as toasters and refrigerators, can choose the best brands when they buy. They are often able to save money again by making repairs themselves. In learning how to make an everyday product, a student learns how to tell good quality from poor quality. For example, someone who knows how to make a chair can tell whether a chair for sale in a store was made well and is worth its price.

Many communities provide vocational high schools where students take industrial arts courses to prepare them for jobs in industry immediately after graduation. For example, a boy or girl who has studied the graphic arts might get a job in a printing shop. Other students go on to technical schools to improve

their skills or to learn new ones before getting a job. TV repairmen, for example, usually have attended a technical school. Still other students go to college to prepare for a profession, such as architecture or engineering, that will require the knowledge and skills learned earlier in industrial arts.

Many people, however, study industrial arts to learn new hobbies. Someone with a knowledge of woodworking may refinish furniture for a hobby. A man with some experience in design and construction and a fondness for sailing might take up boat-building. Knowledge of the industrial arts can make possible a hobby—or a career—that brings pleasure and satisfaction.

ALSO READ: ARCHITECTURE, CAREER, CONSTRUCTION, ELECTRICITY, ELECTRONICS, ENGINEERING, GRAPHIC ARTS, IRON AND STEEL, MANUFACTURING, MECHANICAL DRAWING.

INDUSTRIAL REVOLUTION

People have always manufactured weapons, tools, clothing, and other goods that they need. For many centuries, these things were made mostly by hand. They were manufactured in the home or by individual craftsmen. Most people also produced their own food on farms. About 200 years ago, this system began to change. Men began to produce manufactured goods in large quantities in factories. They did not have time to tend their farms, and so they began to buy their food in stores. This great change in the way men lived is called the Industrial Revolution.

England was the birthplace of this revolution. In that country, where *textiles* (cloth) were a major source of wealth, a new method of manufacturing was started, called the *domestic system*. Merchants would distribute large quantities of wool to be spun and woven by the people who wished to earn money by working in their homes. The merchants

▼*An industrial arts class is a wonderful opportunity for all those who want to develop manual skills.*

then paid the people for their work and sold the cloth at a profit.

In the mid-1700s, a Scotsman called James Watt invented the first workable steam engine. This invention created a vast new source of power. A machine was invented which could spin several threads at one time. Then a mechanical loom was perfected for weaving the thread. The machines made large quantities of a product quickly and very cheaply. This process became known as *mass production*. The merchants who had grown rich from the domestic system began to buy the new machines. They built factories to house the machines, and employed workers to run them. By the mid-1800s, hundreds of factories had been built in England. Machines were also invented for making other products, such as pottery. The making of the machines themselves became a major industry.

Large amounts of iron were needed to make the new machines. Charcoal had always been used to *smelt* (melt) iron ore. But iron workers now discovered that iron ore could be smelted much more efficiently with coal. The mining industry grew with the need for coal and ore. A method soon was discovered for making steel from iron. Much stronger and more accurate machines could be made from this new metal. Manufactured goods and raw materials had to be transported to and from the factories. The shipping industry flourished. Railroads, canals, and new roads were built. The telegraph was invented, quickly speeding up the communications industry.

As the Industrial Revolution spread through Europe and the United States, people's lives began to change. The factories created many new jobs. But they also took some jobs away, by replacing people with machines. People came from far away to work in the factories, hoping to make more money than they could on the farms. They crowded into the new towns that were growing up around the factories. Living conditions were terrible in these towns. People had to work long hours, often in dangerous conditions. They were paid very little money. Many women and children were employed, even in the mines. Workers began to rebel against these injustices. They formed groups that were later called *labor unions*. They gathered to protest against their employers, and sometimes fights broke out, with violence on both sides. Eventually, laws were passed to correct many of the harsh conditions, and the unions gained great strength.

The Industrial Revolution brought enormous wealth and power to England, parts of Europe, and the United States. But this wealth and power was mainly in the hands of the people who owned the industries.

Today, other nations throughout the world are going through their own industrial revolutions. The change from an agricultural to an industrial economy can now take place rather quickly. Modern industry has raised the standard of living in many countries, but it has also created many serious problems. Factory work is often dull and unrewarding, and workers need more responsibility. Too many people are still crowded into the cities. Waste

▲*The invention of the cotton gin by Eli Whitney was one of the most important events of the Industrial Revolution in the United States. Whitney's machine made it possible to remove seeds from cotton much faster than removing them by hand.*

▲*An early typing machine. The development of the typewriter was an important aid to business as it grew and prospered during the Industrial Revolution.*

products of factories have polluted the air and the water. But industry and governments everywhere are beginning to be aware of these evils and are using scientific methods to improve the kind of life people can have in a modern, industrial society.

ALSO READ: AIR POLLUTION; CAPITALISM; CHILD LABOR; CITY; COAL; FULTON, ROBERT; IRON AND STEEL; LABOR UNION; MANUFACTURING; PETROLEUM; STOCKS AND BONDS; WATER POLLUTION; WATT, JAMES; WHITNEY, ELI.

INFECTION see DISEASE.
INFLATION see ECONOMICS.
INFRARED see HEAT AND COLD.

INK Whenever you read anything that is printed, such as a newspaper, book, or poster, you are reading something printed with ink. If you write with a pen, you are writing with ink. Ink is any liquid that is used for writing or printing. The first inks, thousands of years ago, were probably made from berry juice.

There are many kinds of ink, and most of them are made of coloring materials (dyes) dissolved in liquid. The kinds of dyes and liquids depend on what an ink is to be used for. For example, the ink used in ballpoint pens is a thick jelly-like liquid. A ballpoint pen puts very little ink on paper, so the dye in the ink must have a very strong color. On the other hand, ballpoint ink would not work in a fountain pen. Fountain pen ink is more watery.

The liquid part of most printing inks dries very quickly. This quick drying is necessary because paper moves through modern printing presses very fast. Immediately after printing, the paper is stacked, cut, and folded. The ink would smear and run if it did not dry rapidly.

Invisible, or *sympathetic*, ink becomes invisible when it dries. Something must then be done to the dried ink to make it visible. It may be dipped in or sprayed with chemicals

▼*The rollers on this printing press have had green ink applied to them.*

or it may be heated. Invisible ink used to be a favorite of spies, but modern ways of making invisible ink visible are so good that no invisible messages are really secret any more.

You can make invisible ink—just write your message with lemon juice. The writing will disappear as soon as it dries. But you can bring the message back by placing the paper on a warm heater for a few minutes or by moving it back and forth several inches over a candle flame.

ALSO READ: DYE, PRINTING.

INQUISITION see SPANISH HISTORY.

INSECT Insects make up three-quarters of all the animals on Earth. More than 900,000 kinds of insects are known, and entomologists—scientists who study insects—discover about 7,000 new kinds of insects each year.

Insects' Survival
Several reasons explain why insects are so plentiful. First, they are able to live in more different environments than any other animals. Insects live on every part of the Earth, including the coldest polar regions, the hottest deserts, and the middle of the ocean. They live outdoors everywhere, and also in every kind of human dwelling place, from grass huts to brick apartment houses.

Secondly, most insects are small, needing little space and little food. About 21 acres of Earth's surface grow only enough food for one human being for a year, but the same space can feed more than a billion insects. One bread crumb can provide a day's food for several ants. Most insects eat plants or other insects. Termites eat wood. Some insects, such as mosquitoes, live on the blood of human beings and other animals.

Thirdly, insects reproduce so rapidly. For example, a single housefly lays 120 to 160 eggs. The eggs hatch in a few hours, and in 3 to 6 days these flies are full-grown, ready to produce another generation.

Harmful Insects

Fortunately, only a few of the hundreds of thousands of kinds of insects are harmful to man. Perhaps the greatest harm is done by crop-eating insects, which destroy millions of tons of grains, vegetables, and fruits every year.

A number of insects are household pests. Clothes moths damage wool clothes. Silverfish damage clothes, books, and leather. Weevils live in flour and other foods, and cockroaches invade all kinds of food.

Some insects carry serious diseases from one person to another, or from animals to people. Certain mosquitoes carry malaria and yellow fever. Rat fleas carry bubonic plague. Lice carry typhus. Ordinary houseflies carry more than 40 serious diseases including typhoid, tuberculosis, and dysentery.

Helpful Insects

Many insects are helpful to man. Some are important pollen carriers. Bees, wasps, moths, and other insects that feed on nectar carry pollen from one flower to another, pollinating the flowers. The pollinated flowers eventually become fruits.

Some insects produce materials useful to man. Bees make honey and wax. Silkworms make silk.

Among the most helpful insects are those that prey on other insects harmful to man. Ladybird beetles eat great numbers of aphids, which are harmful to food and flower crops. Several kinds of wasps lay their eggs in caterpillars that eat food crops. The wasp larvae that hatch from the eggs eat the caterpillars. Certain flies, called tachinas, destroy squash bugs, mealy bugs, gypsy-moth larvae, and other harmful insects. Praying mantises eat grasshoppers, and dragonflies eat mosquitoes.

The Structure of Insects

Although there are many different kinds of insects, all of them have bodies that set them apart from other kinds of animals. Every insect's body is divided into three main parts—a head, a thorax, and an abdomen. And every insect has three pairs of jointed legs. The head of an insect is, of course, at the front, the thorax is in the middle, and the abdomen is at the rear.

Knowing the body structure of insects, you can see that spiders are not insects, because spiders have only two main body parts and four pairs of legs. Centipedes ("hundred-leggers") have too many legs to be insects, and their bodies are made up of many more than three major segments. Are earthworms insects?

On an insect's head is a pair of antennae, which are for touch, taste, and smell. Every insect also has a pair of compound eyes, usually one on each side of the head. Each compound eye is made up of thousands of tiny lenses. Most adult insects also have three simple eyes that form a triangle on the forehead. The mouthparts of insects are either jaws used for chewing, or tubes used for piercing and sucking. A grasshopper has jaws, a housefly has a sucking tube, a horsefly has a rasping tongue and a sucking tube, and a mosquito has a tube for piercing and sucking.

An insect's six legs are attached to

▲*Aphids (plant lice) suck juice from plants through their tube-like mouths.*

▼*A ground beetle attacking an ant. Some insects are helpful to man because they eat destructive insects.*

major insect groups

▼*A dragonfly. Dragonflies and damselflies have two pairs of wings and chewing mouth parts. The larvae live in water. Some of them have wings with lovely colors.*

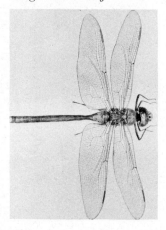

▲*Cicadas have wide heads with large compound eyes. They are related to grasshoppers, leaf hoppers, tree hoppers, and scale insects. Cicadas make a chirping sound at night.*

▼*A hairy moth. Butterflies and moths have four large, light wings that are often brightly colored.*

▼*The adult mayfly, which lives for just a day or so, has large compound eyes but a weakly developed mouth.*

▼*A mantis, like grasshoppers, crickets, and roaches, is a primitive insect with two pairs of wings and chewing mouth parts.*

▼*The red bug belongs to the group of true bugs. Some bugs have wings, while others do not. Red bugs often stain cotton fibers in the field and cause damage to fruit.*

▲Beetles are related to lady bugs and fireflies. This large beetle has horns.

▲A honeybee's tongue. Bees, wasps, ants, and hornets are closely related. Many of them are social insects. Many of the insects in this group are very useful to man.

▼A greenbottle fly. Flies, mosquitoes, and gnats are closely related. Some of them are pests and can carry serious diseases. They have mouth parts for sucking, piercing, or rasping.

▲The ascalaphid, like the lacewing, dobson fly, and ant lion, has four slender, veined wings.

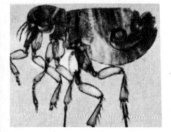

▲Fleas pierce the skin and suck the blood of mammals and birds. A dog flea is shown here.

▼Silverfish are primitive insects with no wings. They have chewing mouth parts, and can cause damage to bookbinding and clothing.

▼Like ants, termites are social insects. The queen termite of a colony is surrounded by sexless workers.

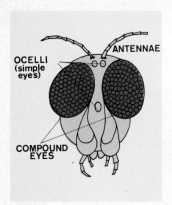

▲ *An insect has two types of eyes—simple and compound.*

▼ *One of the worst insect pests is the potato beetle. The adult beetle chews the leaves of the potato plant. The leaves also provide food for the larvae which hatch from eggs, such as these (lower right).*

▼ *Caterpillars, the larvae of moths and butterflies, can cause widespread destruction to plants.*

the thorax in three pairs. Each leg has five parts connected by joints. In some insects, the legs may look different and have different purposes. The front legs of a praying mantis are spiny and strong for grasping prey. The rear legs of a grasshopper are very long and strong for jumping.

Many insects have two pairs of wings, which are attached to the thorax. In some insects, such as beetles and grasshoppers, the front pair is thick and tough, and serves as a cover that protects the other pair. A beetle's heavy front wings protect most of his body, too. An insect's wings may be transparent, as in dragonflies, or covered with brightly colored scales, as in moths and butterflies. Some insects' wings carry them long distances. Others are used only for short, quick flights from danger. Some kinds of insects, such as fleas, have no wings.

An insect's abdomen is made up of ten sections, or segments. The abdomen contains some of the organs for digesting food, as well as the organs of reproduction.

The outer part of an insect's body is made up of a tough material called *chitin*. This is the insect's skeleton. It covers and protects the insect's inner organs.

In an insect's head, there is a knot of nerve tissues that serves as a kind of brain. From this brain, pairs of nerves run the length of the body, connecting smaller knots of nerves called *ganglia*. From ganglia, nerves go to, and return from, the organs.

Along both sides of an insect's body are rows of openings, called *spiracles*, through which an insect breathes. Air entering a spiracle goes through a tube called a *trachea*. This tube divides into smaller and smaller branches that carry air to inner parts of the insect's body. In insects, blood does not carry oxygen. However, insect blood does carry special chemicals (hormones) that control growth.

Many kinds of insects have developed special organs. Insects that make sounds—grasshoppers (including katydids) and crickets—have organs of hearing. These are located either on the front legs or in the first segment of the abdomen. Some moths, too, have organs of hearing. Insects have short hairs that are organs of touch, especially around the mouth. Other insects have special glands that produce poisons. And some insects have special organs, such as stingers, to defend themselves or attack others.

Reproduction and Growth

A female insect has organs called *ovaries* that form and store eggs. At the rear of the abdomen is a tube called an *ovipositor*, through which the female lays the eggs. Some insects, such as queen termites, lay hundreds of thousands of eggs. A male insect has *testes*, organs that produce *sperm*, male sex cells. A male insect also has an organ used to deposit the sperm on the eggs.

All insects hatch from eggs. Some look much like adults when they hatch. Newly hatched grasshoppers look like "grown-ups," except they have no wings. These young insects are called *nymphs*. Periodically, the nymph's glands release hormones, which cause the skeleton to crack apart. The nymph sheds the old skeleton and grows larger. Other glands release other hormones which help form a new, larger skeleton. This process is called *molting*. The usual number of molts before a nymph becomes full-grown and grows wings, is four to six, but there may be more. The process of growing by molting is called *incomplete metamorphosis*.

Many kinds of insects go through major changes in body form on their way to becoming adults. In this process, a worm-like creature called a *larva* hatches from the egg. Grubs, maggots, and caterpillars are three kinds of larvae. The larva feeds and grows for a period lasting from a day or two to many months. When fully grown, the larva produces a liquid that hardens when it comes into contact with air. The larva completely covers itself with the liquid. The hardened covering is called a *pupa case,* and the insect inside it is a *pupa.*

The pupa undergoes great changes, and finally breaks out of the pupa case as a fully developed insect, called an *imago.* This process of growth in four main steps—egg, larva, pupa, and imago—is called *complete metamorphosis.* Moths, butterflies, mosquitoes, and flies are some insects that go through complete metamorphosis.

ALSO READ: ANIMAL, ANIMAL KINGDOM, ANT, BEE, BUTTERFLIES AND MOTHS, DRAGONFLY, FLY, GLAND, HORMONE, INSECT PEST, LOUSE, METAMORPHOSIS, MOSQUITO, PARASITE, WASPS AND HORNETS.

INSECT-EATING PLANT

Insects destroy many, many plants each year. You have probably seen many trees, flowers, bushes, and vegetables spoiled by insects. But what is surprising is that some plants "fight back"—by eating insects. The plants trap the insects and then digest them. Insects are not the only food of these plants. Like other green plants, their leaves produce starch, which the plants use as food. Insect-eating plants live in wet places, where the soil lacks nitrogen, which is important to plant growth. These plants get nitrogen from the insects' bodies.

The largest insect-eating plant is the *pitcher plant.* The leaves of this plant form a pitcher-shaped container that holds rainwater. The rim of the pitcher has scales or stiff hairs pointing downward. Insects that enter the "pitcher" are unable to climb out because of the hairs or scales. In their struggle, the insects fall into the water and drown. They are digested by the plant.

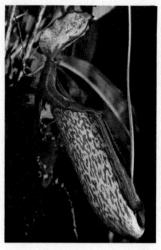

▲*Venus's-flytrap* (left) *has strong, blade-like leaves that snap closed around insects. The small monkey cup* (above) *in a pitcher plant of tropical Asia.*

Another insect-eating plant, the lovely *sundew,* has stalks covered with sticky material. When an insect lands on a stalk, the insect fights to free itself. The fight signals other stalks to slowly bend. The stalks secrete acid that digests the insect.

The *Venus's-flytrap* has leaves folded in the middle, so that each leaf looks like a clamshell. Around the edges of each leaf are tooth-like spikes, and on the surface of each half of the leaf are sensitive bristles. When an insect touches one of these bristles, the halves close suddenly, like a mouth snapping shut. The spikes form a cage that traps the insect. Venus's-flytraps catch mostly crawling insects, because most flying insects are fast enough to escape.

▼*The pitcher plant looks very inviting to any passing insect. But an insect that enters the "pitcher" is sure to meet its death. The "lids" on the pitchers keep out rain. This kind of pitcher plant is found in southeastern U.S.*

▲*Speed spray equipment being used to dust orange trees with insecticide.*

▲*Roses should be sprayed with insecticide about once a week to keep them free of insect pests and disease.*

▼*Spraying crops with insecticide is often done by airplane.*

The *bladderwort* is a water plant that has many one-eighth-inch-long bladders, each with a trap door equipped with sensitive bristles. When an insect touches a bristle, the trap door swings inward with a rush of water that sweeps the insect into the bladder.

ALSO READ: FLOWER, PLANT.

INSECTICIDE Any substance that kills insects is an *insecticide*. (The suffix "-cide" means "killer of.") Insecticides that destroy crop-eating insects have helped to increase the world's food supply. Cattle and other farm animals can be washed or dusted with insecticides that protect them from harmful or annoying insects. These farm animals grow larger and are healthier than unprotected animals. Before the use of the insecticide called DDT, many people in tropical countries died each year from malaria, a serious disease carried by certain mosquitoes. DDT is the most effective way to kill these mosquitoes and end this terrible disease.

Insecticides kill insects in various ways. Some insecticides are poisonous to insects that eat them. Others kill insects that touch, or come into contact with the poison. Still other insecticides prevent insects from reproducing. Some insecticides are bacteria—germs that attack and kill certain kinds of insects. Japanese beetles, for example, can be controlled by bacterial insecticides.

The world today depends on insecticides to protect crops and animals and to help man avoid many serious diseases. But insecticides can cause many serious problems, and they must be used carefully and wisely. For example, DDT sprayed on crops is carried by rainwater into streams and lakes. The chemical is taken into fish's bodies. Then two things happen. First, if the fish absorb (take up) too much DDT, they die. Second, animals that eat the fish—including man—get DDT in their bodies, and they may die, too. DDT can even cause birds' eggs not to hatch.

The world needs many kinds of insects, such as honeybees. Often, an insecticide kills these useful insects at the same time that it kills pests. And if the wrong insecticide is sprayed on plants or animals, it may kill them, not protect them.

For all these reasons, it is extremely important to be careful with *any* insecticide. Never play with or near these substances.

ALSO READ: INSECT PEST, POISON.

INSECT PEST Of all the animals that share the Earth with man, insects do him the most harm. Insects destroy crops of all kinds, as well as great numbers of other useful plants. Most insects that share man's dwelling places do damage to his property or his health. Many insects, such as mosquitoes, carry disease from one person to another.

Only one of about every 50 kinds of insects is a pest. But there are so many different kinds of insects that even this tiny fraction adds up to many thousands of different kinds of pests. About 1,000 kinds of insect pests make their homes in the United States. Among them are enough crop-eating insects to destroy up to one-tenth of all crops.

Plant Pests
Many plant pests, including grasshoppers, destroy plants by eating the leaves. All grasshoppers are pests, but the locusts (a kind of grasshopper) are worst of all. Locusts sometimes travel in swarms so large that they can block out the sun. A swarm of locusts may destroy every green plant in thousands of acres. This destruction of food crops has caused starvation to people in different parts of the world, at different times.

The larvae (young) of many insects eat green leaves and stems. The larvae of *geometrid moths,*

called canker worms, and the larvae of *Colorado potato beetles* do much damage to the leaves of crops. The larvae of *tussock moths* and *gypsy moths* can quickly ruin acres of trees by eating all the leaves.

Many insects destroy plants by sucking the juices from leaves and stems. Among these pests are aphids, leafhoppers, squash bugs, and chinch bugs. These insects may also carry virus diseases from one plant to another.

The larvae of Japanese beetles, cicadas, and striped cucumber beetles are among insects that harm plants by feeding on their roots.

Many kinds of moths lay eggs on fruit trees. When the larvae hatch, they bore into the growing fruit, living in and feeding on the fruit. Codling moths do much damage to apple crops. When you find a worm inside an apple, it probably is the larva of a codling moth. Other moths lay their eggs on vegetable and grain plants, so that the larvae can feed on the vegetable or grain.

Household Pests

Many insects seem very comfortable in man's houses. Some of these insects eat human food, others destroy clothes and household articles, and some feed directly upon humans.

Fleas and lice live on the bodies of human beings, hiding in their clothes. Bedbugs live in bedclothes and mattresses. These three pests live on human blood, and they may carry diseases among people.

Silverfish eat wool clothing and the starch from bookbindings and wallpaper. If you ever pick up a book and see all of its pages fall out, you can guess that silverfish have been dining there.

The larvae of clothes moths do much damage by eating holes in wool clothing. You can help protect your clothing by cleaning all items before storage. Insects do not damage clothes made of cotton, rayon, nylon, Dacron, or Orlon.

The housefly is a disease carrier. It feeds and lays eggs in garbage. Thousands of germs stick to its legs and mouthparts. When a fly crawls over food it spreads the germs, some of which may cause serious diseases.

Cockroaches eat almost everything—meat, fruits, vegetables, grain, sugar, starch, glue, leather, paper, and other cockroaches. These insects are not usually disease carriers, but they crawl in filth where they may pick up disease germs and carry them to food.

The best way to defend against household pests is to make sure that they have nothing to eat. If they find no food in a house, they will move on. Keep the house clean, and do not leave dirty dishes or empty food containers lying around. Close all food containers tightly. Keep clothes and beds clean. If you want to get rid of insect pests already in a house, you may need an insecticide. But be sure to get one that will kill the pests you have, and be sure you use it carefully.

Disease Carriers

Some very serious diseases can be carried from one person to another, or from animals to people, by insects that feed on blood.

Certain mosquitoes carry malaria. When such a mosquito sucks blood from a person who has this disease, malaria germs go into the mosquito's stomach. They go through the stomach walls, and some of the germs end up in the mosquito's salivary glands. When the mosquito pierces the skin of another person to suck blood, some saliva goes into the

▲ *The Japanese beetle, one of the most damaging of insect pests, destroys leaves, fruits, and even lawns. It was accidentally imported into the U.S. in 1917.*

◄ *Cockroaches will eat almost any food. They are more likely to be found in buildings that are unclean and damp.*

The black scientist Benjamin Banneker, of Washington, D.C., was the first man to determine that swarms of locusts appear in seventeen-year cycles.

▼ *Carpet beetle larvae feasting on a carpet. They eat only the woolen pile, leaving the rest of the carpet untouched.*

▲*A swimsuit heater for deep-water divers. Heated water is pumped through tiny tubes in the net garment worn underneath the diver's rubber suit. The heater is attached to the outside of the suit.*

human being's bloodstream. Along with the saliva go the germs, which give the bitten person malaria. Yellow fever is carried by other mosquitoes in the same way.

African sleeping sickness is carried by the tsetse fly. Rocky Mountain spotted fever is carried by a tick. Many other diseases of plants, animals, and people are carried by insect pests.

ALSO READ: FLY, INSECT, INSECTICIDE, LOUSE, MOSQUITO.

INSULATION A ski jacket keeps you warm in winter. It "insulates" your body and prevents heat from escaping into the cold air. Mammals that live in cold climates grow thick coats to protect them from cold weather. Woolen and fur clothing insulate people from the cold. The air trapped in fur or wool provides excellent insulation. The word "insulation" comes from the Latin word *insula*, which means "island." Insulation surrounds an object and prevents the passage of not only heat, but also electricity and sound.

Asbestos, cotton, wool, rubber, and wood are good *insulators*. Glass and porcelain also insulate. Metals are very poor insulators but are very good *conductors* (substances that carry heat, electricity, or sound).

A house must be insulated to keep the heat in during cold weather and out during hot weather. Thick stone or brick walls are good for this purpose. Wooden frame houses must have both outside walls and inside walls. The air space between these walls provides some insulation, but it is better to fill this space with an insulating material such as rock wool. The roof of a house must be well insulated to keep hot air, which rises, from escaping from the top of the house in cold weather. Roof insulation also keeps the hot rays of the summer sun from piling up heat in the house.

Metal wires, which are good conductors, are used to carry electricity. To keep a person from getting a severe shock when he touches them, the wires are insulated with a covering of rubber, plastic, or tightly woven cotton fabric.

A home or apartment is insulated for sound in much the same way it is heat insulated. Single walls must be thick enough, or double walls must have enough space between them, to keep sound out. Many people who live in thin-walled apartments can hear sounds from the next apartment. Sound insulation is also used in many places to keep sounds from becoming too loud and too confusing. Theaters, concert halls, restaurants, and other large rooms have special coverings on their walls and ceilings. These coverings, such as fiber board, absorb much of the sound in a room. Sound bounces off hard stone and plaster walls. Curtains and draperies are also effective in absorbing sound and reducing noise level.

You can see how insulation works by performing an experiment. You will need a very large cardboard carton and two smaller boxes, such as salt or cereal boxes, with the tops removed. You will also need a small table lamp with a 40 or 60 watt bulb, two thermometers, and some shredded newspaper.

Stuff one of the smaller boxes with the newspaper, placing one thermometer in its center. Place the other thermometer into the other small box, which has no newspaper stuffing. Now put both small boxes

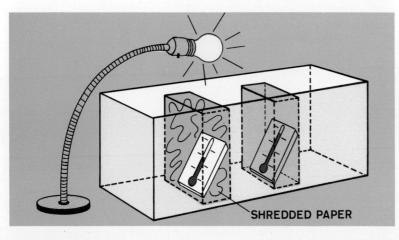

SHREDDED PAPER

into the carton with the lighted lamp between them.

Allow the thermometers to be exposed to the heat of the lamp for one-half hour. Then check them. What has happened? If you extend the time to one hour, what will happen? Can you explain this method of insulation?

ALSO READ: ELECTRICITY, HEAT AND COLD, SOUND.

INSURANCE An accident can cause severe injury to people and costly damage to property. Safety measures are the best protection against accidents. But when accidents do happen, you can be protected against extreme hardship by having insurance.

Insurance is a kind of protection sold by insurance companies. It is based on the fact that a lot of people share the risks (and costs) of losses. For example, a person wishing to buy automobile insurance will pay a certain amount of money, or *premium*, to an insurance company. In return the insurance company will issue a *policy*, or contract, to the individual. The company agrees to pay for all or part of the losses or damages to, or caused by, that person's car. At the same time, thousands of other people are also paying the company for the same kind of insurance. Most of these people will never have an accident, so the insurance company will never have to pay them money for any damages or losses. But the money that these thousands of people have paid to the company is more than enough to cover the losses or damages that some of them will have.

The remainder of the money received by the insurance company is used by them in much the same manner as a bank handles a savings account. Some of the money is kept for a constant supply of cash. Some of the money is used for operating expenses—salaries, rent, supplies. And some is invested for profit.

The *premium rate*, or cost of insurance, is based upon averages. This means that the company will figure out how many times something happens, or is likely to happen, during a given time in a certain place. Then the company decides what chance the policy holder has of being involved in such an event. For example, an automobile owner living in a big city will be more likely to have an accident than one who lives in a small town where traffic is lighter. So the automobile insurance costs more in and around big cities.

People can buy many other kinds of insurance. Many musicians are insured in case anything happens to injure their hands. People who plan to vacation in a sunny place can be insured against rain that could spoil their vacation. Someone who supports a family can buy life insurance so that when he or she dies, the company will pay money to the family. Fire insurance is bought so that if a house or apartment is damaged or destroyed by fire, the owner will have enough money to replace any losses. Health insurance helps to pay doctors' and hospital bills. Many farmers also buy insurance against crop losses caused by nature, such as earthquakes and floods.

ALSO READ: CHANCE AND PROBABILITY, STATISTICS.

INTEGRATION see CIVIL RIGHTS MOVEMENT, NEGRO HISTORY.

INTELLIGENCE Scientists define *intelligence* as the ability to learn or to understand. Someone who is intelligent learns what he or she is taught easily and quickly. An intelligent person also remembers what he has learned. This knowledge can then be used in new situations or problems. An intelligent person faced with some problem or situation that he has never met before will use his knowledge and memory of situations in the past to solve the problem.

The first fire insurance company in America was organized in Charleston, South Carolina, in 1736. The company hired its own fire-fighters. When half of Charleston was destroyed by fire in 1740, the insurance society was financially ruined.

Many psychologists believe that intelligence can be measured with various kinds of tests. These scientists believe that if a person can deal intelligently with some problem in a test, he will also deal intelligently with problems in everyday life.

Psychologists express the results of an intelligence test in a number called an IQ (intelligence quotient). To determine this number, they first give tests to find the person's mental age. Two boys of 8 and 16 may both have a mental age of 12. The younger boy has obviously developed faster than the older boy. But their mental age does not show the difference in their rates of mental growth. The mental age of the younger boy is far above his chronological age (age in years). But the older boy's mental age is far below his chronological age. Therefore, psychologists developed the formula

$$IQ = \frac{MA \text{ (mental age)}}{CA \text{ (chronological age)}} \times 100.$$

This means that the person's mental age is divided by his chronological age. The quotient is multiplied by 100, and the number that results is the IQ. This number represents the way that someone's intelligence compares with that of other people of his age. The 8-year-old boy's IQ is 150; the 16-year-old boy's is 75.

But many people believe that intelligence tests do not really measure someone's ability. Many tests seem to measure *what* someone has learned rather than how quickly or slowly he can learn. Other people think that intelligence cannot be measured accurately.

What makes one person intelligent and another not so intelligent? Are people born with the basic intelligence that they will have all their lives? Is intelligence affected by a person's home life or the number of books he reads? Scientists are still studying these questions.

Human beings are the most intelligent animals. Man has built cities, written books, and flown to the moon. Since man is certainly not the biggest animal, or the animal with the biggest brain, intelligence cannot be measured by size. But studies of other animals are showing that man is definitely not the *only* animal with intelligence.

Other animals can communicate with each other, but they cannot read. They cannot do mathematics or build complicated things like automobiles or airplanes. Still, animals learn very quickly the things they have to know in order to stay alive and healthy. Animals also remember things they have learned.

An animal in the jungle behaves very "intelligently." An animal knows who its enemies are and it keeps out of their way. It knows what foods are good for it and how to find these foods. Animals teach these things to their young.

Many people believe that animals are not intelligent at all. These people say that animals have "instincts," not "intelligence." An "instinctive" act is something done automatically without having to learn it. For example, a newborn baby knows automatically how to suck milk from its mother's breast. No one has to teach the baby how to suck milk. Sucking is an instinct.

Monkeys in the jungle live together in large groups. Sometimes there are hundreds of monkeys living together. Yet, each baby monkey knows its own mother. The mothers can always tell their own babies from the other babies.

Some animals can act in very intelligent ways. Dolphins even have a language. They can "talk" to each other by making whistling and clicking sounds. If a dolphin is in danger, it can call other dolphins to help it. Dolphins can even work together and get a complicated job done that one dolphin alone could not do. They often work together without seeing each other. They talk to each other in their language over long distances and coordinate a "plan."

Many animals possess intelligence. This is shown by the fact that they can be trained to do things that they do not otherwise do. Dogs can be trained to do tricks and to perform useful tasks such as leading blind people or herding sheep. Lions, tigers, seals, bears, and chimpanzees may be trained to perform in circuses. Rats use intelligence to get at food that seems out of their reach. They also learn to avoid food that has been poisoned.

If you have a pet animal, try to teach it to do something it has never done before. You may be able to see how it uses intelligence to find a good way to do that something.

ALSO READ: LEARNING, MEMORY, REASONING.

INTERIOR DECORATING
Interior decorating is the art of making rooms attractive. Interior decorating is successful when a room is comfortable to those who use it.

People who make a living decorating rooms for others are called *interior decorators*. They are usually trained in the use of space, color, light, fabrics, and furniture. Most people, however, do their own interior decorating. They learn about decorating by looking at different styles of furniture in stores and in other people's homes. Decorating magazines and catalogs also give many good ideas.

History
No one knows when people first thought of making their homes beautiful. In ancient Egypt, Greece, and Rome, the upper classes had colorfully decorated homes. The walls and ceilings were often painted with scenes or brightly colored designs. Soft cushions and various textiles were used to cover long sofas and wooden chairs. The ancient Romans carefully planned their rooms according to how these rooms were used. They used great artistic skill in making furniture and room decorations.

After the Roman Empire fell, interior decoration became unimportant in Europe. Furniture was simple—usually just stools, tables, and storage boxes. Europeans traveling to the Middle East during the Crusades discovered the beautiful decorations and carved furniture of the Orient. Trade routes with the Middle East were set up. By the 1400s, wealthy Europeans were

◀ A citron-yellow color scheme has been used for this dining room, which is furnished with Chinese Chippendale furniture.

▶*A bed-sitting room with a luxurious red and green decor. Notice the unusual way in which the bed is draped.*

buying Oriental furniture and copying Oriental designs. Ruling families became *patrons* of decorators. They supported the decorators in exchange for having rooms beautifully furnished. Walls were hung with velvet draperies, mirrors, tapestries, and handmade wallpaper. Some furniture was *gilded* (covered with gold). Fine woods were used for chairs, tables, beds, and chests. Some pieces of furniture were beautifully carved.

During the 1600s and 1700s the wealthy people of France introduced decorated plaster ceilings, delicate fabrics, and huge glass chandeliers that held many candles. The French used fancy woods, such as teak and rosewood, and furniture styles became light-looking, rather than large and heavy. As trade with the Orient expanded, styles of decoration from China and Japan became popular.

In the 1800s, decorators began to discover American styles. The Early American style was simple and practical. The Federal style, using light carving, dark woods, and straight lines, also became popular.

After the Industrial Revolution, a lot of furniture could be factory-made at lower prices. Many people, not just the wealthy, could then afford at least some beauty at home.

Techniques of Decorating

Planning is a very important part of interior decoration. The decorator must first list the activities that take place in each room. Will the living room be used to entertain friends? Will people read and relax there? Will people gather together in the living room at night to watch television? The answers to these and other questions will help the decorator decide how to arrange the room. If the room is used for entertaining friends, comfortable chairs should be arranged so that people can talk together easily. If the room is used for reading, it will need good lighting. If people will be watching television in the living room, the television must be placed so that everyone will be able to see it.

The decorator must also study the shape of the room. How long is it and how wide? How many windows and doors does it have? What is the easiest way for people to pass through the room? (This is called the *traffic pattern*.) These things decide where furniture goes.

The decorator must think about the floor, too. Is it made of hard polished wood or linoleum tiles? Wood floors are attractive, but walking on them can be noisy. If the room is in an apartment with people living below, rugs or carpeting will probably be needed to lessen the noise.

When the decorator has studied the room and how it is used, he then decides what colors would be best in it. The choice of color is important because colors are connected with moods or feelings. Reds and oranges usually have a warm feeling, while blues and blue-greens have a cool feeling. Bright colors often put people in a happy mood, while dark, dull colors put them in a sad mood. Also, light colors make rooms seem larger, and dark colors make them seem smaller. The decorator must consider all these things when choosing a *color scheme.*

Color schemes can be a set of blending colors or contrasting colors. *Blending colors* are those that are nearly alike, such as yellow and orange. *Contrasting colors* are those that are quite different from each other, such as red and green. Different shades of the same color can also be used. A decorator usually uses some light and some dark colors in every room.

A decorator picks furniture that fits the activities and tastes of the people who use the room. Many people like modern, *contemporary* furniture, which has plain, undecorated lines and can be made of wood, metal, fabric, or plastics. Other people feel more comfortable with traditional furniture modeled after furniture styles of the past. Traditional furniture is usually made of wood and fabrics only. Decorators will often combine different styles of furniture in one room.

Accessories are the ornaments used in a room to give it "personality." They include lamps, cushions, vases, pieces of pottery, and pictures. Accessories also include things such as plants, a display of a collection, or other special objects. Such accessories in a room tell something about the people who live there.

You might like to try decorating your own room. If you share a room with a brother or sister, you can both work as a decorating team. A parent or other adult should help you buy the things you need. To make a desk, get two filing cabinets or small chests of drawers from a store. Those can be topped with a long wide board or an old door. You can then paint the desk to match the color scheme in your room. If you have a collection that you would like to display, you can build your own shelves to put it in. You will need 18 bricks and three boards that are four feet long and one foot wide. First, place the short ends of two bricks against the wall where you want your bookcase. Place these bricks about four feet apart. Then put a board on top. Next pile four bricks at each end of the board, just over the first two. Then put another board on top. Repeat this until you have a bookcase with three shelves. Try using your own ideas, too, to decorate your room.

ALSO READ: ANTIQUE, CARPETS AND RUGS, COLOR, FURNITURE, INDUSTRIAL REVOLUTION, LIGHTING.

▼*A boy's bedroom decorated in pirate style. Sheet vinyl flooring with a pebble design gives the effect of beach stones smoothed by the pounding surf. The middle of the floor has a map of a treasure island.*

INTERNATIONAL DATE LINE

If you look at a map of the world, or a globe, you will see lines that extend north and south between the poles. These are the lines of *longitude*. They are also called *meridians*. The globe is divided into 360 parts, or *degrees*. Each degree of longitude represents 1/360 of the distance around the globe. These imaginary lines make it possible to tell the location of a place east or west from the *prime meridian*. The prime meridian, which runs through Greenwich, England, is regarded as zero degrees. Every place in the world is located a certain number of degrees east or west of the prime meridian. Pittsburgh, Pennsylvania, for example, is 80 degrees west longitude, or 80 degrees west of the prime meridian.

Starting from any place on Earth and moving in a straight line east or west, you must cross 360 degrees of longitude to get back to where you started. As the Earth rotates, the path of the sun seems to move from east to west. This means that the sun seems to move 15 degrees west every hour. When it is noon in England, it is five hours before noon (7 A.M.) on the east coast of the United States. When it is noon on the east coast of the United States, it is three hours before noon (9 A.M.) on the west coast.

But where does the date change? The nations of the world have agreed that the date changes at 180 degrees longitude, the 180th meridian. This imaginary line is called the International Date Line. It runs from pole to pole, mostly through the Pacific Ocean. The Date Line does not exactly follow the 180th meridian. It bends to the east to include Siberia with Russia. Then it bends to the west to include the Aleutian Islands with Alaska. It bends to the east to keep all the Fiji Islands on one side of the line.

Each date begins on the west side of the date line and ends on the east side. If you could stand just east of the line and a friend could stand just west of it, he would be one whole day (24 hours) ahead of you. You could watch him open his presents and eat Christmas dinner—but for you, it would still be Christmas Eve. And as he watched you open your presents and eat Christmas dinner, his calendar would tell him it was December 26!

ALSO READ: LATITUDE AND LONGITUDE, MAP, TIME.

INTERNATIONAL LAW

Nations, like people, are guided by certain customs and rules. The rules that guide the way nations try to get along together are known as international law.

The idea of international law was developed in the 1600s by the Dutch statesman Hugo Grotius. Grotius described certain rules that he thought all nations should obey. These rules would be based on custom—the way nations usually act. They would also be based on treaties—written agreements signed by two or more nations. In the 1800s and early 1900s, the major Western nations of the world met together and agreed upon a system of international law. The laws they made guide the behavior of countries in both peacetime and wartime. For example, these laws state that in peacetime every nation has a right to govern its own territory within its legal boundaries, and to control its

▼*The International Court of Justice sits at the Hague in the Netherlands. This court decides cases involving international law.*

ambassadors and embassies abroad. A nation must declare war before attacking another nation. Soldiers wounded in war must be given medical care. Warring armies must not pass through the land of a *neutral* nation, or one that favors neither side in war.

If nations do not obey international laws today, they may be urged to do so by an international organization, the United Nations. *Sanctions* (penalties for disobedience) may be applied against the offending country. For example, other countries may be forbidden to trade with that country. The International Court of Justice, which was set up by the United Nations, also helps to settle international disputes by the rules of international law.

ALSO READ: INTERNATIONAL RELATIONS, LEAGUE OF NATIONS, TREATY, UNITED NATIONS, WAR.

INTERNATIONAL RELATIONS

Relations among nations are somewhat like those among members of a family. Most family members want to get along with each other. Most nations want to get along with other nations. Family members want to feel secure in their home. Nations want to feel secure. No nation wants to live in fear of attack by another country. Each nation wants to govern itself as it wishes, without interference from other nations.

The guiding factor in family relationships is usually love. Members of a family are concerned about and help one another because they love each other. The guiding factor in international relations is usually *self-interest*. Nations help each other if it will benefit themselves in some way to do so. Each nation looks out for itself and is mainly interested in its own welfare.

How Does Self-interest Work?

A nation may protect its own interests in several ways. The most

obvious way is to build a large, well-trained army, with modern weapons. Even if the army never goes into battle, its very existence keeps other nations from interfering in that country's affairs or invading its land. Some nations have gained a great deal for themselves through international trade. If a country has a much-needed product, such as oil, or if its industry is very strong, it can make agreements to supply other nations with products that they need. This increases a country's income. The strong trading nation can stop supplying needed products (or threaten to stop supplying them) in order to get what it wants from other nations. A nation that buys a great deal from one country can threaten to start buying from some other country if the nation from whom it buys begins to interfere.

Probably the best place to see national self-interest at work is in international negotiations. Nations come together to discuss their differences and try to reach an agreement that is acceptable to all of them. In the early stages of negotiations, each nation usually states its position. It tells the others what it wants. As negotiations progress, each nation sees that it cannot have *everything* it wants. Each must decide what *concessions* it will make. Each nation must *concede* (give up) some things it wants in order to come to agreement on other things. Each nation tries to concede only the less important things. A nation will not concede anything that is important to it or that seems to affect its welfare. Each nation looks out for its own self-interest—trying to get as much out of the negotiations as possible, while conceding as little as possible.

Economics

All nations want wealth, because wealth means power. The search for wealth often brings nations into contact with one another. In earlier

▲*The General Assembly of the United Nations is the meeting ground for most of the world's nations.*

▶*International conferences help settle disputes between nations. Here, representatives of the U.S. and the U.S.S.R. are negotiating an agreement on armaments.*

▲*An ambassador is his country's representative to another country. Here, the U.S. Secretary of State, William Rogers (left), discusses U.S.-Korean relations with William Porter, who was ambassador to the Republic of Korea.*

times, this search led some nations to establish colonies in other lands. These colonies provided raw materials for the industries of the colonizing nation and markets for its goods. Throughout history, countries have increased their wealth by trading with one another. Today, nations in the same geographic area have formed associations to increase their economic or political power. One of these is the European Economic Community, or "Common Market."

History

International relations have been conducted in many ways. In ancient times, strong nations such as Rome conquered territories and built great empires. During the Middle Ages and Renaissance, most of western Europe was made up of small territories ruled by princes. These rulers were continually struggling for power among themselves. European nations, as we know them, began to be formed in the 1300s. They were based on the idea of *national sover-*

eignty. This meant that each nation was independent and had the right to govern itself.

Nations tried to keep peace by preventing any one nation from getting so much power that it was a threat to the other nations. This system is called a *balance of power.* When one nation showed signs of becoming too powerful, other nations would form an *alliance* against it. The allied nations agreed to help one another in case of political interference, military attack, or even for economic reasons. An alliance on one side often led to a *counteralliance* on the other. Each side tried to become stronger than the other. In the 1800s, Great Britain kept a balance of power in Europe by allying itself first with one side, then with the other.

Since World War II, a new power balance has been formed, based on three groups—the United States and western European nations, the Soviet Union and eastern European Communist nations, and the People's Republic of China. The three powers compete for the friendship of the underdeveloped countries in Asia, Africa, and Latin America (so-called "third world" nations). Many underdeveloped nations have vast resources of raw materials and manpower.

International relations today have been influenced by the United Nations. The United Nations serves as a meeting place where countries can argue their disagreements and sometimes find solutions that may avoid their going to war. The United Nations also tries to persuade countries to obey international law in their relations with one another.

Official relations among nations are carried on by *ambassadors* and their staffs of foreign service officers. An ambassador is an official representative of his government in a foreign country. An ambassador must keep informed of the policies and decisions of his country's government. He must be able to explain his government's policies to officials of the foreign government. He must also be good at persuading the foreign government to agree with his country's policies. An ambassador must be well informed about the country in which he is stationed. He must report to his government on the policies and actions of the foreign country. And he must be ready to advise his government in any dealings it has with that country. Relations between countries are sometimes carried out by heads of government, as when the President of the United States meets with the leaders of other nations.

For further information on:

International Alliances, *see* COMMON MARKET, COMMONWEALTH OF NATIONS, NORTH ATLANTIC TREATY ORGANIZATION, ORGANIZATION OF AMERICAN STATES, WARSAW PACT.

International Diplomacy, *see* FOREIGN SERVICE.

International Organizations, *see* LEAGUE OF NATIONS, UNITED NATIONS.

International Relations and Economics, *see* COLONY, ECONOMICS, INTERNATIONAL TRADE, NATION.

International Travel, *see* PASSPORTS AND VISAS.

Relations between Countries, *see* INTERNATIONAL LAW, TREATY, WAR.

INTERNATIONAL TRADE Every country engages in international trade. A country sells some things that it produces to other countries. Products sent out of the country are called *exports.* A country also buys products that it needs from other countries. Products brought into the country are called *imports.* International trade takes place because countries generally produce more of certain things than they need, and not enough of other things. For example, Great Britain is a leading manufacturer of cloth. It exports cloth and other goods to other nations. But Britain cannot

raise enough food to feed its population, so it imports food from nations that raise great amounts of agricultural products.

Why do nations produce large amounts of some products and not enough of others? Nature is one reason. Oranges, for instance, grow best in hot climates. Some metals, such as copper, are found only in certain areas of the world. Each nation concentrates on the products it can produce best with the resources it has. A nation imports goods that it cannot produce at home, or that it can produce only at a higher cost than the import price. Some nations, such as the United States, are able to produce most of the things they need. But every country, no matter how wealthy, needs to do some trading. The United States must import items such as coffee, tea, natural rubber, sugar, and tropical fruits.

Trading nations try to keep a good *balance of payments.* The balance of payments is the comparison between the amount of money coming into a country when others pay for its exports, and the amount of money going out when a country buys imports. When a country exports more than it imports, more money comes into the country than goes out of it. This is considered a favorable balance of payments.

Governments sometimes set up *tariffs* (taxes on imports) or *quotas* (limits on the amount of goods that may be imported). Tariffs and quotas raise the prices of products coming into a country. The higher the prices on products, the less trade takes place. People will not buy the imports if they cost more than products made in their own country. Tariffs and quotas are usually set up by a government to protect the farmers and manufacturers of its own country. For example, if the United States puts a tariff on imported cars, the prices of these cars become higher than the prices of U.S. cars. Since the American-made

▼*Fruits picked at noon in Hungary are transported by air to Denmark to be sold in the supermarkets of Copenhagen the next morning.*

cars are then cheaper, people are more likely to buy them.

Some nations have joined together in "trading communities" in order to do away with tariffs and quotas and to promote free trade among the member nations. The Common Market is a trading community in western Europe. Members of the Commonwealth of Nations also have trade agreements.

ALSO READ: COMMON MARKET, COMMONWEALTH OF NATIONS.

INTRODUCTION   When someone wants two people to meet, he introduces them. This can usually be done very simply by telling each person the other's name.

There are some rules about introductions that are best to follow in certain situations. It is more important, however, to say the names correctly in a polite and friendly manner than it is to follow the rules.

One rule is that the more important name should be mentioned first. Everybody is important as a person, however, so it is usually correct to say the name of the older person first. For example, if you are introducing your teacher to a child, say the teacher's name first—"Mr. Silva, this is my friend, Bob Edwards." If a man and woman are being introduced, the woman's name is mentioned first, unless the man is much older or is a distinguished person. Once two people are introduced, it is polite to help them start a conversation with each other.

The handshake originated during the Middle Ages, when men would hold out their right hands as a sign to each other that they were friendly and not carrying weapons. In Japan, people bow instead of shaking hands.

▼*Important inventions of the 1800s can be seen in this print made in 1876. The steamboat and locomotive are on the right of the picture. Can you spot the telegraph and the powered printing press?*

When you have been introduced, you should say, "How do you do?" or "Hello." It is also courteous to repeat the name of the person to whom you have been introduced. For example, if you have just been introduced to Mr. Silva, you might say to him, "How do you do, Mr. Silva." This will also help you to remember the name of your new acquaintance. Men and boys stand up for all introductions and shake hands with each other. But a man does not put out his hand to a woman unless she offers her hand first. Women and girls in their own homes stand up to meet guests. But outside their homes, they do not rise unless they are being introduced to the hostess, the guest of honor, a very old woman, or a great person.

If you have not been introduced to the others at a party or other gathering, you may walk up to someone and introduce yourself.

ALSO READ: MANNERS.

INVENTION   Look around your home or classroom and observe the tools and other objects that you use every day. You will begin to see how much you depend on inventions in your daily life. The books you read in school would not have been possible without the invention of paper and ink—or of printing itself. Pencils, pens, staplers, and pencil-sharpeners are also useful inventions. Both your school and home have electric lights and heating systems that came about through the work of inventors. At home you also have a refrigerator, telephone, radio, and other useful things. Countless other inventions are vital to industry, business, medicine, farming, and other fields.

An invention may be the creation of something completely new or an improvement of something made before. Many important inventions have resulted from the work of one hard-working individual. Inventors often owe much to discoveries and inventions made by others before them. For instance, James Watt invented the first workable steam engine, but his invention was based on earlier models built by others. Samuel F. B. Morse's telegraph, however, was a completely original invention.

At times, two or more inventors, working independently, have come up with the same invention. For example, Elisha Gray and Alexander Graham Bell both applied for a patent on the telephone on the same day in 1876. (A *patent* gives an inventor the legal rights to his invention and forbids anyone else to copy it or claim to have invented it.) Gray made his application a few hours later than Bell, so Bell received credit for the invention.

Many modern inventions have been created not by one person, but by many people working together as a team. The atom bomb, for instance, was developed during World War II by a large group of scientists and technicians. Today, research teams in government, industrial, and university laboratories work hard to create new inventions or to improve existing inventions.

Not all inventors have been scientists or experts in their fields. Ordinary people have invented useful objects. Some inventions have even come about by accident. Charles Goodyear, the inventor of vulcanized rubber, was a hardware salesman with no formal education. He was trying to find a way to treat natural rubber so that it would not become brittle when cold, or soft and sticky when hot. He had made hundreds of unsuccessful experiments, mixing rubber with different materials. Then one day in 1839, Goodyear accidentally dropped some rubber, which he had treated with sulfur, into the fire. The heat gave the mixture the elastic quality he wanted. This method of treating rubber, *vulcanization*, is still the basis of rubber manufacturing.

▲ *Thomas A. Edison was one of the most important inventors of all time. The electric light and the phonograph were among his many inventions.*

History of Inventions
The earliest inventions were tools and weapons that helped people to build shelters and get food. Prehistoric men chipped stones with other stones to make simple hammers and axes. They also shaped stones into

SOME IMPORTANT INVENTIONS

YEAR	INVENTION	INVENTOR(S)	NATIONALITY
About 1447	Movable Type Printing	Johannes Gutenberg	German
1593	Thermometer	Galileo Galilei	Italian
1608	Telescope	Hans Lippershey	Dutch
1642	Adding Machine	Blaise Pascal	French
1705	Steam Engine	Thomas Newcomen	English
1769	Steam Engine for Power	James Watt	Scottish
1793	Cotton Gin	Eli Whitney	American
1800	Electric Battery	Alessandro Volta	Italian
1804	Steam Locomotive	Richard Trevithick	English
1807	First Practical Steamship	Robert Fulton	American
1819	Stethoscope	René Laënnec	French
1821	Electric Motor	Michael Faraday	English
1837	Telegraph	Samuel F. B. Morse	American
1846	Sewing Machine	Elias Howe	American
1852	Elevator	Elisha Otis	American
1866	Dynamite	Alfred Nobel	Swedish
1876	Telephone	Alexander Graham Bell	American
1877	Internal Combustion Engine	Nikolaus Otto	German
1885	Gasoline Automobile	Karl Benz, Otto Daimler	German
1888	Kodak Camera	George Eastman	American
1893	Motion Picture Machine	Thomas Edison	American
1895	X-ray Machine	Wilhelm Roentgen	German
1896	Wireless Telegraph	Guglielmo Marconi	Italian
1903	Airplane	Orville and Wilbur Wright	American
1907	Radio Vacuum Tube	Lee De Forest	American
1923– 1928	Television	Vladimir Zworykin	American
		John L. Baird	English
		Philo T. Farnsworth	American
1928	Jet Engine	Frank Whittle	English
1935	Radar	Robert Watson-Watt	English
1942	Atomic Reactor	Enrico Fermi	American
1947	Polaroid Camera	Edwin Land	American
1960	Masers and Lasers	Charles H. Townes	American
		Theodore H. Maiman	American
1966	Artificial Heart	Michael DeBakey	American

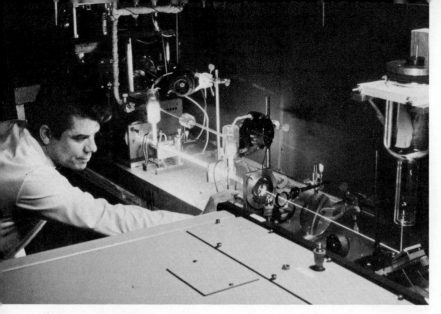

▲ *A scientist adjusts a laser used in experiments to learn about the atomic structures of transparent liquids and solids.*

▼ *A weather radar is used to spot storms. Radar was invented in 1935 by the English scientist Robert Watson-Watt.*

crude knives and spear points for hunting. These stone tools later gave way to tools made of bronze and iron, as men learned to use metals. Early men also learned to make clothing, first from animal skins and later from plant materials. Men invented plows and learned how to plant and harvest grains and other foods. They also dug out logs to make crude boats.

One of the most important of early inventions was the wheel. The wheel made carts and wagons possible, as well as inventions such as the potter's wheel and the water wheel. The water wheel, believed to have been invented by the Romans about 100 B.C., was a large wheel with paddles attached to the rim. The wheel was put under a waterfall so that the wheel turned when the water struck the paddles. The turning axle of the wheel, attached to a machine, gave the machine power to operate. Water wheels were long used for such jobs as grinding grain and pumping water. Windmills came into use in Europe in the 1100s. Just as the water wheel used moving water as a source of power, the windmill used the force of moving air.

For further information on:

Inventions, *see* AIR CONDITIONING, AIRPLANE, AUTOMOBILE, BICYCLE, CALCULATOR, CAMERA, CLOCKS AND WATCHES, COMPUTER, ELEVATORS AND ESCALATORS, EXPLOSIVES, GEIGER COUNTER, GUNS AND RIFLES, GYROSCOPE, HEATING, HELICOPTER, LENS, LIE DETECTOR, LIGHTING, LOCKS AND KEYS, MATCH, MICROSCOPE, MOTION PICTURES, PAPER, PARACHUTE, PENS AND PENCILS, PHONOGRAPH, PHOTOGRAPHY, PLASTIC, PRINTING, RADAR, RADIO, RUBBER, REFRIGERATION, SEWING MACHINE, SUBMARINE, SYNTHETIC, TELEGRAPH, TELEPHONE, TELESCOPE, TELEVISION, THERMOMETER, X-RAY, ZIPPER.

Inventors, *see* BELL, ALEXANDER GRAHAM; EDISON, THOMAS ALVA; FARADAY, MICHAEL; FERMI, ENRICO; FRANKLIN, BENJAMIN; FULTON, ROBERT; GALILEO; GODDARD, ROBERT H.; GUTENBERG, JOHANNES; LEONARDO DA VINCI; MC CORMICK, CYRUS; MARCONI, GUGLIELMO; MORSE, SAMUEL F. B.; NEWTON, ISAAC; VON BRAUN, WERNHER; WRIGHT BROTHERS.

INVERTEBRATE see ANIMAL KINGDOM.

ION see ATOM.

IOWA The state of Iowa got its name from an Indian tribe that lived in the region before the white man came there. This tribe originally called themselves the Pahotcha. If they had continued to be called by that name, you would probably be reading about the state of Pahotcha.

The Land and Climate

Iowa lies in the plains that curve west and south of the Great Lakes. Minnesota is north of its straight northern boundary. Missouri is south of its almost-straight southern boundary. Its western boundary line is not straight at all. It is formed by the Missouri River and the Big Sioux River, which flows into the Missouri. Nebraska and South Dakota are Iowa's western neighbors. Its eastern boundary is wavy, too. It is formed by the Mississippi River, which separates Iowa from Illinois and Wisconsin.

Most of Iowa is a gently rolling plain. The state is highest in the northwest. It is lowest in the southeast. But it really slopes in *two* di-

▲*Baling hay in Iowa. This midwest state has millions of acres of rich, fertile farmland and a climate that is good for farming.*

rections. The rivers prove that it does. The Des Moines River and the other rivers in the eastern two-thirds of Iowa flow southeast toward the Mississippi. The rivers in the western third of the state flow southwest.

Iowa is wonderful farming country. No other state has so much top-grade soil. Most of the Iowa region was covered with tall prairie grass for hundreds of years. The long grass roots added to the plant food in the soil as they decayed. Iowa also has a very good climate for crops. There is usually enough rain for the crops during the six warm months. It is brought by winds from the south. The hot sunshine of long summer days helps the crops ripen. Winter winds blow from the cold, dry north. They give Iowa bright days and sparkling, frosty nights.

History

The Indians liked this prairie region. The women raised vegetables in the rich soil, and the men hunted the plentiful game. The land was so good that tribes fought one another for it.

Prehistoric Indians called Mound Builders once lived in Iowa. They built large mounds of earth as burial places or as bases for houses and temples. Most of their mounds are cone-shaped. But some, called *effigy*

mounds, are in the form of huge birds or beasts. These interesting mounds can be seen in Effigy Mounds National Monument, a park near the town of Marquette on the Mississippi River.

The mounds were already old when the first white men arrived. These men were French explorers, led by Louis Joliet and Father Jacques Marquette. They spent two days with friendly Indians of the Illinois tribe in Iowa in June, 1673.

Several Indian tribes played important parts in the history of this region. One was the warlike Sioux. Another was the Sauk. These and other tribes, including the Fox and the Winnebago, occupied most of the state until the 1800s.

Iowa was a small part of the huge French territory called Louisiana. France let Spain control Louisiana Territory for a time. But the men who entered the Iowa region during the 1700s were French.

The first one to start a settlement was Julien Dubuque. He asked the Fox Indians to let him mine lead near the Mississippi. The chiefs granted his request in 1788. Dubuque and the Indians became good friends. Today a city and a county in Iowa have his name. They mark the place where his trading post, farm, and mines were once located.

The United States bought the

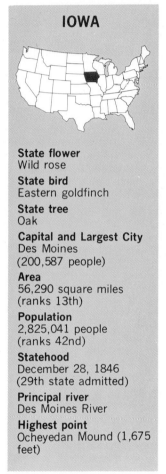

IOWA

State flower
Wild rose

State bird
Eastern goldfinch

State tree
Oak

Capital and Largest City
Des Moines
(200,587 people)

Area
56,290 square miles
(ranks 13th)

Population
2,825,041 people
(ranks 42nd)

Statehood
December 28, 1846
(29th state admitted)

Principal river
Des Moines River

Highest point
Ocheyedan Mound (1,675 feet)

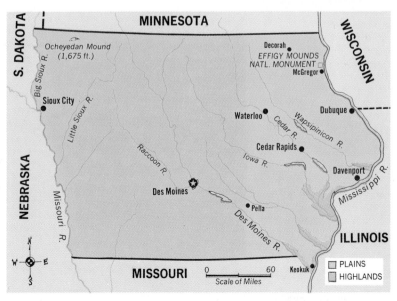

whole territory of Louisiana from France in 1803. Americans found, as the French had, that the Iowa region was rich in fur-bearing animals. The American Fur Company started trading posts there to buy furs from the Indians. Keokuk (in Iowa's southeastern corner) is one of several towns that began as trading posts.

The Indians liked traders who treated them fairly. They liked being able to exchange furs for wool blankets and other goods. But some settlers cheated the Indians to get their land. For this reason, a number of tribes sided with Great Britain in the War of 1812. Their leader was Black Hawk, a Sauk chief. Black Hawk made peace with the white Americans after the war. But unjust treatment led him to fight them again in the Black Hawk War of 1832. He was defeated. During the years that followed, almost all the Indians were pushed out of Iowa.

Iowa became a state in 1846. By this time, a flood of settlers was pouring in. They came by wagon from the East and the South. Most of them had oxen. They had heard that horses and mules weren't strong enough to pull plows through the thick prairie sod (grass-covered earth). The early farmers there became known as *sod busters*.

Once the sod was broken, all was well. The farmers then had excellent cropland. News of the fertile soil spread around the world. Many European farmers came to Iowa. Most came from Germany, Norway, Sweden, Denmark, the Netherlands, and Ireland. The Amanites, a religious group from Germany, founded seven villages near Iowa City in 1855. Some of the villagers there still produce old German handicrafts. Many Dutch families settled in Pella, in southeastern Iowa. Their descendants dress up in traditional Dutch costumes each spring for the annual Tulip Festival. Historical museums in Decorah, in the north-

▼*Iowa has many fine lake resort areas, especially in the northern part of the state. In this region, sailing is a popular pastime.*

▲*Iowa winters are long and cold. But these hardy outdoorsmen are having a good day's ice fishing.*

east, show how the early Norwegian farm families of this region lived and worked.

Iowans at Work

Iowa is still a farm state. Agriculture brings the state more than three billion dollars' worth of business every year. This makes Iowa second only to California in the value of its agricultural products. Iowa is the nation's leading producer of corn. Soybeans are important, too. But livestock brings in more money than crops do. Much corn is not sold. The farmers who raise it feed it to pigs and cattle instead.

Although Iowa is a leading agricultural state, it is also a manufacturing state. Machinery is the number-one product of Iowa's manufacturing industry. Much of it is farm machinery. Food products are second in value. Both agricultural and industrial products are exhibited at the Iowa State Fair, held in Des Moines every summer.

ALSO READ: BLACK HAWK, GREAT LAKES, LOUISIANA PURCHASE, MOUND BUILDER, PRAIRIE.

IRAN Did you ever hear of a flying carpet? Colorful hand-made carpets, like the flying carpets in fairy tales, are still made by skillful weavers in the country of Iran today. Wandering tribes of shepherds, living in the deserts and mountains, practice this ancient art. Each tribe has its own rug design. Most Ira-

IRAN

Capital City: Teheran (2,720,000 people).
Area: 628,000 square miles.
Population: 27,892,000 people.
Languages: Persian and Kurdish.
Export Products: Oil and carpets.
Unit of Money: Rial.

nians, however, are farmers who live in small villages. Others live in houses surrounded by gardens in the cities. Most people are Muslims.

Iran's northern boundaries are the Soviet Union and the Caspian Sea. Waters of the Gulf of Oman and the Persian Gulf lap its southern shores. Iraq lies to the west, and Afghanistan and Pakistan lie to the east. Teheran, a Muslim city, is the capital. (See the map with the article on the MIDDLE EAST.)

Iran is mainly a plateau, 4,000 feet above sea level, surrounded by mountain ranges. A vast desert stretches 800 miles across the central part of the country. Much of Iran receives ten inches or less of rainfall each year. However, the area near the Caspian Sea gets as much as 50 inches.

Iran is an agricultural country. Most of the land suitable for farming is irrigated. Wheat, barley, and rice are grown. Other crops are tobacco, tea, dates, apricots, sugar beets, cotton, and corn. The country has coal, lead, copper, chromite, and iron. However, oil is Iran's most important natural resource.

The country's industries depend upon agricultural production and natural resources. Silk, cotton, and wool are woven. Hides, tobacco, and sugar beets are processed. Oil is refined, and copper is smelted.

The Iranians are descendants of the Medes and Persians. These people came to the area of present-day Iran about 900 years before the birth of Christ. Cyrus the Great, an ancient statesman and warrior, conquered the Medes and Persians in about 550 B.C. He united the area now called the Middle East and built it into the Persian Empire.

Alexander the Great, a great Greek general, conquered the Persian Empire in 331 B.C. Other invaders came and went, including Arabs, Mongols, and Turks. Great Britain and Russia also fought to control Iran during the 1800s.

In 1925, Mohammed Reza Shah Pahlavi became shah (king) of Persia. Reza Shah made many reforms. He gave royal lands to the peasants. He demanded that parliament make laws establishing education for all, women's voting rights, and profit-sharing for workers in industry. In 1941, the shah abdicated (gave up the throne) and his son, Mohammed Reza Pahlavi, became shah. The new shah was officially crowned on October 26, 1967, after his first son was born. Today, the shah chooses the premier to head the elected members of parliament.

ALSO READ: ALEXANDER THE GREAT, PERSIA.

IRAQ The word "Iraq" comes from an Arabic word meaning "origin." The name probably refers to the fact that this fertile valley between the Tigris and Euphrates

▲*Modern and traditional modes of transport compete on Iran's highway network. Here, a heavily loaded truck passes a camel train.*

The official throne of Iran was stolen from India in the early 1700s. The jewel-encrusted throne is called the Peacock Throne because its back is shaped like the spread feathers of that bird.

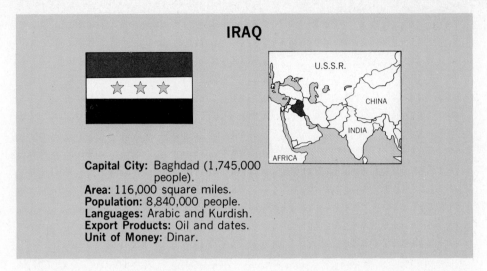

IRAQ

Capital City: Baghdad (1,745,000 people).
Area: 116,000 square miles.
Population: 8,840,000 people.
Languages: Arabic and Kurdish.
Export Products: Oil and dates.
Unit of Money: Dinar.

rivers may have been the birthplace of civilization. Iraq is bounded on the north by Turkey, on the east by Iran, on the south by Saudi Arabia, and on the west by Syria and Jordan. The only outlet to the sea is a narrow strip of coast on the Persian Gulf. The ancient city of Baghdad is the capital. (See the map with the article on the MIDDLE EAST.)

The climate in Iraq varies according to location. The northern part of the country has cold winters and cool summers. The central area has short, cool winters and long, hot summers. The country gets ten inches of rainfall or less each year.

Most of the Iraqi people are Muslims who live on farms or in small villages or towns. Some of them, however, are *nomadic* (wandering) shepherds who live in the mountains. Their leaders, called *sheiks*, are sometimes very rich and powerful. About three-quarters of the Iraqis are Muslims.

Iraq supplies about 80 per cent of the world's supply of dates and grows other fruits, tobacco, cotton and grain crops. Oil is the nation's most important natural resource. Small deposits of various minerals are found, including iron, gold, lead, copper, silver, platinum, and zinc.

The nation's most important industry is the production of oil. Other industries include the manufacture of glass, cigarettes and other tobacco products, vegetable oils, soap, woolen textiles, brick, and tile.

Records of civilization in Mesopotamia go back 6,000 years. The area was conquered by Persia in 538 B.C., and then invaded and ruled by several other conquerors. Iraq was under Turkish rule from 1638 until World War I, when it came under British control. Iraq became independent in 1932. Political disputes and military take-overs have marked Iraq's years as an independent state. Major General Ahmed Hassan al-Bakr headed a military group that took over the government in 1968. ALSO READ: MESOPOTAMIA, MIDDLE EAST, TIGRIS-EUPHRATES RIVER.

IRELAND Ireland is a land of wild seacoasts and misty rolling hills—so green that it is sometimes called the Emerald Isle. Whitewashed cottages with thatched roofs dot the countryside. The Irish people are known for their wit, imagination, and spirit.

Ireland lies west of Great Britain, between the Irish Sea and the Atlantic Ocean. The island is divided into two parts. Most of the island is the independent Republic of Ireland, often known as Eire (the Irish name for the whole island). The northeastern region, Northern Ireland (Ulster), is part of the United Kingdom. The capital of Eire is the ancient city of Dublin. (See the map with the article on BRITISH ISLES.)

A gentle region of hills, *loughs*

▼*Oil is a source of great wealth to Iraq. Here an Iraqi technician checks the valve on an oil pipeline.*

(lakes), and rivers stretches across central Ireland to the west coast. Here, massive granite cliffs and rugged headlands face the storms of the Atlantic Ocean. The Shannon River, the longest river in the British Isles, flows southward across central Ireland. The climate of the island is moderate and moist.

The Irish people are descended mainly from Celtic tribes that settled in Ireland more than 2,000 years ago. The Irish encourage the use of the ancient Celtic language, *Gaelic*, but most people also speak English. The major religion in Ireland is Roman Catholicism.

Ireland has few natural resources. Farming and food processing are the most important industries. A rapidly-growing tourist industry is bringing new wealth to the country. Visitors love the friendly people, good fishing, quaint countryside, and ancient castles. Irish dairy products, woolen goods, stout (a heavy, dark beer) and whiskey are exported to other parts of the world. Homes and small industries in Ireland burn peat (a soft form of coal) from the Irish bogs for fuel. Peat diggers, with their ponies and carts, and farmers with their donkeys are familiar sights.

Saint Patrick, the patron saint of Ireland, converted the Irish to Christianity in the 400s. After the barbarians overran Europe in the 500s and 600s, devout Irish monks kept Christianity alive. They copied down the religious scriptures by hand in beautifully decorated books, such as the famous *Book of Kells*. Ancient Celtic folklore survived in ballads and legends. Later Irish writers sometimes used these legends as themes for their stories and poems. Many modern Irish authors, including William Butler Yeats, James Joyce, Oscar Wilde, and George Bernard Shaw, have become famous throughout the world.

The high kings of Ireland ruled from a great palace at Tara, near Dublin, in the Middle Ages. In the 1100s, the first English invasions began from the east. In the 1500s, English settlers began to seize land throughout Ireland. These Protestant settlers brutally persecuted the Roman Catholic Irish. The Irish had no political rights and were forced to live in poverty on the poorest land. Their diet was mainly potatoes. In the 1840s, a disease destroyed the potato crop for several years and millions of Irish people died of starvation. Others left to go to the United States.

In 1916, a revolution known as the Easter Rebellion broke out. It was led by a group of Irish patriots called the *Sinn Fein* ("We Ourselves"). The Irish fought for many years to free themselves from English rule. In 1949, the British finally recognized the independence of the Republic of Ireland, but kept con-

▲*Fishing is a popular pastime in Ireland. These fishermen are trying their luck near Galway Bay on the west coast of the country.*

IRELAND (EIRE)

Capital City: Dublin (650,000 people).
Area: 26,601 square miles.
Population: 2,291,000 people.
Languages: English and Irish (Gaelic).
Export Products: Live animals, meat, and textiles.
Unit of Money: Irish Pound.

trol of the northern counties. The Irish Catholics continue to fight Ulster's Protestants for control of the area. This struggle has caused much violence and bloodshed. The Republic of Ireland is now governed by a president, a prime minister, and a parliament.

ALSO READ: BRITISH ISLES; ENGLAND; NORTHERN IRELAND; PATRICK, SAINT; UNITED KINGDOM.

IRON see VITAMINS AND MINERALS.

▲Molten iron is poured into molds. In these molds the metal cools and hardens in the shape of bars, or ingots.

▶Cold, hard steel ingots are heated and softened and then rolled into long bars in a rolling mill. Rolling strengthens the steel.

▼An ingot being rolled into the shape of a slab, a rectangular piece of steel. Some ingots are shaped into blooms or billets, which are squared pieces of steel.

IRON AND STEEL Have you ever seen a shooting star? It makes a fiery trail across the sky and suddenly vanishes. A shooting star is not a star at all. It is a *meteor*. Meteors are white-hot chunks of metal and stone from outer space. The metal is mostly iron, mixed with nickel. When a meteor enters the earth's atmosphere, the friction of its movement through the air creates great heat. Most meteors burn up completely, but those that hit the earth are called *meteorites*.

Thousands of years ago, men used tools made of stone, copper, or bronze. When people began to find pieces of iron meteorites, they discovered that the iron was heavier and harder than stone, copper, or bronze. By hammering the iron, men could shape it into knives, arrowheads, and spear points, and it could even be made into jewelry. The iron was believed to have magic powers because it came from the heavens. In some ancient languages,

the word for iron meant "metal from the sky." Iron was considered more valuable than gold, silver, copper, or bronze.

Copper, gold, silver, and some other metals were obtained when men learned that rocks of certain colors, or *ores*, were changed by fire. Fire caused the metal ore in the rocks to melt. The melting of ore to obtain metal is called *smelting*. The metals are poured off and cooled so they would harden. Then the hardened metals were made into tools.

No one knows when or where man first discovered that he could make iron by smelting iron ore. The discovery was certainly made several thousand years ago, possibly in several different areas. The Bible mentions iron and other metals. Iron was used in China, Egypt, the Middle East, and Europe long before the time of Christ.

There is much iron ore in the ground. After it was discovered in large quantities, iron was no longer considered so valuable as some of the rarer metals. During the Industrial Revolution, iron was needed for thousands of new machines and engines. Iron ore is now mined in most countries of the world. One of the largest iron ore regions in the United States is in Minnesota, near Lake Superior. Most of the high-grade ore has been mined, but a method has been developed to process a low-grade ore called *taconite*.

The iron mines in Minnesota are *open-pit* mines. This type of mine is used when the ore is near the surface of the ground. Big loads of ore are scooped up from the open ground by giant steam shovels, to be hauled away for smelting. This digging makes a huge open pit. In other iron ore ranges, the ore is sometimes deep underground. A tunnel, or *shaft*, is dug downward into the ground until the ore is reached. Miners go down into the shaft and dig out the ore, which is then hoisted to the surface.

For many years, iron ore was smelted by placing it on a fire of charcoal. The iron had to be hammered and reheated several times before it was free of *impurities* (the other materials in the ore). The first *blast furnaces* were made in Europe in the 1300s. A blast furnace is a tall, cylinder-shaped building with a hearth inside, on which the iron ore is smelted. Modern blast furnaces may be more than 200 feet high.

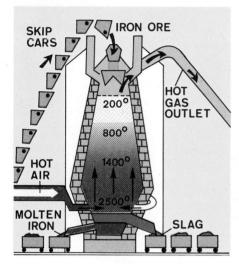

Blasts of heated air make the fire in a blast furnace so hot that most of the impurities in the ore are burned away the first time it is heated. The melted iron sinks to the bottom of the furnace and the impurities are collected as *slag* or burned off as gases. In the 1700s, people discovered that *coke* (a by-product of coal) smelted iron much faster than charcoal. Coke has been used for smelting ever since. Crushed limestone is also added to the fire in a blast furnace. Chemicals in the limestone help to purify the iron. After the iron has been smelted in a blast furnace, it is poured into bar-shaped molds, or *pigs*. It then hardens into *pig iron*. The pigs are shipped to a *foundry*, where they are reheated and *cast* (poured into molds) to make iron products. This type of iron is called *cast iron*. Cast iron is brittle, hard, and extremely heavy.

To make a different kind of iron, the pigs are reheated and mixed with a glass-like sand. The iron is then cooled. After it hardens, it can be put between rollers and squeezed into desired sizes. This kind of iron is called *wrought iron*. It can be bent or twisted without breaking. Wrought iron is used to make such things as iron gates, garden furniture, and pipelines.

In the 1850s, different discoveries made by three men, working separately, showed how iron could be cheaply and easily made into *steel*. The men were William Kelley, an American, Robert F. Mushet, a Scot, and Sir Henry Bessemer, an Englishman. Their inventions created the steel industry.

Steel is an *alloy*. An alloy is a mixture of two or more metals. Steel is made by mixing melted iron with measured amounts of other substances, such as carbon, manganese, chromium, tungsten, molybdenum, and nickel. Different alloys make different kinds of steel. For example, *stainless steel* is mostly an alloy of steel and chromium. But all steel begins with iron ore. Steel is much stronger than iron and can be shaped more accurately. Many of the products of modern technology, from suspension bridges to razor blades, could not have been made without steel.

The United States, Great Britain, Germany, France, the Soviet Union, and Belgium produce millions of tons of iron and steel each year. Great quantities of this iron and steel are sold to other countries that do not have enough iron mines or steel mills to meet their own needs. Iron and steel are used in the building of skyscrapers, automobiles, steamships, airplanes, rockets and space ships, bicycles, railroad tracks, trains, toys, typewriters, computers, knives, guns, and thousands of other goods. The iron and steel industries are among the most important in the world.

ALSO READ: ALLOY, INDUSTRIAL REVOLUTION, METAL, MINES AND MINING.

▲*Railroad lines are made of very strong steel to withstand the impact of heavy locomotives. The rail ends are connected by two pieces of special steel called* angle bars.

▼*A view of a plate mill where steel sheets up to a width of 13 feet are produced. Plate steel is strong and is used in industries such as shipbuilding and bridge building.*

▲*An Iroquois false face made of carved and painted wood. The Iroquois hung it up to keep evil spirits and sickness away.*

IROQUOIS INDIANS In part of what is now New York State, five Indian tribes (the Mohawk, Oneida, Onondaga, Cayuga, and Seneca) united to form the Iroquois Confederacy, or the Five Nations. The life of the Iroquois was highly organized and culturally advanced.

The Iroquois lived in villages defended by *palisade fences,* or fences of tall, pointed pieces of wood tied closely together. They lived in long wooden structures called "long houses." Several related families lived in each house. Each family had its own part of the long house.

The Iroquois grew corn *(maize),* squash, and beans. The women of the tribes tended the fields and picked wild fruits and vegetables. Maple sugar was also enjoyed by the Iroquois. Collected elm bark was used for covering the walls and roofs of the long houses and for making containers. The men and boys went on hunting and fishing expeditions.

Women had a very important place among the Iroquois. The head of each family was an elderly woman. Women owned the long houses, the fields, and the crops. An Iroquois traced his ancestors through his mother's family. The matrons at the head of the most important Iroquois families were responsible for choosing the chiefs, or *sachems,* who sat in the tribal council. The sachems governed the tribes, but if they did not govern wisely the women dismissed them.

Religion was an important part of Iroquois life. Any man or woman who was thought to have magical powers could become a priest. The major religious festival was celebrated in midwinter. Ceremonies at this time were supposed to encourage the growth of the new year's crops. The members of the False Face Society danced wearing frightening masks. These masks were believed to destroy evil spirits.

The Iroquois believed in justice, healthful living, and cooperation and respect between people. Some of their ideas may have helped to inspire the men who drew up the Constitution of the United States. ALSO READ: FIVE NATIONS.

IRRIGATION For thousands of years, farmers have taken water from rivers to make up for lack of rain. At first, farmers simply dug narrow channels from the river to their fields. This was irrigation, but it had limitations. The irrigated fields had to be downhill from the river and close to it, because there were no pumps to carry the water uphill or over long distances. These problems have been solved by modern irrigation methods.

Irrigation plays an important part in agriculture today. In the United States, irrigation makes it possible for farmers to use about 37,000,000 acres of land normally too dry for farming. The Columbia, Sacramento, San Joaquin, and Missouri rivers supply water for the largest irrigation systems in the U.S. Other large irrigation systems are along the Nile River in Egypt, the Yellow River in China, the Indus River in Pakistan, the Ganges and Brahmaputra rivers in India, and the Tigris and Euphrates rivers in Iraq.

The pumps of a modern irrigation system can move millions of gallons of water a day. Some irrigation systems take water from underground wells. But most systems get water from rivers. In this case, a dam is built and the water is taken from the lake formed behind the dam.

Pumps carry water from the river into canals or concrete channels. Special tunnels are dug to carry the water under hills and mountains. Along the way are pumping stations that keep the water moving over long distances. Smaller canals, called *feeders,* branch off from the main canal, and *laterals,* still smaller canals that take the water into the crop fields, branch off from feeders.

There are several ways of bring-

▼*A farmer in India is using water-filled ditches to irrigate his field of winter wheat. He obtains water from a well.*

▲*Sprinklers are used here to irrigate land on which potato plants are in bloom. The pipes can be moved wherever they are needed.*

ing the water to the growing plants. Water may be allowed to flow from the laterals by gravity through the ploughed furrows in which the crops are growing. In *underbedding*, the plants are grown on rows of small hills, and the water flows along the rows. The water seeps down to the roots of the plants. Sometimes a whole field is simply flooded at regular intervals.

Rows of sprinklers may be built in a field. The water is pumped through the sprinklers and "rains" on the crops.

ALSO READ: AGRICULTURE, CANAL, DAM, PUMP.

IRVING, WASHINGTON (1783–1859) Washington Irving has been called the father of American literature. He was the first important fiction writer in the United States and one of the first American authors to use the short-story form. His humorous stories and other writings won him fame in Europe as well as at home.

Irving was born in New York City. As a young man, he began a career as a lawyer. But he preferred writing and soon began to publish amusing little articles and essays. He published a humorous *History of New York* in 1809, under the made-up name Diedrich Knickerbocker. This book poked fun at history and at American government.

Irving traveled to Europe in 1815 for his family's business. Money troubles caused the business to fail a few years later, and Irving turned to writing as a full-time occupation. His next work was *The Sketch Book*, which included his two most popular stories—*The Legend of Sleepy Hollow* and *Rip Van Winkle*. Both these stories were based on old legends that Irving had heard from Dutch-Americans in New York. *The Legend of Sleepy Hollow* is the tale of a timid schoolmaster, Ichabod Crane, and his terrifying meeting with the Headless Horseman. *Rip Van Winkle* is the story of a man who falls asleep for 20 years in the Catskill Mountains of New York. He wakes up after the American Revolution and finds that life in his town has changed completely.

▲*Washington Irving, an American author.*

▲*"Rip Van Winkle" was one of Irving's most beloved stories. Here, old Rip returns home after his 20-year sleep in the mountains. His dog does not recognize him.*

Irving was appointed U.S. minister to Spain and was sent to Madrid in 1826. There he wrote several books, including a biography of Christopher Columbus. He later served as a diplomat in England, and again in Spain. He returned to America in 1846 and retired to Sunnyside, his country home in Tarrytown, New York.

ISABELLA AND FERDINAND Spain became a strong nation under the rule of Queen Isabella (1451–1504) and King Ferdinand (1452–1516). In the early 1400s, Spain was a group of kingdoms. In 1469, at

▲*Isabella and Ferdinand receive Christopher Columbus after his first voyage to America.*

the age of 17, Ferdinand of the kingdom of Aragon married Isabella of Castile. She was just 18. Their marriage combined the two largest kingdoms in Spain. Isabella was a strong queen. She wanted to drive the Moors out of Spain. The Moors were Arabs who had come over to Spain from Africa. The Moors were forced to give up their last stronghold in the south, Granada, in 1492. In that same year, Isabella and Ferdinand gave Christopher Columbus the money he needed to make his first voyage in search of a westward route to India.

Isabella and Ferdinand wanted all of Spain to be Roman Catholic. They supported the Inquisition—special courts that tried anyone suspected of not believing the teachings of the Roman Catholic Church.

Ferdinand was a good soldier and good at negotiating with other leaders. He brought all of the land south of the Pyrenees mountains, except Portugal, under control of Spain. He also conquered Corsica, the island of Sardinia, and Naples, Italy.

ALSO READ: COLUMBUS, CHRISTOPHER; SPAIN; SPANISH HISTORY.

ISLAM   Islam is one of the world's great religions. Its greatest prophet (proclaimer) was an Arabian named Muhammad, who lived from about 570 to 632 A.D. The people who believe in Islam are called *Muslims*, or *Moslems*. Today, there are 700 million Muslims throughout the world. Most of them live in the Middle East, in Africa, and in Asia.

Islam in Arabic means "peace, purity, and obedience to God." According to Muslim belief, Muhammad saw the angel Gabriel in a vision. Gabriel told Muhammad that he was to be God's messenger to teach the words of God to the world. Those words became the holy writings of Islam, the book called the *Koran*.

Muhammad lived in Mecca, a great Arabian trading city. At that time, the Arab tribes worshiped many gods. Muhammad preached that there was only one God. He urged the people to give up their wicked ways and live virtuous lives. The people of Mecca did not wish to change their ways and persecuted Muhammad. The prophet fled to another city, Medina, in 622 A.D. His flight, called the *hegira,* is holy to Islam. Muslims date their calendar from this year. In Medina, Muhammad became a powerful leader. Before his death, the people living in Mecca became Muslims, too.

After Muhammad died, belief in Islam continued to spread. Its Arab followers *(Moors)* carved out an empire. They conquered Persia, Syria, and Egypt, and invaded Spain and France. However, internal struggles for power and European opposition helped to break up the Muslim empire after the 1200s.

Muslims believe that "There is no god but Allah (God), and Muhammad is the prophet of Allah." They believe in the same God Christians and Jews believe in, and in the religious teachers of the Old Testament, such as Abraham, Isaac, and Jacob. Muslims think of Jesus Christ as a

▼*Muslims kneel in the direction of Mecca when they pray to God. The faithful pray several times each day.*

great teacher, and believe that there will be a Judgment Day when the good will go to heaven and the wicked to hell.

Muslims pray five times each day, always facing toward Mecca. A *muezzin*, or crier, calls the people to pray in the *mosque*, or temple. An *imam*, or chief religious official, leads the people in prayer. Every able man must give *alms* (money) to the poor. During the holy month of *Ramadan*, adult Muslims must *fast* (go without food or drink) between sunrise and sunset. Once during his lifetime, every Muslim is supposed to make a *hadj*, or visit, to the holy city of Mecca. Muslims are not supposed to drink liquor, eat pork, or gamble.

ALSO READ: BLACK MUSLIMS, KORAN, MOSQUE, MUHAMMAD.

ISLAND An island is a body of land entirely surrounded by water. In a way, even the continents are islands because they are surrounded by oceans. Australia is often called the "island-continent." But all the continents are very large, and the word "island" is most often used to mean a smaller body of land. You can find islands in the oceans, in rivers, and in lakes.

In the ocean, islands may be part of a continental shelf. These islands formed at the end of the last ice age,

▲*San Giorgo Maggiore, one of the islands on which Venice is built. This city of islands lies close to the mainland of Italy.*

▼*An isthmus connecting two parts of an island. This narrow strip of land was probably formed by deposits of sediment in the ocean.*

when the level of the ocean rose and covered low-lying areas at the edges of the continents. Newfoundland, off Canada's east coast, was formed this way. So were the British Isles. Ocean islands far from continents are often the tops of underwater volcanoes. Each time the volcano erupts, lava piles up higher and higher, until the cone of the volcano finally reaches above the surface of the ocean. The Hawaiian Islands are volcanic islands. Other oceanic is-

▼*A cluster of small Japanese islands close to the mainland. The coastline probably subsided, leaving mountain peaks as islands.*

▼*The Guttenberg islands in Iowa were formed by collections of sediment that piled up on the bottom of the Mississippi River.*

The ten largest islands in the world are:

GREENLAND (North Atlantic)
839,999 square miles

NEW GUINEA (South Pacific)
345,054 square miles

BORNEO (Pacific)
289,859 square miles

MADAGASCAR (Indian)
241,094 square miles

BAFFIN (North Atlantic)
183,810 square miles

SUMATRA (Indian)
164,148 square miles

GREAT BRITAIN (North Atlantic)
88,745 square miles

HONSHU (North Pacific)
87,426 square miles

ELLESMERE (Arctic)
82,119 square miles

VICTORIA (Arctic)
81,930 square miles

lands formed when earthquakes pushed up pieces of the Earth's crust. Many small islands are simply large circular coral reefs called *atolls*.

Islands in rivers are sandbars or areas of hard rock that have resisted the action of the water that cut the river bed.

Islands in lakes are usually higher parts of the lake bed sticking above the surface of the water.

ALSO READ: CONTINENT, CORAL, GREAT BARRIER REEF, MOUNTAIN, VOLCANO.

ISOTOPE see ATOM.

ISRAEL In the brief period of time that the modern-day state of Israel has been in existence, the Israeli people have managed to change a barren, non-productive land into one of the most modern and industrialized nations in the world. Since gaining independence in 1948, Israel has made remarkable progress in making the rocky Negev Desert "bloom."

Israel is located in part of the area that was once Palestine. Ancient Israel was the traditional homeland of the Jewish people. It is also the birthplace of Christianity—the land where Jesus Christ lived. Jerusalem, the capital, is a holy city for the Muslims, as well as for Jews and Christians. Tel Aviv, the largest city, is the diplomatic capital. (See the map with the article on the MIDDLE EAST.)

▼*Most of the Arabs who have remained in Israel get along peacefully with their Jewish neighbors.*

Israel is a narrow country, somewhat larger than the state of New Jersey. The land in the north and east is hilly, but it is flat along the coast of the Mediterranean Sea. The Negev Desert, in the southern part of the country, occupies more than half of the total land area. The Jordan River Valley lies in the eastern part of the country. The lowest point of land in the world, the Dead Sea, is located there.

Israel has a warm climate throughout the year. Most of the rain falls in the winter. The northern part of the country receives more rain than the southern desert.

Israel is primarily an agricultural nation. The principal crops include citrus fruits, olives, barley, wheat, tomatoes, potatoes, figs, and corn. One type of farming community frequently found in Israel is the *kibbutz*. People live and work together on a *kibbutz*, sharing the farm equipment and the money earned from the produce.

Large factories are located in Haifa and Tel Aviv. The principal industrial products are glass, bricks, ceramics, tiles, tires, metal goods, pharmaceuticals, agricultural products, and textiles.

In the 1800s, mass killings of Jews in Russia and other parts of Eastern Europe caused thousands of Jews to emigrate to Palestine. Great Britain received control of Palestine from the League of Nations after World

ISRAEL

Capital Cities: Tel Aviv (838,000 people) and Jerusalem (275,000).
Area: 7,978 square miles.
Population: 2,822,000 people.
Languages: Hebrew and Arabic.
Export Products: Diamonds, textiles, processed foods, and citrus fruits.
Unit of Money: Israeli Pound.

War I (1918). The British and the League promised to make Palestine a "national homeland" for Jews. The Arabs living in Palestine and the surrounding countries were violently against having a Jewish nation there.

Nazi persecution in the 1930s forced thousands of Jews to flee from Germany and other European countries. Many settled in Palestine. Thousands more arrived after World War II. The Palestinian Arabs began to attack the Jewish settlements. In order to stop the fighting, the British announced that only a small number of Jews could enter the country. This satisfied the Arabs, but the number of Jewish immigrants kept growing. Thousands of refugees waited on ships in the harbor at Haifa, hoping to be admitted.

The British government submitted the problem to the United Nations in 1947. The UN voted to divide Palestine into two separate states—one Arab and one Jewish. The British left Palestine in 1948, and the Jewish state of Israel was established. Many Palestinian Arabs left Israel to live in refugee camps. The fate of these 200,000 people has never been settled.

Israel is a parliamentary democracy. The elected legislative body, the Knesset, elects the president and the prime minister. The nation has no written constitution, and authority lies with the legislature.

The tiny nation has had to defend its borders from its Arab neighbors since its birth. Border clashes, acts of sabotage, and a constant atmosphere of hostility have been the general state of affairs between Israel and the Arab states since 1945. There have been bitter disputes over the land, the water supply, and the use of the Suez Canal.

On June 5, 1967, Israel attacked threatening Arab forces. The fighting lasted only six days. Israel captured territory from Syria, Jordan, and Egypt. Israel and the Arabs

▲ *A modern, tree-lined boulevard in Tel Aviv, Israel's diplomatic capital.*

have not yet made a peace treaty. The Israelis continue to occupy the land taken from the Arabs.

ALSO READ: BEN-GURION, DAVID; DEAD SEA; EGYPT; ISLAM; JERUSALEM; JEWISH HISTORY; JORDAN; JUDAISM; MIDDLE EAST; PALESTINE; SYRIA; UNITED NATIONS.

ITALIAN see ROMANCE LANGUAGES.

ITALIAN HISTORY The Italian peninsula in Europe has a history of almost ceaseless warfare within its shores and countless invasions from abroad. For most of its history, Italy was not united as one nation.

About 1,000 years before the birth of Jesus Christ, many different tribes lived in the Italian peninsula. The most powerful people were the Etruscans. Their homeland was a region in central Italy. They conquered lands to the north and south, but were never able to take over the whole peninsula.

The Italian city of Rome succeeded where the Etruscans had failed. The Roman people not only conquered the whole of Italy, but by 27 B.C., they had also created a huge empire in Europe and the Middle East. The Roman Empire prospered for about 500 years. But in the 300s A.D., German tribes from the north began to invade the western part of the empire. The last

▼ *This group of statues show Marcus Aurelius, a Roman emperor, talking with his soldiers.*

Roman emperor of the west, Romulus Augustulus, was defeated by a German barbarian, Odoacer, in 476 A.D. From that date until the mid-1800s, Italy was for the most part divided into a group of small states. These states fought continually among themselves. They found it difficult to combine, even against a foreign invader. Italy was overrun again and again by more powerful peoples from other parts of Europe.

Ever since the Roman Catholic Church was founded, Rome had been the headquarters of its leader, the pope. In 572, Italy was invaded by a fierce German tribe, the Lombards, who conquered many regions and threatened to attack Rome. The pope appealed for help to the most powerful ruler in Europe, the King of the Franks. Later, the Frankish king, Charlemagne, finally drove the Lombards out of Italy. He was crowned Emperor of the Romans in 800 by Pope Leo III. The Franks gave the pope a large area of land in central Italy. This area became known as the Papal States. The popes soon became strong enough to resist attempts by invaders to take over the Papal States.

After the death of Charlemagne, the Franks and the Germans struggled for control of Italy. In 962, northern Italy was captured by a powerful German king, Otto the Great. Otto was crowned Holy Roman Emperor by the pope. For the next 500 years, Italy was dominated by the Holy Roman emperors and the popes. By this time, many Italian cities had become important trading centers. They grew wealthy and powerful, and some became self-governing states. Among the greatest of these city-states were Florence, Genoa, Milan, Pisa, and Venice. Genoa and Venice were ruled by powerful magistrates, called *doges,* who were similar to today's mayors. Wealthy merchants in the cities encouraged the work of artists and scholars. The Italian cities became the birthplace of the great movement of new ideas known as the Renaissance.

Italy was invaded by France in 1494. Shortly afterward, the Holy Roman Empire was split between Spain and Austria. For the next 400 years, Italy became the battleground for struggles among these three powers. At one point, northern Italy was united as the Kingdom of Italy by the French emperor Napoleon I. But after Napoleon was defeated at the Battle of Waterloo in 1815, Italy was once again divided among several rulers.

By the mid-1800s, the Italian people began to speak of fighting for a free and united Italy. Several revolutions were organized against the Austrians, who ruled Italy at that time. By 1860, Count Cavour, the prime minister of the Kingdom of Sardinia, had united most of northern Italy against Austria. The same year, the Italian patriot, Giuseppe Garibaldi, led his army of "red

▶*Giuseppe Garibaldi, the man who was most responsible for uniting Italy* (far right).

▶*The Lion of Saint Mark, emblem of the Republic of Venice, which was one of the richest and most powerful of the Italian city-states.*

shirts" to victory in southern Italy. By 1870, the whole peninsula had been united as the Kingdom of Italy. The first king was Victor Emmanuel II of Sardinia.

The long years of war had left the Italian people poor and hungry. The people became dissatisfied with the new government when it did very little to help them. Italy's rulers were more interested in gaining power and influence abroad. During World War I (1914–1918), Italy fought with Great Britain and France against Austria-Hungary and Germany. The Italian people became even poorer, and when a new leader, Benito Mussolini, promised to bring back the wealth and glory of the Roman Empire, many people supported him. Mussolini became premier of Italy in 1922. He organized a fascist government with himself as dictator. In 1936, he signed a treaty with the German dictator, Adolf Hitler. Italy and Germany were defeated by Great Britain and her allies in World War II (1939–1945), and Mussolini was killed.

In 1946, free elections were held in Italy. The people voted to end the monarchy, and Italy became a republic. The government began programs to improve the lives of the Italian people. Northern Italy is now one of the most prosperous regions of Europe. But the Italian people are still split by fierce strug-

gles between different political parties. The Communist party in Italy has become one of the largest Communist parties outside of the Soviet Union and China.

ALSO READ: CHARLEMAGNE; DANTE ALIGHIERI; DICTATOR; ETRUSCAN; FASCISM; HOLY ROMAN EMPIRE; MUSSOLINI, BENITO; NAPOLEON BONAPARTE; POPE; RENAISSANCE; ROMAN EMPIRE; ROME; VENICE; WORLD WAR I; WORLD WAR II.

ITALY Visitors love Italy for its scenic landscapes, ancient ruins, beautiful architecture, and great art museums. Tourism has become an important industry in this sunny, mild country. The Italian peninsula is shaped like a boot and reaches far into the Mediterranean Sea. The snow-capped Alps Mountains rise along its northern border, which is shared with France, Switzerland, and Austria.

A chain of mountains, the Apennines, runs down the center of Italy. The mountains often rise from the very edge of the sea. Many of Italy's coastal towns are crowded into narrow spaces between cliffs and the sea. Italy's major valley lies just south of the Alps, where the Po River cuts through the land. The Mediterranean islands of Sicily, Sardinia, Elba, Capri, and Ischia are also part of Italy.

Rome is the capital of Italy. It also is the world capital of the Ro-

▲*King Victor Emmanuel III* (left) *riding with Benito Mussolini* (center), *the man whom the king allowed to become dictator of Italy.*

▼*Many Italians live in old buildings made of stone and covered with stucco, a cement-like material.*

ITALY

Capital City: Rome (2,656,000 people).
Area: 116,286 square miles.
Population: 53,170,000 people.
Language: Italian.
Export Products: Citrus fruits and other foods, textiles, and automobiles.
Unit of Money: Lira.

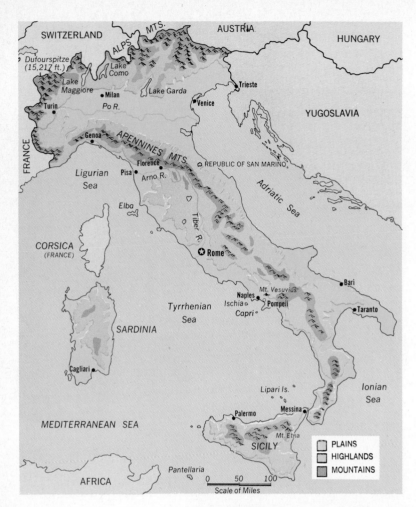

man Catholic Church. The pope rules Vatican City, a tiny independent church state located in the heart of Rome.

Before World War II, most Italians were farmers. After the war, many factories were built and Italy became an important industrial nation and a member of the European Common Market. The most important farming and industrial area is the Po Valley. Textiles, chemicals, machinery, and automobiles are produced in factories in the valley's cities. Cattle graze in lush pastures, and orchards produce peaches and apples. In parts of western and southern Italy, farmers grow oranges, lemons, and olives. Grapes for wine are cultivated throughout the country. After France, Italy is the biggest wine-producing country in the world.

In southern Italy, the soil is poor and farming is difficult. Most rivers dry out during the hot summers. Farmers work very hard to earn a living. They often plant their crops on steep hillsides where the soil is held in place by stone walls. Most Italian farm families live in small towns. They go out to work in the fields in the mornings and return home at night.

Before 1870, Italians were not ruled by one national government. The region was a patchwork of small kingdoms, independent territories, and Papal States (areas governed by the pope, or Roman Cath-

▶No matter where you are in Italy, you are never far away from the sea. This small fishing village is located on the western coast near the city of La Spezia.

olic Church). When the country was finally united it was ruled by a king. Benito Mussolini, a fascist dictator, became his country's leader in 1922, although the king still reigned. Italy became a republic after World War II. A president, prime minister, cabinet, and parliament form the government today. Italy has had more than 30 prime ministers since the second world war.

ALSO READ: ADRIATIC SEA; ALPS MOUNTAINS; COMMON MARKET; FASCISM; FLORENCE; HOLY ROMAN EMPIRE; ITALIAN HISTORY; MEDITERRANEAN SEA; MUSSOLINI, BENITO; ROMAN EMPIRE; ROMANCE LANGUAGES; ROME; VATICAN CITY; WORLD WAR I; WORLD WAR II.

IVORY COAST When European explorers first visited West Africa, they set up trading posts for ivory in a particularly fertile region of the coast. This region became known as the Ivory Coast. Today the country located there is an independent republic, about the size of the state of New Mexico. It is on the southern coast of the West African bulge, on the Gulf of Guinea. The Mali Republic and Upper Volta lie to the north. Guinea and Liberia are its western neighbors, and Ghana lies to the east. (See the map with the article on AFRICA.)

In the Ivory Coast, thick rain forests spread inland from the coastal capital, Abidjan. Further north, grassy plains rise to an area of rolling hills and mountains. The climate is hot and humid in the coastal region and cooler in the north.

The people of the Ivory Coast are called Ivorians. The official language is French, but most people speak one of the local African languages. About two-thirds of the people follow African tribal religions. A smaller number are Muslims or Christians.

The Ivory Coast has long been one of the most prosperous West African nations. Numerous crops thrive on the fertile soil. Bananas, coffee, cocoa, oil palm, rice, cotton, and coconuts are raised. Timber is also an important source of wealth. The ground holds important mineral resources, including diamonds, manganese, bauxite, and copper. Rich fisheries exist along the coast. Although most people earn their living by working in agriculture, others work in food processing plants and textile mills.

The first Europeans to visit the region of the Ivory Coast were Portuguese explorers in the 1400s. French missionaries and traders arrived in the 1600s. The French claimed the region as a colony of France in 1893. The Ivory Coast gained its independence in 1960. It is governed by a president and his cabinet of ministers. A national assembly is elected by the people.

ALSO READ: AFRICA.

▲*Old-fashioned ways are still common in many parts of the Ivory Coast. This woman is working with grain to make flour.*

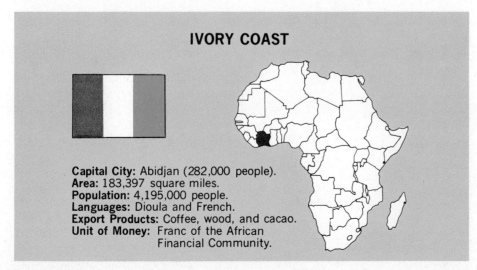

IVORY COAST

Capital City: Abidjan (282,000 people).
Area: 183,397 square miles.
Population: 4,195,000 people.
Languages: Dioula and French.
Export Products: Coffee, wood, and cacao.
Unit of Money: Franc of the African
　　　　　　　　　Financial Community.

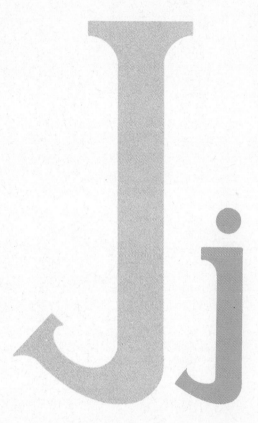

JACKS This game is played with a small rubber ball and ten small metal objects, called *jacks*. (You can buy these at many stores.) Two or more people can play. Sit on the floor and toss the jacks out in front of you. Begin by throwing the ball up in the air, but don't throw it too high. While the ball is in the air, pick up one jack very quickly with the hand you used to toss the ball. Catch the ball with the same hand. Don't let the ball bounce more than once before you catch it. When you have caught the ball, set the first jack to one side. Continue tossing the ball and picking up jacks one at a time until you have picked up all ten. If you miss catching the ball or picking up a jack, you lose your turn to the next player. If you get all ten jacks picked up without missing, your turn continues.

You now throw the jacks out in front of you and begin picking them up *two* at a time. If you make any of these mistakes, you lose your turn: (1) let the ball bounce more than once; (2) miss picking up a jack; (3) pick up the wrong number of jacks. When your turn comes again, you must continue picking up the number of jacks that you were trying for when you made your last mistake. You cannot start picking up the jacks three at a time until you have picked up all the jacks two at a time perfectly. The winner is the first to pick up all ten at once.

When you have picked up all ten at once, you can begin some more difficult ways of playing. To play "Pigs," cup your hand over the floor and shoot the jacks across the floor into the "cup" before catching the ball. Shoot one in at a time to begin, then two at a time, and so on. "Cherries in a Basket" is played by picking up a jack with one hand and putting it in the other hand while the ball bounces once. In "Knocks" the player must knock on the floor once, pick up the jack, and catch the ball. "Double Bounce" is played, as the name tells you, by letting the ball bounce twice before you catch it. "Around the World" is difficult. Throw the ball in the air, pick up a jack, and circle the ball with your hand before you catch it!

Probably every one of your friends will have a different way to play jacks. Why not try to make up a few ways of your own?

JACKSON, ANDREW (1767–1845) Jackson's admirers called him "The People's President." The six men who were Presidents before him had been well-to-do educated men from Virginia and Massachusetts. Jackson, however, came from a poor South Carolina frontier family. He was born a few days after his father died. Young Andy had little schooling, but he had a lot of courage. He was 13 when British soldiers invaded the Carolinas during the American Revolution. He joined the American volunteers. Andy and his brother Robert were captured by the British. A British officer ordered Andy to clean his boots. The boy refused. The officer cut Andy's head and hand with a sword. Robert also refused and was wounded. The two boys were marched 40 miles to a prison. In prison they both caught smallpox. Andy got better, but Robert died. Their mother later died of a fever she caught while caring for wounded American soliders. Andy's only other brother had been killed earlier in the war. At the age of 14, he was left without a family.

He stayed with relatives and tried various jobs, including saddle-making and teaching school. He finally turned to studying law and became a lawyer at the age of 20. He was appointed attorney general for the area which was soon to become Tennessee, and he moved to Nashville. There, he met and married Rachel Robards. At the time of the marriage, Mrs. Robards thought that her previous husband had divorced

SEVENTH PRESIDENT   MARCH 4, 1829—MARCH 3, 1837

ANDREW JACKSON

Born: March 15, 1767, Waxhaw, South Carolina
Parents: Andrew and Elizabeth Hutchinson Jackson
Education: Mostly self-educated
Religion: Presbyterian
Occupation: Lawyer and army officer
Political Party: Democractic (formerly the Democratic-Republican Party)
State Represented: Tennessee
Married: 1791 to Rachel Donelson Robards Jackson (1767–1828)
Children: 1 adopted son
Died: June 8, 1845, The Hermitage, Nashville, Tennessee
Buried: The Hermitage, Nashville, Tenn.

▲*Andrew Jackson's inauguration as President was celebrated with a White House party in which a gigantic cheese was offered to the guests.*

her. But the divorce did not go through until she had been married to Jackson for two years. The two were remarried. But Jackson's enemies often criticized his wife. Mrs. Jackson was hurt by the attacks, and avoided public life. After his marriage, Jackson became a landowner and one of the leading citizens of the new state of Tennessee. He served briefly in the U.S. House of Representatives and the Senate, but returned home to Tennessee in 1798 to become a judge.

Jackson became a military hero during the War of 1812 against the British. His soldiers called him "Old Hickory" because he was so tough. He led the Americans to the greatest victory of the war at the Battle of New Orleans. The battle was fought after the peace treaty had been signed, but word of this had not yet reached New Orleans.

In 1818, Jackson led a raid on the Seminole Indians in Florida, which was still owned by Spain. He became the first governor of Florida after Spain sold it to the United States in 1821, but he resigned after a few months.

Jackson ran for President in 1824. He received more electoral votes than the other candidates, but he did not have the necessary majority.

The election was decided by the U.S. House of Representatives, according to the election rules of the Constitution. They decided that John Quincy Adams should be President. Jackson ran again in 1828. This time he won the necessary majority and was elected President. After the inauguration, Jackson invited the crowd into the White House. In their haste to shake hands with their hero, the people overturned chairs and tables, broke dishes, and tore curtains. Jackson escaped through a window.

Jackson gave many government jobs to his political associates. This was called the "spoils system." Under this system, the winner in an election gives jobs to his friends. He can fire the people who previously held these jobs in order to do this.

In 1832, Congress passed a bill to renew the charter of the Bank of the United States. This bank, in which government funds were deposited, was controlled by private individuals. The bank was accused of favoring rich people. Jackson vetoed (refused to sign) the bill. He said he was opposed "to the advancement of the few at the expense of the many." He was re-elected President that year.

Jackson also took a firm stand when the South Carolina legislature voted to *nullify* (set aside) an import tax law that Congress had passed. The President threatened to use force if necessary to make sure the law was obeyed. He believed that the Union would be in danger if one state was permitted to nullify a law passed by the Federal Government. He said in his last address as President, "By every sacrifice, this Union must be preserved."

After his Presidency, Jackson returned to Tennessee. He lived at The Hermitage—a handsome house he had built near Nashville.

ALSO READ: ADAMS, JOHN QUINCY; CALHOUN, JOHN C.; CLAY, HENRY; SOUTH CAROLINA; WAR OF 1812.

JACKSON, MAHALIA (1911-1972)

This gospel singer brought her music to churches and concert halls across America and other lands. Mahalia Jackson, granddaughter of slaves, was born in New Orleans, Louisiana. As a child, she sang in the choir of the Baptist Church in her home town. She also enjoyed the rhythmic songs that she heard at a nearby Holiness Church and the music of street singers. Young Mahalia soon developed her own style of gospel singing.

Mahalia went to Chicago at the age of 15 and began to sing with a group there a few years later. She then went on to sing alone, reaching wider and wider audiences. She sang on radio and television and made many recordings. Her powerful contralto voice and the strong religious feeling she brought to her songs won her many admirers throughout the nation. She sang *Negro spirituals*—religious folksongs handed down from generation to generation—as well as *gospel songs* —religious songs written by composers. In 1963, Mahalia Jackson sang for the people who marched in Washington, D.C., to demand equal rights for America's black citizens. She also sang at the funeral of the great civil rights leader, Martin Luther King, in 1968.

JACKSON, THOMAS JONATHAN ("STONEWALL") (1824-1863)

Stonewall Jackson was one of the best Confederate Army generals during the Civil War. He was born on January 21, 1824, in Clarksburg, Virginia (now West Virginia). He graduated from the U.S. Military Academy and taught at Virginia Military Institute for ten years.

When the Civil War began, he joined the Confederate Army. He fought in the first Battle of Bull Run at Manassas, Virginia, in July, 1861. A Confederate officer said that Jackson and his men stood "like a stone wall" against the Union Army. The

South won the battle, and Jackson won the name of Stonewall.

Serving under General Robert E. Lee, Jackson and his troops were victorious in the Shenandoah Valley, at Fredericksburg, and at the second Battle of Bull Run. Jackson became famous for the speed with which his men could march from place to place. He was respected by his men and his fellow officers.

In May, 1863, Jackson's men helped defeat a northern army at Chancellorsville, Virginia. But as Jackson returned from the front lines on horseback at twilight, southern troops thought he was an enemy officer and shot him. His last words were, "Let us cross the river and rest in the shade."

ALSO READ: CIVIL WAR.

JAGUAR see CAT, WILD.

JAI ALAI The fast and dangerous game of *jai alai* is a spectator sport. That means it is a game which many people watch a few others play. Jai alai began in Spain.

The game is similar to handball, except that the players use basket-like *cestas*. The cesta is made of a wooden frame and light, tough reeds, woven together to form a curved scoop. The cesta, attached to the player's forearm, permits the player to catch the ball and throw it against the wall at high speed.

The jai alai ball, called a *pelota*, is slightly smaller than a baseball. In a jai alai game, the ball sometimes reaches a speed of 150 miles an hour. The ball is made of a special, very hard rubber, and is covered with goatskin.

Jai alai is popular in Miami, Florida. It is also played in Cuba, France, Italy, Mexico, Spain, and the Philippine Islands. The game is played on an indoor court, called a *fronton*. The spectators enjoy the fast action of jai alai matches.

Jai alai players are trained in special schools in the Basque section of northern Spain. There, young boys

▲*Mahalia Jackson, American gospel singer.*

▼*Stonewall Jackson, Confederate general.*

▼*A jai alai player jumping to scoop the ball with his basket-like cesta.*

▲*James VI of Scotland became James I of England.*

▼*James II of England.*

▼*A ceremony at Jamestown aboard a replica of one of the ships that carried the first colonists to America.*

learn the game when they are between eight and thirteen years old. The best ones become professionals and play jai alai all over the world.

ALSO READ: HANDBALL.

JAMAICA see WEST INDIES.

JAMES, JESSE see OUTLAW.

JAMES, KINGS OF ENGLAND

James was the name of two kings of England.

James I (1566–1625) was the son of Mary, Queen of Scots, and a cousin of Queen Elizabeth I of England. When he was one year old, his mother was forced to give up the throne of Scotland, and he became King James VI of Scotland. When Queen Elizabeth died without any children in 1603, James VI was also crowned King James I of England. In this way, England and Scotland were joined under one ruler.

James believed that God, and not the people, gave the kings the right to rule. This belief, known as the "divine right of kings," made him very unpopular with the English people. While James I was king, the first permanent English settlement in America, Jamestown, was founded (1607) and named after him. James I is also remembered for the poetic English translation of the Bible, the King James Version.

James II (1633–1701) was the grandson of James I. His father, King Charles I, was beheaded after being defeated in the English Civil War. When James became king, he organized the British expedition that seized the Dutch colony of New Amsterdam, in America. In his honor, the colony was renamed New York, because he had been the Duke of York and Albany before becoming king. Fort Orange, on the Hudson River, became Fort Albany.

James II became king of England and Scotland in 1685, after the death of his older brother, Charles II. James II believed in the divine right of kings, just as his grandfather and father had. James was a devout Roman Catholic, and most of the English people were Protestants. James tried to force them to become Catholic like himself. He persecuted and imprisoned those who refused. The English Protestants finally asked William, Prince of Orange, to lead a rebellion against the king. William was a Dutch prince who had married James's daughter, Mary. William landed in England with an army in November, 1688. James II fled to France without fighting. William and Mary were then crowned king and queen of England.

ALSO READ: CHARLES, KINGS OF ENGLAND; MARY, QUEEN OF SCOTS; WILLIAM AND MARY.

JAMESTOWN Would you have wanted to be one of the first American colonists? You would have sailed on the *Discovery*, the *Susan Constant*, or the *Godspeed* across the Atlantic Ocean in 1606. The passengers aboard these ships had been ordered to set up a colony in the part of the New World called Virginia. In 1607, these ships sailed up the James River, named in honor of the English king, James I. The colonists came ashore on a wooded peninsula. They built a fort to protect themselves from Indian attacks. The new community was called "King James His Towne." This name was later shortened to Jamestown.

The area chosen for the new colony was low and damp. Many of the colonists became ill. All would have starved, but their leader, Captain John Smith, got the neighboring Indians to sell them food. He also made the colonists work to grow some of the needed food. The winter of 1609–10 was called the "starving time." Many of the colonists died from hunger and disease.

Lord De La Warr, the new governor, arrived after that disastrous winter ended. He encouraged the remaining colonists to stay, and the town began to prosper. The colonists began raising tobacco, a plant they learned about from the Indians. This crop became the community's most important product.

Jamestown was the capital of the new colony of Virginia, until the capital was moved to Williamsburg in 1699.

Today, part of Jamestown lies within the Colonial National Historical Park. Exact copies of the fort and other early buildings have been built. Visitors can tour the buildings and watch people performing crafts and chores the way the early colonists did them. Anchored off shore are models of the ships that brought the colonists to the New World.

ALSO READ: POCAHONTAS; POWHATAN; SMITH, CAPTAIN JOHN; VIRGINIA.

JAMS AND JELLIES Foods stay fresh for a short time. Then bacteria, yeasts, and molds from the air cause them to spoil. The more water and the less sugar a food contains, the more quickly it spoils. Many fruits contain 75 per cent water and 10 to 15 per cent sugar. They can be preserved (kept from spoiling) by reducing the water in them and adding sugar. Preserved fruits, made into jams and jellies, are among children's favorite foods. Many people like to make them at home. But most jams and jellies in the United States are now made in factories.

Jelly is made by boiling fruit and water together until the fruit is soft. A special jelly bag, or a cheesecloth bag, is then placed over a bowl. The mixture is poured or pressed through the bag into the bowl below. The juice within the bag can be pressed out or hung above the bowl so that the juice can drip into it. The collected juice is measured, and a certain amount is put into a pot on the stove. Sugar is added. *Pectin*, a natural fruit substance, may also be added. It thickens the mixture. Some fruits, such as apples, currants, grapes, and blackberries, contain large amounts of pectin. They may not need additional pectin when made into jelly.

The mixture is boiled and stirred until the sugar dissolves. The pot is then removed from the stove, and the mixture is skimmed to remove the white foam that has collected on top. The jelly is poured into clean jars. Each jar is sealed with a special cap, or one-eighth of an inch of wax is poured over the jelly. The lid is put on after the wax hardens.

Jam is made from whole or crushed fruit. The fruit and sugar are placed in a pot on top of the stove. The mixture is boiled, stirred, and skimmed.

You can make strawberry jam with the help of an adult. Crush two quarts of ripe washed berries. Measure four cups of berries into a large pot. Add one-half cup of lemon juice for a sharper taste. Stir in seven cups

▲*Jars of jelly being capped in a factory.*

▼ *Some of the steps in making apple jelly at home. Add water to the cut-up fruit* (left), *and bring it to a boil on high heat* (center). *Finally, at the end of the process, the cook pours the jelly into sparkling clean jars* (right).

of granulated sugar, and bring the mixture to a full boil. When it has boiled hard for one minute, remove the pot from the heat. Stir for five minutes. Skim the white foam off the top. Pour the jam into clean glasses and cover it with melted wax.

ALSO READ: FOOD.

JANE see GREY, LADY JANE.

DATES OF SPECIAL EVENTS IN JANUARY

1 ● New Year's Day.
  ● Paul Revere was born (1735).
  ● First federal income tax (1862).
  ● Abraham Lincoln issued the Emancipation Proclamation, freeing the slaves in the Confederate states (1863).
  ● The Commonwealth of Australia was formed (1901).
  ● Fidel Castro became leader of Cuba (1959).
6 ● Joan of Arc was born (1412).
7 ● First United States Presidential election was held (1789).
  ● Transatlantic telephone service between London and New York began (1927).
8 ● The Eleventh Amendment to the U.S. Constitution was adopted, restricting powers of U.S. Supreme Court (1798).
  ● U.S. troops under Andrew Jackson defeated the British at the Battle of New Orleans (1815).
9 ● President Richard M. Nixon was born (1913).
10 ● First subway system in the world opened in London (1863).
  ● The first great oil strike occurred in Texas (1901).
  ● The League of Nations was established (1920).
  ● First United Nations General Assembly meeting, in London (1946).
11 ● Alexander Hamilton, American statesman, was born (1755).
  ● Sir John A. Macdonald, first prime minister of Canada after confederation, was born (1815).
12 ● John Hancock, first signer of the Declaration of Independence, was born (1737).
  ● Albert Schweitzer, jungle missionary and philosopher, was born (1875).
17 ● Wassailing the apple tree, an old custom, takes place every year in Carhampton, England. Villagers gather round the largest tree and sing, "Old apple tree, old apple tree, we've come to wassail thee." The custom was originally carried out in the hope of a good apple crop.
  ● Benjamin Franklin, American statesman, was born (1706).
18 ● Daniel Webster, American statesman, was born (1782).
19 ● Robert E. Lee, Commander in Chief of the Confederate Armies, was born (1807).
  ● Edgar Allan Poe, American author, was born (1809).
20 ● Inauguration Day for U.S. Presidents (every four years). Established 1937.
21 ● *Nautilus*, first atomic submarine, was launched (1954).
22 ● Lord Byron, English poet, was born (1788).
24 ● Gold was first discovered in California (1848).
25 ● Robert Burns, Scottish poet, was born (1759).
  ● Martin Luther King, Jr., American civil rights leader, was born (1929).
  ● Transcontinental telephone service began in U.S. (1915).
27 ● Lewis Carroll, author of *Alice in Wonderland*, was born (1832).
  ● United States Coast Guard was established (1915).
29 ● First successful gasoline-powered car was patented by Carl Friedrich Benz (1886).
  ● American League in professional baseball was formed (1900).
30 ● President Franklin D. Roosevelt was born (1882).
  ● Adolf Hitler was named chancellor (head) of Germany (1933).
  ● Mahatma Gandhi, Indian political leader, was assassinated (1948).

JANUARY January is named for the Roman god Janus. He was a god with two faces—one face looking forward, and one looking backward. He was the god of doors and gates, and also the god of beginnings.

January did not always begin the year. In ancient Rome it was probably the eleventh month. Julius Caesar ordered the calendar to be changed. As a result of those changes, January became the first month of the year. The month was then named after Janus.

January's special flower is the carnation, and the garnet is its birthstone. January occurs in winter in the Northern Hemisphere (north of the equator), but in the Southern Hemisphere, January is a summer month. The first day of January is New Year's Day, and on that day many people make New Year's resolutions. January sixth, 12 days after Christmas, is the feast of Epiphany, the day the Three Wise Men came to visit the infant Jesus. It is the last day of the Christmas season. The evening before Epiphany is called Twelfth Night. Twelfth Night, rather than Christmas, is the time for gift-giving in Mexico and some other countries. An old legend warns that if you do not take down your Christmas decorations by Twelfth Night, elves will get in and mess up your house.

ALSO READ; CALENDAR, MONTH.

JAPAN Japan, the "land of the rising sun," has a land area smaller than the state of California, but it is the third-ranking industrial power of the world. This Asian nation is made up of four large islands—Hokkaido, Honshu, Shikoku, and Kyushu—plus more than 3,000 smaller islands. Tokyo, the capital, is located on the largest of the islands, Honshu.

Land and Climate

Japan is covered with mountains. Many of them have volcanoes. The

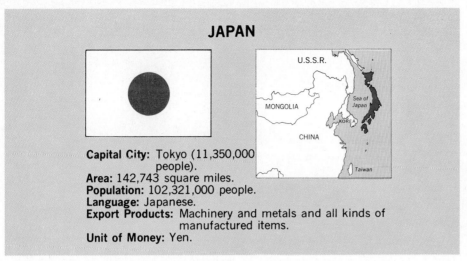

JAPAN

Capital City: Tokyo (11,350,000 people).
Area: 142,743 square miles.
Population: 102,321,000 people.
Language: Japanese.
Export Products: Machinery and metals and all kinds of manufactured items.
Unit of Money: Yen.

▲ *An actor of the kabuki theater, a popular Japanese entertainment. Costumed performers take part in both tragedies and comedies which include elaborate singing and dancing.*

most famous mountain, Fujiyama (Mt. Fuji), is topped by snow most the year. The country also has many lakes, waterfalls, and rivers.

The climate of Japan varies greatly from one end of the island chain to the other. Kyushu, the southernmost island, has a subtropical climate like that of northern Florida. Hokkaido, in the North, has cool summers and snowy winters. The islands get at least 40 inches of rain each year, with much more in some areas.

Less than one-fifth of the land in Japan is suitable for farming. But the Japanese have learned to cultivate carefully the soil that can be farmed, so that their crop yields are among the highest in the world. Japanese farms produce most of the food needed by the entire nation. Additional food is imported.

Japan has been a fishing nation for many centuries. The waters around Japan are rich with fish, but Japanese fishing boats sail all over the Pacific Ocean. Japanese ships also sail the waters of the Arctic and Antarctic searching for whales. Japanese fishermen catch more fish than the fishermen of any other country but Peru. Fish is an important part of the Japanese diet and a major export.

People

Most Japanese belong to the Buddhist or Shinto religions. Shinto is an ancient religion of Japan in which the spirits of nature and of ancestors are worshiped. Some Japanese today are Christians.

The Japanese had no system of writing their language before the 700s. Then they learned to use a form of writing similar to the Chinese. *Characters*, or small line drawings, are used to represent entire words or ideas. Today nearly all

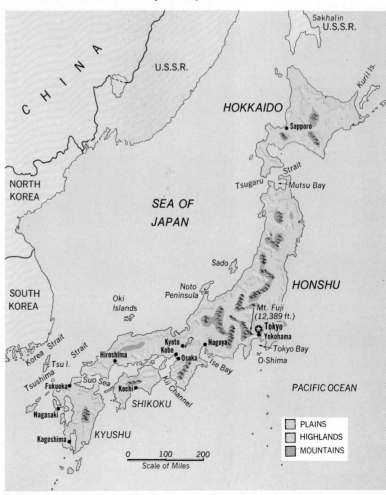

JASON

▲ *A sure sign of spring in Japan is the blossoming of the beautiful cherry trees. The pagoda adds even more charm to this enchanting river scene.*

▼ *These Japanese workers are making cameras, an important industry in Japan. Since World War II, Japanese cameras have become known for their fine quality.*

Japanese can read as well as write.

The Japanese appreciate beauty in everything around them. This love of beauty has produced some of the world's greatest works of art. Japanese artists and craftsmen excel in wood carving, flower arranging, delicate paintings, and architecture.

History

Marco Polo, the Venetian who went to China, heard about Cipangu (Japan) and wrote about it in his travel diaries in 1229. The first Europeans to go to Japan were Portuguese sailors in 1543. Six years later the Roman Catholic missionary, Saint Francis Xavier, arrived and began to teach Christianity. At first missionaries were welcomed, and some Japanese became Christians. After some years, the rulers became afraid that the Europeans might send soldiers to conquer Japan. In 1637, they killed many Christians and closed the country to all foreigners except the Dutch (who had sent no missionaries). Japan was isolated from the rest of the world for more than 200 years.

In 1853, Commodore Matthew Perry was sent to Japan to establish diplomatic and trade relations. He persuaded the Japanese to open two ports for American trade. Soon other nations began to trade with

Japan. The Japanese learned much from these countries, and developed industries and military forces. Japan became one of the world's great powers by the end of World War I. During the next 20 years the Japanese expanded their empire by conquest. In 1941 the Japanese carried out a surprise bombing attack on the U.S. Navy fleet at Pearl Harbor, Honolulu, bringing the United States into World War II. Japan had to give up all its occupied territories after its defeat by the U.S. in 1945.

Since World War II Japan has become a great industrial power, in spite of having very few mineral resources. It is third in the world in steel production, yet the iron ore and most of the coal needed to make steel are brought from other countries. Almost all its oil comes from the Middle East. The Japanese are highly skilled in technical fields. Japan is the largest shipbuilder and the second-largest automobile manufacturer in the world. The Japanese electronics industry is important, too. Millions of television sets, radios, cameras, and other electrical products are exported to many countries of the world.

Japan was ruled by emperors for thousands of years. The emperors were believed to be descended from the sun god, and had absolute power. After World War II the emperor was forced to give up most of his power. Today Japan is a constitutional monarchy. This means that it has an emperor, who has no real power, and a democratic form of government.

ALSO READ: ASIA, PERRY FAMILY, WORLD WAR II.

JASON In the myths of ancient Greece, one of the bravest men was Jason. He was the son of Aeson, king of Iolcus, whose throne had been stolen by Pelias, Jason's uncle. Pelias promised Jason the throne if he would bring him the marvelous Golden Fleece—golden wool cut

▲ *A scene from a vase painting shows Jason as he attacks a monster.*

from a magic ram. Jason sailed off in a ship named the *Argo*, accompanied by the bravest men he could find. He and his crew were called the *Argonauts*. They survived several dangerous adventures during their trip, including an encounter with monsters called Harpies, who were half human and half bird. But at last the Argonauts reached Colchis, where the king forced Jason to fight two fire-breathing dragons and a bull. Medea, the king's daughter, helped Jason destroy the monsters and capture the fleece. Jason left Colchis with Medea, whom he later married. Some years later, however, Jason tired of her, and went off to marry the princess of Corinth. Medea was so furious that she killed the princess and then murdered her own children, in revenge. Jason, in deepest grief, killed himself.

ALSO READ: GREEK LITERATURE, MYTHOLOGY.

JAVA see INDONESIA.

JAVELIN   A javelin is a long, light spear. In modern times the javelin is used only for sport, but at one time it was an important weapon. Rocks and sticks were the earliest weapons of prehistoric man. Then man learned to sharpen one end of a long stick and kill for food and defend himself against his enemies by stabbing them. He then found he could kill at a distance by throwing a pointed stick, or spear.

Throwing a javelin was a popular sport in ancient Greece. At the first Olympic Games, in 776 B.C., javelin throwing was one of the events.

Today, nearly 3,000 years later, the javelin throw is still an Olympic sport. It is also part of school and college track and field meets.

In competition, the Greeks used a javelin that was 8 to 10 feet long. The modern javelin is still about the same length. In throwing the javelin, the hurler grips it in the center, gets a running start, and heaves the javelin into the air. Expert javelin throwers can hurl the spear more than 300 feet.

ALSO READ: SPORTS, TRACK AND FIELD.

JAZZ   Jazz began in the early 1900s as the music of poor black people. Since then it has gained worldwide popularity and is played in night clubs and concert halls. The most truly American music, jazz began as a form of folk music created and played by ordinary people, rather than by professional musicians. *Improvisation* (impromptu, spur-of-the-moment playing by a solo instrumentalist who is backed up by the other players) is an important part of jazz.

Early History
Following the Civil War, many Negroes came to New Orleans. With them they brought their folk music—spirituals, work songs, and *blues*. Blues are popular songs about sadness or loneliness. The music used B-flat and E-flat in the scale, called *blue notes*. The music of the blacks got mixed with styles of music that were popular with the Spanish and French people. There was much musical activity in and around New Orleans, including street-singing, brass bands that played for parades and funerals, and popular music in nightclubs.

An early form of jazz, called *ragtime*, became popular in the early 1900s. The rhythm was fast and sometimes stressed a weak instead of a strong beat, giving the music a kind of "jerk." This is called *synco-*

▲ *It takes great strength and skill to throw the javelin in competition.*

▲Duke Ellington, composer, bandleader, and pianist (above). Thelonius Monk, composer and pianist (right).

▼Dizzy Gillespie, composer and trumpet player (below). He has played in big bands and small groups. Ella Fitzgerald and Louis Armstrong (right), brilliant jazz singers. Armstrong was also a great trumpet player.

pation, and is an important part of jazz. Although ragtime music is not so popular today as it once was, "Twelfth Street Rag," "Alexander's Ragtime Band," and "Tiger Rag" are still well known.

Many musicians, white as well as black, were playing the new music. Since this was folk music rather than formal concert music, musicians began improvising, adding blues melodies (especially the blue notes), and making up new ways to play the melodies. This music began to be played in other big cities in the South such as Atlanta, St. Louis, and Memphis. Many popular musicians and musical groups came from these cities. Chicago finally became the center for this music, with King Oliver, Louis Armstrong, and others moving there from New Orleans. One group from Chicago went to New York in January, 1917. Called the Original Dixieland Jazz Band, they were a great hit and soon made

the first phonograph recording of jazz. This new, exciting music was well liked, and the 1920s were called "The Jazz Age."

Changes in Jazz

A smoother jazz style, called swing, became popular in the 1930s. This was played by big bands, especially those of Glenn Miller, Tommy and Jimmy Dorsey, and Benny Goodman. Swing was followed in the 1940s by bebop or bop (which used different rhythms and harmonies to play well-known tunes). Thelonius Monk was one of several jazz musicians who, in jam sessions (informal playing after work), developed bop.

Since the 1920s, jazz music has become popular all over the world. Composers of great symphonies and concert works have used jazz or jazz ideas in their creations. One of the most famous jazz groups, the Modern Jazz Quartet, has played jazz in concert halls throughout the world. And Duke Ellington has written serious sacred jazz music, performing it in churches with great success. Many colleges offer jazz courses.

Instruments of Jazz

Early jazz combos (instrumental music groups) featured the trumpet, trombone, and clarinet to play the melody. Drums, string bass, piano, and guitar or banjo kept the rhythm going. Saxophone and other instruments have also been added. Jazz singers usually use their voices as

another instrument, singing notes without using words. This is called *scat singing*. Ella Fitzgerald and Louis Armstrong made this style popular. Blues and gospel singers, such as Billie Holliday and Mahalia Jackson, sang in jazz style.

Try comparing jazz to some of the modern music (such as *rock*) that has developed from it. A librarian or other adult will be able to find some jazz and rock records for you. Play them and listen carefully to the sound of each. What instruments do you hear? Is there any singing? Which style of music do you like better, and why?

ALSO READ: ARMSTRONG, LOUIS; BRASS INSTRUMENTS; JACKSON, MAHALIA; PERCUSSION INSTRUMENTS.

ginia. He was a brilliant student. He attended William and Mary College, where he read books by great English and French authors who wrote about liberty for all people. This was not a common belief in those days. After Jefferson graduated from college, he studied law. He became a member of the Virginia legislature and was a delegate to the Continental Congress in 1775. The Continental Congress adopted the Declaration of Independence which Jefferson largely wrote. When the Congress ended, Jefferson returned to Virginia to work for the passage of laws that would make his own state more democratic.

When Virginia was an English colony, a law had been passed that

THIRD PRESIDENT   MARCH 4, 1801—MARCH 3, 1809

THOMAS JEFFERSON

Born: April 13, 1743, Goochland County, Virginia (now Albemarle County)
Parents: Peter and Jane Randolph Jefferson
Education: William and Mary College, Williamsburg, Virginia
Religion: Deism (belief in God but not in any organized religion)
Occupation: Lawyer and writer
Political Party: Democratic-Republican
State Represented: Virginia
Married: 1772 to Martha Wayles Skelton Jefferson (1748–1782)
Children: 5 daughters, 3 of whom died in childhood
Died: July 4, 1826, Monticello, Charlottesville, Virginia
Buried: Monticello, Charlottesville, Virginia

JEFFERSON, THOMAS (1743-1826) Twenty-five years before he became President, Thomas Jefferson was the principal author of the Declaration of Independence. Two years before that he had written *A Summary View of the Rights of British America*, protesting laws passed by the British Parliament.

"Let no law be passed by any one legislature," he wrote, "which may infringe on (step on) the rights and liberties of another. . . . The God who gave us life gave us liberty at the same time."

Thomas Jefferson was born at Shadwell, a farm in western Vir-

forbade people to attend any church except the Church of England. Jefferson suggested a new law to the state legislature, stating that "all men should be free to have their own religious opinions and that people should not be molested (harmed), restrained, or . . . otherwise made to suffer on account of their beliefs."

Jefferson also felt that slavery was wrong. He believed that a man has the right to freedom no matter what his abilities, education, or social status might be. He tried to keep slavery out of the new lands that were added to the United States. Even though he believed that owning

▲ *Monticello, Thomas Jefferson's home, is located in Charlottesville, Virginia. This fine building was designed by Jefferson himself, as were many objects in it. It is now open to visitors.*

▼ *A jellyfish looks soft and harmless. But its tentacles are able to sting very painfully.*

human beings was wrong, Jefferson owned slaves all his life. But he left instructions that they were to be freed after he died.

Jefferson served his country as minister to France (1785–1789), as secretary of state (1790–1793), and as Vice President (1797–1801). Jefferson became President in 1801. Soon afterward, his ministers in France made an agreement with the French government to buy the vast region between the Mississippi River and the Rocky Mountains. This was called the "Louisiana Purchase." It doubled the size of the United States. Jefferson was curious to know more about this huge area of western land. He sent the Lewis and Clark Expedition to explore these lands all the way to the Pacific Ocean.

No President ever had more varied interests and talents. He loved horseback riding, and even in his last years he rode as often as he could. Jefferson was not only a musician and a fine writer, but he was also an architect and inventor. He designed Monticello, his beautiful home near Charlottesville, Virginia. You can still visit it today and see his various inventions. Jefferson also founded the University of Virginia and designed the original buildings, which still stand. Jefferson set up a telescope at Monticello to watch those first buildings being built. Visitors to Monticello can still see the university through that same telescope. Jefferson arranged for good students from poor families to be admitted to the university free. At Monticello, where he spent his last seventeen years, Jefferson tried new ways to improve his crops.

During his lifetime, Jefferson saw his new nation successfully carrying out the ideals that had inspired the Declaration of Independence. "All eyes," he wrote, "are opened or opening to the rights of man." He wrote those words a few days before he died. The words Jefferson wrote

for his own tombstone tell us the accomplishments of which he was most proud: "Here lies buried Thomas Jefferson, author of the Declaration of Independence, of the Statute of Virginia for Religious Freedom, and father of the University of Virginia." He did not mention the many government offices that he had held.

ALSO READ: AMERICAN REVOLUTION, CONTINENTAL CONGRESS, DECLARATION OF INDEPENDENCE, LEWIS AND CLARK EXPEDITION, LOUISIANA PURCHASE.

JELLYFISH Have you ever seen a jellyfish washed up on a beach? It is hard to believe that an animal that looks like a blob of jelly can give such a painful sting. Some jellyfish stings are not just painful; they can be deadly.

A jellyfish, or medusa, is a simple, primitive sea animal. Its body is only two cell layers thick. Between these two cell walls is jelly. The jelly acts as a float to keep the animal near the water's surface. Jellyfish move with the tide, but they are not good swimmers. They are often washed up onto beaches after storms or high tides.

The main part of a jellyfish's body looks like an umbrella. Hanging down from the umbrella are string-like tentacles. In the tentacles are tiny cells that contain a small amount of paralyzing poison. If a fish brushes against a jellyfish's tentacle, the poison cells on the tentacle "explode," shooting poison into the victim. Then the tentacles pull the victim up to the mouth, at the bottom of the umbrella.

Jellyfish are *coelenterates*, one of a large group of water animals with tube-shaped stomachs. Many coelenterates need two generations to complete a life cycle. The first generation is the free-swimming jellyfish. From the jellyfish's eggs come tiny *polyps*, animals that cling to rocks or plants on the ocean floor.

The polyps then produce a third generation, which are jellyfish again.

One of the most common of the many types of jellyfish is the *moon jelly.* Another type that is found in many areas is the *sea nettle,* which often bothers swimmers with its stings. The world's largest jellyfish is the *Arctic sea blubber* that lives in the cold waters of the north. It grows to be eight feet across, and its tentacles can grow to be 200 feet long. The kind of sea blubber that lives in warmer waters is only about one foot across. Its tentacles often give swimmers painful stings.

The most famous jellyfish is the *Portuguese man-of-war.* This is not a true jellyfish, but a colony of animals that live together. A man-of-war is a beautiful purple-blue color, but its dangerous tentacles are often more than 60 feet long.

ALSO READ: COELENTERATE, CORAL, MARINE LIFE.

JENNER, EDWARD (1749–1823)
An English doctor, Edward Jenner, discovered a vaccine to protect people from smallpox. As a result of Jenner's discovery, smallpox—which was one of man's worst enemies—has almost disappeared.

Jenner noticed that people who got the mild disease cowpox never got that disease again, nor did they ever get smallpox. (Both cowpox and smallpox produce large pimple-like sores all over a person's body.) Jenner thought about this strange fact and decided that if a person were purposely given cowpox, then that person would not get smallpox.

On May 14, 1796, Jenner took some pus from a cowpox sore on the arm of a milkmaid. He made a small cut in the arm of an eight-year-old boy, and rubbed cowpox pus into the cut. This was the first vaccination. Four weeks after the boy recovered from cowpox, Jenner rubbed smallpox pus into a cut in the boy's arm. The boy did not get smallpox.

At first, other doctors showed no interest in Jenner's discovery, but before his death, Jenner was honored throughout the world as the conqueror of the dreaded smallpox. Other doctors, using Jenner's ideas, have developed vaccines to protect people from many other diseases.
ALSO READ: DISEASE, IMMUNITY.

JERUSALEM Jerusalem is among the oldest cities in the world, and has played a leading role in history. Jews, Christians, and Muslims alike consider it a holy city. It is built on the hills of Judea (in Israel), about 35 miles east of the Mediterranean Sea coast. About 300,000 people live there.

Jerusalem was an important city when King David of the Jews made it his capital around 1000 B.C. His son, King Solomon, built a great temple there. The Jews held the city for about 500 years, but were then conquered by the Babylonians. The Romans occupied the city in 65 B.C. About 90 years later, Jesus Christ was tried there by the Roman governor, Pontius Pilate, and was crucified. The Jews revolted against the harsh Roman rule in 66 A.D. and the Roman Emperor, Titus, savagely destroyed the city. Constantine, the first Christian Roman emperor, rebuilt Jerusalem in the 300s. He built the Church of the Holy Sepulcher on the spot where Christ was believed to have been buried.

Muslim Arabs conquered the city in 637 A.D. They believed that their greatest teacher, Muhammad, rose to heaven from the same spot where King Solomon's temple once stood. They built the Dome of the Rock, an important shrine, on the site.

Muslim Arabs, Christian Crusaders, Turks, and finally the British occupied the city in the hundreds of years before 1948.

The country of Israel was created in that year. Its border with Arab Jordan went right through the middle of Jerusalem. But Israel occu-

▲*A Portuguese-man-of-war rests on the surface of the sea by means of a bright blue, bladder-like float.*

▲*Edward Jenner, discoverer of vaccination.*

▼*A view of Jerusalem looking toward the Mount of Olives.*

pied the rest of the city during the war of 1967 and declared all of Jerusalem part of Israel. No final settlement has been made.

Jerusalem today is a fascinating mixture of old and new, East and West. The historical area of the city, now called the "Old City," is surrounded by a huge stone wall built by a Turkish sultan in the 1500s. This area's narrow cobblestone streets throb with colorful activity. Most of Jerusalem's great religious landmarks are located in the Old City. Jews worship at the Wailing Wall, the remains of King Solomon's great temple. Christians visit the Church of the Holy Sepulcher, built over the tomb of Christ. Muslims visit the Dome of the Rock. The so-called "New City" consists of modern apartments and office buildings built outside the Old City's walls. Interesting sights here include Hebrew University, the Orthodox Jewish quarter, and King David's Tomb on Mount Zion.

ALSO READ: CHRISTIANITY, ISLAM, ISRAEL, JEWISH HISTORY, JORDAN, JUDAISM, MIDDLE EAST.

JESUS CHRIST (about 4 B.C.-about 29 A.D.) Christianity was founded on the teachings of Jesus Christ. Much of our knowledge of Jesus comes from the writings of the New Testament of the Bible. The parts that tell the story of Jesus are the Gospels (from the Old English words, Good Spiel, meaning "good news") of Mark, Matthew, Luke, and John. The good news these writers wanted to tell was that Jesus is the Christ, the son of God, and to explain his ideas. This may be why they tell us so little about the life story of Jesus. The Gospels in the form we have them today appeared 35 to 70 years after Jesus' death.

Jesus comes from a Hebrew word meaning "God is Salvation." Christ comes from a Greek word translating the Hebrew word "Messiah"—the anointed (chosen) one.

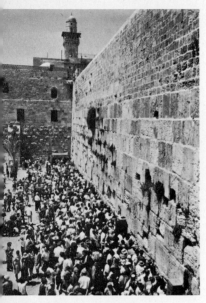

▲Jews gather before the Wailing Wall in Jerusalem, all that remains of the Holy Temple of biblical times. Prayers are said here to express sorrow for the destruction of the temple, and this is how the Wall gets its name.

▲The three Wise Men visiting the infant Jesus in Bethlehem. They brought him gold, frankincense, and myrrh.

The name Jesus Christ expresses the faith of the early Christians that Jesus is the Messiah, or Savior.

Jesus was born to a devout Jewish couple in the ancient country of Judea (now parts of Israel and Jordan). According to the Gospels, Jesus' mother Mary was told by an angel that she would give birth to the son of God. Soon afterwards, Mary was married to Joseph of Nazareth, a carpenter. Joseph and Mary traveled to the little town of Bethlehem to register for a tax list. The small town was so crowded that the only room left for them was a stable.

▼The Baptism of Christ, by Master of the Life of St. John the Baptist. National Gallery of Art, Washington, D.C., Samuel H. Kress Collection.

▲*Jesus calling Peter and Andrew to serve him and become his first disciples. Jesus filled their net with fish after they had fished all night without success.*

It was there in the stable that the baby Jesus was born.

Little is known about the early years of Jesus' life. The Gospels agree that Jesus probably began preaching at about the age of 30. He chose 12 of his followers to be his apostles and help him in his work. Jesus was a good speaker and storyteller, and he attracted huge crowds of people. The Gospels tell how he could make sick people well with the power of faith and could make miracles happen. He taught men that God is our father and that we are brothers and should love one another as he has loved us. He taught that God forgave men to the degree that they forgave one another, and that the father would grant them eternal life.

Fear on the part of civil and religious authorities of what Jesus said and did led to his arrest and execution in Jerusalem, the capital city. At the last supper, the night before he died, Jesus celebrated the Passover feast with his disciples. He took the bread and wine and said, "This is my body; this is my blood," and told them to do this with bread and wine after his death and resurrection. This is what the churches do when they have a communion service, or the Mass.

Jesus was arrested and brought to trial. Pontius Pilate, the Roman governor, sentenced him to die on the cross. (Crucifixion was a common way of execution at that time.) After Jesus died, his body was placed in a tomb. On the third day afterward, the tomb was found open, and Jesus was gone. The Gospels report that he appeared to several of his followers after he had risen from the dead. He was with his disciples until the day that they saw him taken up into heaven.

The Gospel or "good news" of Jesus' resurrection and his teachings were carried first to the Jews and then to the Gentiles. His followers took his teachings to other people and other nations. Christianity became one of the major religions of the world. The calendar in use today is dated from the birth of Jesus. "B.C." means "before Christ." "A.D." stands for *anno domini* (in the year of our Lord) and is used for dates after Christ's birth.

ALSO READ: BIBLE, CHRISTIANITY, CHRISTMAS, EASTER, RELIGION.

▲*Jesus entering Jerusalem on a donkey. Crowds of people waved and cheered and threw palm branches before him. The day is now celebrated as Palm Sunday.*

◀*Jesus and his apostles at the Last Supper, a rite now celebrated as the communion service, or the Mass.*

▲*The air intake of a jet engine. The air, pulled in by the fan when the engine is running, helps make the fuel burn at a high temperature.*

JET PROPULSION   The words "jet propulsion" usually describe how spacecraft and many airplanes move. When you blow up a balloon and let it go, it zooms around the room because it is also jet-propelled. Sir Isaac Newton explained how jets—and balloons—move when he said, "For every action, there is an equal and opposite reaction." This is called the Third Law of Motion. You can see how it describes what happens to the balloon. Air rushes out through the neck of the balloon (action), and the balloon moves in the opposite direction (reaction).

A jet-propelled airplane is more complicated, but the idea is the same. The engine is a long tube. At the front of the tube is a *compressor*, a powerful fan that sucks in air. The compressor pushes the air through pipes to the *combustion chamber*, where fuel is sprayed into the air.

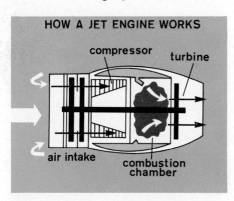

HOW A JET ENGINE WORKS

compressor

turbine

air intake

combustion chamber

When the engine is first turned on, a spark causes the fuel to burn. After that, the fuel burns as soon as it is sprayed into the combustion chamber. The engine stops when the fuel is cut off.

The burning fuel expands (spreads out) very rapidly. The only direction the gases can move is backwards, towards the open end of the tube. The rush of the burning fuel out the back end of the engine (called *thrust*) causes the forward movement of the airplane.

Near the back of the jet engine is a *turbine*, another special fan. The burning fuel spins the turbine as it rushes past. The turbine is connected to the compressor, so that turns too, and more air is pulled into the engine.

A jet engine sucks oxygen from the outside air. This means that it can work only in the atmosphere. A rocket engine carries its own oxygen. This means that it can burn fuel even in outer space, where there is no atmosphere.

ALSO READ: AIRPLANE; ENGINE; MOTION; NEWTON, SIR ISAAC; ROCKET.

JET STREAM see ATMOSPHERE.

JEWELRY   Some experts think the word "jewelry" comes from the French word *joie*, meaning "joy" or "gladness." People have always decorated themselves with beautiful things to make themselves seem important. Long ago, people fastened pretty things on their heads, around their necks and arms, or in their noses and ears. Seashells, animal teeth, carved bone, and birds' feathers made pretty decorations for happy celebrations. Warriors often wore similar decorations to raise their spirits before a battle. People living near the sea used shells for jewelry. Inland tribes used sparkling rocks found on the ground. People discovered pearls in oysters. They also learned how to cut and polish the stones from the ground into beautifully colored gems.

The early Egyptians were familiar with many precious and semi-precious gems. They used amber, amethyst, and crystal in their jewelry, as well as colored glass and porcelain. The ancient Greeks considered gold to be more valuable than gemstones. Their heavy decorations were mostly made of gold, but sometimes they would add a bit of enamel or a few pearls. The people of South Africa became expert at making delicate gold wire jewelry. An ancient skeleton found in Ecuador (South America) has small gold circles set into five of its front teeth.

Greek culture began to spread to Rome in about 200 B.C. An impor-

◀ *A woman of Darjeeling in northeastern India. Her face and neck are adorned with jewelry. Notice the unusual nose ring and ear pieces.*

▶ *A woman from the island of Bali, a province of Indonesia. She is wearing a jewel-studded headdress with two rows of white shells.*

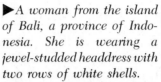

▼ *A golden necklace with a head of a satyr, a mythical god. This piece of jewelry comes from Palestrina, a town near Rome, Italy.*

◀ *A gold collar made by the Hittites, a people of ancient Syria. This piece of jewelry is made of beaten gold.*

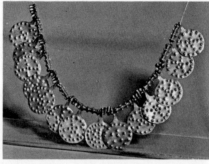

▲ *A gold earring made in ancient Greece. It was made in the shape of an animal's head, a fashionable form of jewelry in ancient times.*

◀ *This gold necklace and brooch made by the Incas is a fine example of pre-Columbian jewelry of the Indians of South America.*

tant Roman, named Cato, thought the Greek love of decoration would ruin his people. He passed laws limiting jewelry. The Romans then began having ordinary things, such as hairpins and mirrors, made by jewelers.

In more recent times French, English, and Italian craftsmen have raised jewelry-making to a real art. Royal crown jewels of various countries are perhaps the finest examples of their work.

In former times, all jewelry was made by hand. Now machines can

do some of the work. If a manufacturer wants to make several bracelets that are all alike, he uses a method called *casting*. First, a model of the bracelet is made out of metal, and this model is covered with melted rubber. When the rubber hardens, it is carefully removed. This makes a rubber mold of the bracelet. A wax model of the bracelet is made with the rubber mold. The wax model is then covered with plaster and put in an oven. As the heat melts the wax model inside the plaster, the wax drains out through a

▲ *A fashion model wearing a modern matching set of jewelry consisting of necklace, bracelet, earrings, and ring.*

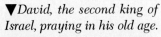

▼ *David, the second king of Israel, praying in his old age.*

small hole. Then the precious metal (gold, silver, or whatever) is poured into the plaster mold through the small hole and allowed to harden. When the plaster is removed, the bracelet is polished.

Jewelry is also made by *stamping*. A flat sheet of precious metal is pressed between two curved pieces of steel, called *dies*. The dies shape the metal into the form of a bracelet, a ring, or whatever is being made. The stamping method is used for very large amounts of jewelry of the same pattern.

Many people collect jewelry because it is rare and will always be valuable. Museums often have exhibits of famous and valuable pieces of jewelry. Many people wear *costume jewelry*, which is made of less valuable stones or glass and less expensive metals. Some attractive costume jewelry is made of plastic.

You might like to try making some jewelry yourself. Simple bracelets, rings, and necklaces can be made by bending and twisting metal wire into various shapes.

You can also make your own gems at home, with an adult's help. First, place a clear round marble in a frying pan and put it on the burner of the stove. Cover the pan and let the marble cook over a high heat for 10 to 15 minutes. While the marble is heating, prepare a bowl of ice water. Then take the marble out of the frying pan with a spoon and quickly place it in the bowl of ice water. The marble will then crack and split on the inside, but it will not break apart. Take the marble out of the water and you will see it sparkle like a real precious stone. You could then set your "gem" in a wire ring.

ALSO READ: CROWN JEWELS, GEM.

JEWISH HISTORY The history of a country, or the people of a nation, is a record of events in the development of that country. Jewish history is even more—it is the thread that has bound the Jewish people together through thousands of years of persecution, landlessness, and wandering.

The Origins of the Jewish People
The Old Testament, the first half of the Bible, tells of the beginnings of the Jews, of their wanderings, and of their establishment of a homeland. The Biblical word "Hebrew" refers to a group of wandering tribes that lived in the Middle East before 1300 B.C. In those days, most people worshiped many gods, who were often represented in statues. But the Hebrews were *monotheistic*, believing that there was only one true God. The word "Jew" originally meant "a member of the Hebrew tribe of Judah," or "a member of the Hebrew state, Judea."

Both the Old Testament and historical theory trace the ancestors of the Jews to the land of Ur, in Mesopotamia. About 2350 B.C., Abraham, a tribal chief who was told by God that he would be the "father of a multitude," made a *covenant*, or agreement, with God. If Abraham and his descendants would worship only this God and follow his laws, God would lead them into "a land of milk and honey" and they would prosper. Abraham led his family and his followers to Canaan in what is now Israel.

Isaac was the son of Abraham, and Jacob was the son of Isaac. God spoke to Jacob, telling him that he would become known as "Israel," and his descendants would be the "children of Israel." Jacob's (Israel's) twelve sons and their descendants formed the twelve Hebrew tribes that became the Jewish people.

Promised Land Won—and Lost
About 1700 B.C. some Hebrew tribes wandered to the borders of Egypt. There they prospered for over 100 years. Then they were forced into slavery by the Egyptians. According to the Bible, a Hebrew prophet

▲*Moses receiving the Tablets of the Law, the Ten Commandments, from God on Mount Sinai.*

named Moses forced the Egyptian pharaoh to free the Hebrew slaves. Moses led the Hebrews out of Egypt, and they became desert wanderers. During this period of wandering, Moses received the Ten Commandments from God.

The Bible says that the Hebrews wandered over the desert for 40 years, joining with tribes that had not been slaves. In the 1200s B.C., they settled in Canaan. There, about 1030 B.C., they founded a kingdom. The greatest kings were Saul, David, and David's son, Solomon. The great temple in Jerusalem was built during the reign of Solomon. There is a wall that stands in Jerusalem today. It is known as the Wailing Wall, and is believed to be a part of Solomon's Temple.

When Solomon died, the kingdom was divided. Ten tribes formed a northern kingdom called Israel. The remaining two tribes created a southern kingdom, Judah.

In the 700s B.C., the kingdom of Israel was invaded by the Assyrians, and Israel was destroyed. The ten tribes living there were scattered over the world, and came to be known as the "Lost Tribes of Israel."

In 597 B.C., the kingdom of Judah was attacked by the Babylonians. Most Judeans were taken to Babylon, where they lived in exile.

When the Persian Empire conquered Babylon, about 539 B.C., the Jews there were allowed to go home. The temple in Jerusalem was rebuilt, and Judah prospered. Around this time, many Jews began to move to other parts of the ancient world. They formed colonies throughout the Mediterranean and Black Sea areas. This great movement was called the "Diaspora," or *dispersion* (scattering).

In the 330s B.C., Alexander the Great of Macedonia conquered the Persian Empire. After Alexander's death, Judah became part of Egypt. The Jews were forbidden to practice their religion and an altar to Zeus (the Greek god) was placed in Solomon's Temple. A rebellion of the Jews was led by a Jewish priest and his sons, who were called the Maccabees. After a bitter military struggle, the Jewish forces defeated Syria. Judah was briefly free again.

In 47 B.C., Judah was made a province of the Roman Empire. The Roman governors of Judah gave little respect to the Jewish religion. In 70 A.D., the Temple in Jerusalem was again destroyed. The Roman emperor, Hadrian, forbade any Jew to enter Jerusalem on pain of death. Over half a million Jews were killed by Roman soldiers in the battles that followed, and Judah was finally crushed in 135 A.D. The Jews no longer had a homeland.

Persecution and Hope
In the centuries following the loss of their homeland, the Jewish peo-

▼*A relief from the Arch of Titus in Rome shows the looting of the Temple in Jerusalem by the Romans.*

▲ *Doctor Chaim Weizmann's inauguration as the first president of the modern state of Israel on February 17, 1949.*

ple were persecuted wherever they went. Usually, when the Jews sought refuge in a country, they would have many years of peaceful prosperity. Then some internal strife would upset the country, and the Jews would sometimes be blamed as the cause of problems. In the Middle Ages and during the Crusades, Christian countries in Europe were especially cruel to Jews.

When the Jews were allowed to remain in a country, they were often forced to live in small, crowded areas, called *ghettos*, and to wear special clothing. They were not allowed to vote, own land, or practice any profession. During the thirteenth and fourteenth centuries, several European kings filled their treasuries by taking things that belonged to the Jews.

For many years, colonies of Jews in Spain existed peacefully under Muslim rule. Spanish Jews were statesmen, doctors, bankers, and scholars. The peaceful Spanish era ended in the thirteenth century, when the Muslims were driven from Spain.

In 1480, the Spanish Inquisition was established in Spain. This court—independent of the church—persecuted persons suspected of heresy (not believing in the doctrines of the church). In order to

save their lives, many Jews converted to Christianity, while secretly practicing Judaism. But all Jews were finally banished from Spain in 1492.

Thousands of Spanish Jews migrated to Turkey, which still followed the Muslim policy of toleration. Jews were expelled from England, France, Germany, and Switzerland and settled in Poland and Russia. In the seventeenth and eighteenth centuries, Jews were again welcomed in England and France. Many also sought refuge in the new colonies in North America. But in Russia and Poland, terrible massacres (*pogroms*) of entire Jewish villages began. In the centuries of wandering, the Jewish people in every land retained their identity as Jews by maintaining their faith. They waited for the coming of a Messiah who would again lead them to the promised land.

THE HOMELAND REGAINED. In 1896, an Austrian who was named Theodor Herzl founded a movement called *Zionism*. The aim of this movement was to regain the Jewish homeland in the Middle East and re-establish the Jewish nation. Meanwhile, a wave of hatred against Jews, called *anti-Semitism*, was rising in Europe. In the 1930s and early 1940s, the German dictator Adolf Hitler and his Nazi followers murdered six million Jews in concentration camps.

In 1948, the State of Israel was established in Palestine. Once again, all Jews had a homeland. Israel is also the home of many Arabs and Christians. Throughout the world there are now about 14 million Jews. Many of them (over six million) live in North America. Israel and the Soviet Union also have large Jewish populations.

ALSO READ: BABYLONIA; BIBLE; DEAD SEA SCROLLS; EGYPT, ANCIENT; HANUKKAH; HEBREW; ISRAEL; JERUSALEM; JUDAISM; MIDDLE EAST; PALESTINE; PASSOVER; TALMUD; YIDDISH.

JIGSAW PUZZLE Working on a jigsaw puzzle is fun for people of all ages. A jigsaw puzzle consists of a picture which has been cut into irregularly-shaped small pieces with a tool called a jigsaw. The jigsaw puzzle worker scatters the pieces on a flat surface and then tries to put the picture together again. Jigsaw puzzles usually come with the completed picture shown on a piece of paper or on the lid of the box. This picture serves as guide to those who are trying to piece the puzzle together. Hiding the picture until the puzzle is completed makes the job harder, but more fun, too. Jigsaw puzzles for very young children usually contain only a few pieces, which are fairly large. More complicated jigsaw puzzles might contain hundreds of small pieces. One person can work on a jigsaw puzzle alone, or it can be entertainment for a group.

You can make your own jigsaw puzzle. Draw a picture on a stiff piece of paper, such as construction paper or cardboard. Color it any way you like. Then use scissors to cut the picture into many pieces with irregular shapes. Now see if you can put the picture back together again. You might enjoy exchanging your puzzle for one a friend has made. See which one of you can put the other's puzzle together faster.

JOAN OF ARC (1412-1431) "I will teach them all to fight that the will of God may be done in France." These words were spoken by Joan of Arc in *Saint Joan*, a play written by dramatist George Bernard Shaw.

Joan of Arc was a French teenager who led her people to victory in battle with the English. She was born in Domrémy, France, to a peasant family. At the age of 13, Joan had visions and heard voices that she said were from heaven. The voices told her she must help free the French from the English. At this time, the English controlled part of France.

Joan went to see Charles (later King Charles VII), the uncrowned leader of the French people. He became convinced Joan had powers given to her by heaven. He put her in charge of his troops. Joan freed the city of Orléans from the English in 1429. After that, she was known as the Maid of Orléans. When Charles was crowned king, Joan had the place of honor at his side.

In 1430, allies of the English, the Burgundians, captured Joan and sold her to the English. The English put her on trial as a witch. She was found guilty and was burned at the stake in Rouen, France. Joan was declared a saint by the Roman Catholic Church in 1920.

Some of the plays about Joan of Arc (besides *Saint Joan*) include *The Maid of Orléans*, by Johann Friedrich von Schiller, *The Lark*, by Jean Anouilh, and *Joan of Lorraine*, by Maxwell Anderson. Mark Twain wrote a historical novel about her, called *The Personal Recollections of Joan of Arc*.

ALSO READ: CHARLES, KINGS OF FRANCE; FRENCH HISTORY; HUNDRED YEARS' WAR; SAINT.

JOGGING see EXERCISE.

JOHN, KING OF ENGLAND (1167-1216) King John of England was an unpopular king, and his enemies called him cruel and dishonest. He was the youngest son of King Henry II. He received no lands from his father, and so he was called John Lackland. His older brother, King Richard I, gave John much English land. But John tried to take the crown from his brother while Richard was a prisoner in Austria. Richard had been imprisoned on his way back to England after the Third Crusade. Richard forgave John, and supposedly made him heir to the throne. John became king after Richard died in 1199.

▲*A gilded statue of Joan of Arc in the Place des Pyramides in Paris reminds the French of their great heroine.*

▼*King John of England.*

The kings of England once ruled over several provinces in France. John lost most of these provinces in a long war with the French king. John also quarreled with the pope. The pope sided with John's greatest enemies, the English *barons* (noblemen). John had forced the barons to pay for the French war with huge taxes. He refused to listen to their complaints. In 1215, the barons presented *Magna Carta* (the Great Charter) to King John. John signed this historic document, which limited the power of the king and gave the barons certain rights. John then went to war against the barons, in spite of the agreements he had made in Magna Carta. The struggle ended with John's sudden death. His nine-year-old son became King Henry III.

ALSO READ: CRUSADES; ENGLISH HISTORY; MAGNA CARTA; RICHARD, KINGS OF ENGLAND.

JOHNSON, ANDREW (1809–1875) Andrew Johnson was the Vice President who became President when Abraham Lincoln was assassinated. He inherited all the problems of Lincoln's administration. Lincoln had wanted to show understanding and mercy to the South after the Civil War. President Johnson wanted to do the same thing. He was strongly opposed by certain Republicans in Congress

▲*The reasons for impeaching President Andrew Johnson being presented to the Senate by Senator Thaddeus Stevens.*

who insisted that the Confederate states be punished. Harsh laws were passed, even though Johnson had *vetoed* (rejected) them. The quarrel between Congress and the President became so bitter that the House of Representatives voted to *impeach* him. This means that they charged him with wrongdoing, hoping to force him out of office. The Senate found him innocent of the charges, however, by the margin of a single vote. Johnson was the only President who has ever been impeached.

Johnson was born in Raleigh, North Carolina, to very poor parents. He never attended school. At age 14, he became an apprentice (student and helper) to a tailor. At 18, he moved to the town of Greeneville, Tennessee, where he set up his own tailor shop. He married Eliza McCardle, a schoolteacher, and she taught him to read and write. She also read aloud to him while he stitched clothes for his customers.

Young Johnson was both well-liked and eager to get ahead. He became interested in politics and was elected mayor of Greeneville. He was later elected to more important offices, and was serving as U.S. Senator from Tennessee when the Civil War began. Tennessee left the Union to fight for the South, but Johnson remained loyal to the United States. In 1864, Lincoln

SEVENTEENTH PRESIDENT   APRIL 15, 1865—MARCH 3, 1869

Born: December 29, 1808, Raleigh, North Carolina
Parents: Jacob and Mary McDonough Johnson
Education: Mostly self-educated
Religion: No special church
Occupation: Tailor
Political Party: National Union-Republican
State Represented: Tennessee
Married: 1827 to Eliza McCardle Johnson (1810–1876)
Children: 2 daughters, 3 sons
Died: July 31, 1875, Carter's Station, Tennessee
Buried: National Cemetery, Greeneville, Tennessee

ANDREW JOHNSON

asked him to run for Vice President. The two men were from different political parties, but they were elected together on the National Union ticket.

Less than two years after Johnson became President, the impeachment trial began. It was held in the Senate and, according to the Constitution, a two-thirds vote would be needed to convict him. After several weeks, the Senate failed by one vote to convict Johnson. He finished his term as President.

In 1875, Johnson returned to Washington as a senator from Tennessee. Many Americans now felt that the charges against him in the impeachment trial had been false ones, made up by his political enemies. Johnson gave a speech in the Senate, denouncing the spirit of hate that he feared might still wreck the Union. And he urged his fellow Senators to concentrate on "this grand work of saving the Constitution," which meant "saving the country." He said, "Let peace and prosperity be restored to the land." Johnson died a few weeks later.

ALSO READ: CIVIL WAR; IMPEACHMENT; LINCOLN, ABRAHAM.

JOHNSON, LYNDON BAINES
(born 1908) The thirty-sixth President of the United States took the oath of office in an unusual place. It was aboard an Air Force jet. Lyndon Johnson was the Vice President under President John F. Kennedy. Johnson was in Dallas, Texas, with the President on November 22, 1963, the day Kennedy was assassinated. Less than two hours after Kennedy died, Johnson was sworn in as President by a woman who was a federal judge. The ceremony was held on the jet plane that carried Johnson back to Washington, D.C.

Lyndon Baines Johnson, often called "LBJ," was born and grew up in central Texas. Johnson taught high school for two years after graduating from college. He then went to Washington as secretary to a congressman. LBJ returned to Texas in 1935 to become a state administrator of the National Youth Administration. He helped many needy young people find work during the Depression when there were very few jobs. Two years later, Johnson was elected to the U.S. Congress as a representative from Texas.

Johnson served in the House of Representatives for 11 years. In 1948, he was elected to the Senate, where he became known as "the man who gets things done." He served as the Democratic Party whip, or assistant leader, and later became the majority leader. Johnson won the Democratic nomination for Vice President in 1960.

After Johnson became President, he addressed a joint session of Con-

THIRTY-SIXTH PRESIDENT   NOVEMBER 22, 1963—JANUARY 20, 1969

LYNDON BAINES JOHNSON

Born: August 27, 1908, Stonewall, Texas
Parents: Samuel Ealy, Jr., and Rebekah Baines Johnson
Education: Southwest Texas State Teachers College
Religion: Christian Church (Disciples of Christ)
Occupation: Teacher and legislator
Political Party: Democratic
State Represented: Texas
Married: 1934 to Claudia ("Ladybird") Taylor Johnson (born 1912)
Children: 2 daughters

▲*President Johnson talks with Russian Premier Aleksei Kosygin. The meeting, designed to further Soviet-American understanding, took place in Glassboro, New Jersey, in 1967.*

gress. He suggested that the best way to honor the memory of John Kennedy was to pass bills the late President had requested. Johnson had great influence with the Congress, having served in both houses for many years. During the next few months, civil rights, anti-poverty, and tax reduction bills were enacted into law. In 1964, Johnson was nominated by the Democrats for the Presidency. He received a larger majority vote in the election than any other President before him.

Mrs. Johnson—named Claudia Taylor but always called "Ladybird"—campaigned actively with President Johnson. A favorite project of hers during his Presidency was beautification of the United States. She led a successful campaign to abolish billboards and junkyards and to plant flowers and trees along roads and parkways.

During Johnson's administration, more troops were sent to fight in Vietnam. Many Americans believed the war was unjust. The country became divided, and Johnson decided not to seek re-election.

After the former President returned to his Texas ranch, he planned and contributed to the building of a huge library at the University of Texas. The Lyndon Baines Johnson Library and School of Public Affairs opened in 1971.
ALSO READ: CIVIL RIGHTS MOVEMENT; KENNEDY, JOHN FITZGERALD; VIETNAM.

▼*Samuel Johnson, English writer.*

JOHNSON, SAMUEL (1709-1774)

"Being in a ship is being in a jail, with the chance of being drowned." These words were spoken by Samuel Johnson, who was one of the wittiest writers of the 1700s.

Johnson was born in Staffordshire, England. His father was a bookseller, and Johnson received much of his early education from reading his father's books. He attended Oxford University for three years, and ran a boys' school for a short time.

Johnson later moved to London, where he became well known for his writing and for his witty comments on people, literature, and life in general. His best-known work is the *Dictionary of the English Language*. It contains such humorous definitions as: "oats—a grain which in England is generally given to horses, but in Scotland supports the people." He also wrote a long poem, called *The Vanity of Human Wishes*, and a series of essays. He became known as a good judge of literature, and published *The Lives of the Most Eminent English Poets, with Critical Observations on Their Works*.

In 1763, Johnson met a young Scottish lawyer named James Boswell, who became his very close friend and companion. Boswell kept a record of almost everything Johnson said and did. After Johnson's death, Boswell wrote *The Life of Samuel Johnson*, a biography that gives us one of the best descriptions of a man that was ever written.
ALSO READ: LITERATURE.

JONES, JOHN PAUL (1747-1792)

"I have not yet begun to fight," declared John Paul Jones, an American naval hero. He made this fighting reply when the captain of a British warship asked Jones to surrender his ship during a naval battle in the American Revolution.

John Paul Jones's real name was John Paul. He was born in Scotland. At the age of 12, he sailed to Virginia as a cabin boy aboard an English ship. He then began his career at sea, sailing on slave trading ships in the West Indies. After John was accused of murdering a man during a mutiny, he escaped to America. There he added Jones to his name to hide his identity.

When the American Revolution began, Jones became an officer in the colonial navy. He commanded the *Alfred,* the first naval vessel purchased by the Continental Congress. He captured many ships filled with valuable cargo, and his fame grew. Jones won his best-known battle with the British in 1779. His ship, the *Bonhomme Richard,* defeated the British ship, the *Serapis.* Congress later awarded Jones the only gold medal given to an officer in the colonial navy.

Jones went to Europe in 1783. He then served as an admiral in the Russian navy during that country's war against the Turks. He later retired in Paris, where he died.

ALSO READ: AMERICAN REVOLUTION, NAVY.

JORDAN Jordan is a new kingdom but also an ancient land described in the Bible. Most of the country lies on a plateau approximately 3,000 feet above sea level. The Jordan River and Dead Sea lie west of the plateau. Amman is the capital and largest city. (See the map with the article on the MIDDLE EAST.)

Jordan's climate has sharp seasonal variations. Temperatures below 39 degrees occur in January, the coldest month. August, the hottest, has an average temperature of 92 degrees. Rain falls mostly in the winter. The eastern part of the country receives the most rain.

Jordanians can cultivate only a small portion of the land because the climate is so dry. The principal crops are beans, peas, grains, citrus fruits, grapes, and bananas. Camels, cattle, and goats are herded.

Natural resources include manganese, iron, phosphates, and potash. Phosphates and potash are made into fertilizer. An oil pipeline, extending from Saudi Arabia to Lebanon, crosses Jordan. Jordanians work in oil refineries near Amman. They are also employed in food processing and leather tanning.

Jordan is an ancient land. It later became part of the Roman Empire until the Arabs pushed out the Romans. In the early 1500s, the Turks took over and held the region for approximately 400 years. The British controlled Jordanian territory after World War I. They recognized Jordan's independence in 1946, and Abdullah became the country's new king. Abdullah was assassinated in 1951 because he seemed to want peace with neighboring Israel, and his grandson, King Hussein, was crowned in 1952.

Ever since Israel became a sep-

▲*John Paul Jones, a naval hero of the American Revolution.*

JORDAN

Capital City: Amman (330,000 people).
Area: 34,750 square miles.
Population: 2,160,000 people.
Language: Arabic.
Export Products: Phosphate rock, salts, and fruit and vegetables.
Unit of Money: Dinar.

▲ *A view of the Jordan River in early summer.*

arate country in 1948, the Jordanians and Israelis have been unfriendly neighbors. More than 200,000 Arabs who once lived in Palestine (now called Israel) have been forced to live in crowded Jordanian refugee camps. These Palestinians have brought great problems to Jordan. In 1967, the Israelis captured Jordanian land west of the Jordan River. The area included that part of Jerusalem where the Dome of the Rock is located. Most Jordanians, who are Muslims, believe that this shrine stands where the prophet Muhammad ascended to heaven. No settlement of the Israeli occupation has yet been made.

ALSO READ: ISLAM, ISRAEL, JERUSALEM, MIDDLE EAST.

JOSEPH, CHIEF (about 1840-1904) The last and most famous leader of the Nez Perce Indians was Chief Joseph. The Nez Perce lived in northeastern Oregon, where they fished for salmon, raised horses, and gathered roots and berries. They had welcomed Lewis and Clark when the explorers reached the Northwest in 1805.

By 1850, white settlers, miners, and gold seekers looked with longing eyes on the beautiful valleys of the Nez Perce. The U.S. government told Chief Joseph to move his people away from their homeland to a reservation in Idaho. But the Nez Perce had already given much of their land to the government. "The earth is our mother," said Joseph. "How can we sell you our mother?"

In 1873, President Ulysses S. Grant agreed that this land belonged to the Indians. Two years

▼ *Chief Joseph, Nez Perce Indian chief.*

later he changed his mind. Chief Joseph refused to move. The U.S. Army was sent to force the tribe off their land. The peace-loving Nez Perce would have to leave—or fight.

Chief Joseph guided his braves to victory in the first two battles. But the soldiers greatly outnumbered the Indians. Joseph ordered a fighting retreat, seeking safety across the border in Canada. It was one of the most remarkable retreats in military history. The soldiers caught the Nez Perce after a 1,000-mile chase. Few of the warriors were still alive. Joseph had to surrender—only 40 miles south of the Canadian border. At the surrender, Joseph made a speech ending with the words: "Hear me, my chiefs. I have fought; but from where the sun now stands, Joseph will fight no more forever."

ALSO READ: INDIANS, AMERICAN; LEWIS AND CLARK EXPEDITION; NEZ PERCE INDIANS.

JOSEPH, SAINT see JESUS CHRIST.

JOSEPHINE see NAPOLEON BONAPARTE.

JOURNALISM How do you find out what happened on the other side of the world today? Or in a state a thousand miles away from where you live? Or even what happened in your own neighborhood? You probably look in a newspaper or news magazine, or tune into a news broadcast on radio or television. How does this information "travel," get written or photographed, and arrive in your home?

The profession and business of collecting and presenting information about current events is called journalism. The word "journalism" comes from the old French word *journal*, which meant "daily." Most journalism is a daily recording of events. We usually think of journalism today as including not only current news, but also feature articles on subjects of public interest and columns of opinions.

The basic form of journalism is news. Most large news publications and radio and TV broadcasting companies employ people to *cover* (go out and see) events as they are happening. Very often these people are assigned to cover specific places or topics, such as social events, local government meetings, or sports events. These *reporters* then report, or write about, what they have seen or heard. Since it is nearly impossible (and very expensive) to have a reporter at every spot in the world, many news publications rely on *news agencies* for much of their news. This is especially true of small-town newspapers. A news agency is a very large organization which employs reporters in many parts of the world. Newspapers pay these agencies for permission to print their news stories. The best-known news agencies in the United States are the Associated Press (AP) and United Press International (UPI). The initials of these agencies appear on the top of their stories. How many of these articles can you find in your newspaper?

Another form of journalism is the *feature*. A feature article can be entertaining, informative, or instructive. Features include comic strips, cartoons, dramatic stories, and humorous articles for entertainment, and they include background material on people and places in the news, weather reports, and articles on art and the theater for information. Instruction is given in articles on cooking, gardening, and such hobbies as stamp collecting.

A third form of journalism is the expression of opinion. Opinions, or a writer's thoughts on a subject, appear in *editorials* (editor's essays), television and radio commentaries, and letters to the editor. A good journalist tries to keep opinions separate from the news so that the reader, listener, or viewer can get the facts in a story and make up his own mind about their meaning.

Journalists must decide which news is to be reported. They must also decide the manner in which stories will be presented. How important is a story? Should it be on the front page or at the beginning of the newscast? Will it get a big headline? In deciding these things, journalists give their opinions about the news stories. You can easily see that journalism plays an important part in forming public opinion.

When people speak of journalists, they are usually thinking of reporters or writers. But many other people are involved in getting the news to you. Some of them are editors, photographers, and cameramen. The person in charge of the entire operation is called a *publisher* (for newspapers and magazines) or a *producer* (for broadcasting). Technicians are often not included in the journalism profession, although they are important to it. They include printers, distributers, broadcasting engineers, and dozens of other specialists required for the complex production of mass communications.

Many young people go to college to study journalism. More than 150 colleges and universities in the U.S. have schools and departments of journalism. To study journalism, a student should have an aptitude for writing, photography, or art. He needs an interest in people and current events. He must be accurate in his writing and be curious about the world.

▲*The editors of a magazine meet to discuss the contents of the next issue.*

▼*Journalists from newspapers, magazines, radio, and television cover important events such as Presidential news conferences. Here, President Nixon is being questioned. The streaks in the photograph are from the television lights.*

▲*Chet Huntley* (left) *and David Brinkley, two popular broadcast journalists, who worked together as a television news team.*

Would you like to be a journalist? You can put out a newspaper at home with some friends, or in school with your class. First, decide what kind of information you want to put in your "journal." Perhaps you would like to write about some important project your class is working on. Did you take a trip that is worth reporting? Is there an interesting person in your community whom you could interview (ask questions)? You could include original stories, poems, riddles, and jokes.

When you have put all the items you have written together, ask a parent or teacher to help you *publish* them. Your school probably has a mimeograph, ditto, or other machine on which you can make copies. You will find it exciting to see your finished writing "in print."

ALSO READ: COMMUNICATION, MAGAZINE, NEWSPAPER, PUBLISHING, RADIO BROADCASTING, TELEVISION BROADCASTING.

JUAREZ, BENITO (1806–1872)

Benito Juarez was one of the great Mexican patriots. He was born of Indian parents, and as a child knew the hardships suffered by the Indians of Mexico.

Juarez became governor of the state of Oaxaca at the age of 40. He was opposed to the harsh methods of the dictator of Mexico, General Santa Anna. He was forced to leave Mexico, but returned to join in a revolution against the dictator.

Finally Santa Anna was defeated. Juarez tried to introduce a constitution which would bring new freedom to the poor. It took a three-year struggle, called the War of the Reform, before Juarez won. Juarez's new constitution took away most of the Roman Catholic Church's traditional powers and gave much of the Church's land to the poor. This displeased some powerful European nations including France. French troops invaded the country. Maximilian, an Austrian archduke, was

▲*Benito Juarez, Mexican political leader.*

made Emperor of Mexico and Juarez fled again.

He set up his own capital in a town now named Juarez in his honor. Within three years his brave resistance to the French brought about their defeat. He entered Mexico City in triumph and was made president. The foreign troops fled and Maximilian was executed. Juarez was re-elected president. He had enormous popular support, and died in office a national hero.

ALSO READ: MEXICO.

JUDAISM

Judaism is one of the oldest religions in the world. The Old Testament, the first part of the Bible, tells of a Hebrew tribal chief, Abraham, who lived in the Middle East about 4,000 years ago. Abraham was one of the first men to believe in one God. The Bible tells how Abraham made a *covenant*, or agreement, with God to worship only him and to obey his laws. In return, the descendants of Abraham would live in "a land of milk and honey" and prosper. God later gave the Ten Commandments to the Hebrew leader, Moses.

The early history and laws of Judaism are found in the *Torah*, the first five books of the Old Testament. The *Talmud*, another collection of ancient writings, includes laws governing everyday life and interpretations of these laws. Both the Talmud and the Torah contain all the beliefs and rules that not only bound the Jewish people together through centuries of wandering, but also form the religious and political laws of the Jewish people wherever they live. They include ideas about the equality of all members of a community, personal liberty and love of freedom, personal morality, property rights, and the rights of all human beings, in addition to the belief in one God who is creator, law-giver, and king.

Judaism teaches that people must be fair and kind to others. A person is supposed to live a good life simply for the satisfaction of being a good human being, without any promise of a reward. Many Jews believe that a leader called the Messiah will someday come to save mankind. Each Jewish community, or congregation, is led by a religious teacher and scholar called a *rabbi*. Many Jews worship and study in a special building called a *synagogue*. A *cantor* sings the prayers when the congregation worships.

Certain days are special to the Jews. One is the *Sabbath*, a day of prayer. It begins at sunset on Friday evening and ends at sunset, Saturday evening. (All days in the Hebrew calendar are figured from sundown to sundown.) *Yom Kippur*, the Day of Atonement, is the holiest day of the year, on which Jews fast and pray. *Rosh Hashanah* is the Jewish New Year.

Judaism has laws governing much of daily life. There are laws (called *kosher* laws) about the preparation of food and what may or may not be eaten. Weddings and funerals are performed as commanded in the Torah and Talmud. All Jewish boys are circumcised when they are seven days old. Boys officially become adults at the age of 13, with all the responsibilities of men, in a ceremony called a *Bar Mitzvah*.

Three main branches of Judaism exist today. People who carefully follow all the ancient traditions and laws are called Orthodox Jews. People less strict in their observance are called Conservative Jews. A third group, Reform Jews, do not always observe traditional laws, but believe in the ideals of Judaism. Approximately 14 million Jews are scattered throughout the world today. Most of them live in the United States, the Soviet Union, Canada, and Israel.

ALSO READ: BIBLE, CHRISTIANITY, DEAD SEA SCROLLS, HANUKKAH, ISLAM, ISRAEL, JERUSALEM, JEWISH HISTORY, NEW YEAR'S DAY, PASSOVER, TALMUD, YOM KIPPUR.

JUDO One of the few sports that began as a method of self-defense is *judo*, a system of fighting without weapons. (The word "judo" means "the gentle way" in Japanese.) Judo was developed in the late 1800s by Dr. Jigoro Kano of Japan, based on an earlier sport called *jujitsu*. Today, all Japanese students receive training in judo. The sport has also become popular in other countries, including the United States.

A judo fighter wears a loose-fitting white jacket and trousers. The color of the belt he wears indicates the amount of skill he has. A beginner wears a white one. The most skillful wear black belts. Fighters may compete in either *randori* (free combat or competition) or *kata* (planned practice of the various movements).

A judo expert can overcome a larger, stronger person. He can do this because judo depends on concentration and the use of balance and leverage rather than on size. A player uses non-resistance to get his opponent off balance. He does not fight back when he is attacked. In this way, his opponent is thrown off balance by the force of his own attack. (You have the same sort of experience if you push hard on a door that opens easily. Your own strength can make you trip or fall.) The non-resisting player can then overcome his opponent.

A judo competitor uses two kinds

▲*Judaic religious symbols are shown in this mosaic wall of an ancient temple in Israel.*

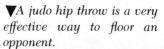

◄*A Japanese judo expert gives a demonstration of how to disarm a man with a sword. The judo expert is about to use a hand throw.*

▼*A judo hip throw is a very effective way to floor an opponent.*

of techniques to overpower an opponent. The first group of techniques offers him several ways to throw his opponent's body. The five kinds of throws are named for the part of the body involved—hand, foot, back, side, and hip. The second group concerns *locks*, or ways to keep an opponent's body from moving. Locks are applied to the legs, arms, or neck.

Do not try to learn judo by yourself or with a friend. Most cities have judo clubs where beginners can learn safely and carefully with qualified instructors.

ALSO READ: EXERCISE, GYMNASTICS, PHYSICAL EDUCATION.

JUGGLING　　One of the most spectacular acts in show business is that of the skilled juggler. Professional jugglers appear in stage shows and on television. The most skilled jugglers can keep ten or more objects in motion at the same time. In addition to balls, jugglers often perform with china plates, plastic hoops, and other objects.

Balancing acts are also part of juggling. A good juggler can balance a long pole on his nose. On top of the pole is a balanced plate, which is spinning around and around. While balancing the plate on top of the pole, the juggler may use both hands to juggle balls or hoops or plates.

For juggling, you need lots of practice and good coordination between your eyes and your hands. The simplest form of juggling is with two round objects—for example, two oranges or two small balls of the same size. Holding a ball in each hand, toss the right-hand ball into the air slightly to the left. At the same time, quickly toss the other ball from your left hand across to your right hand. As soon as the ball is released from the left hand, the hand should be ready to catch the other ball. Continue to toss and catch the two balls, trying to develop a constant rhythm in your juggling.

It shouldn't take you too long to get the knack of working with two balls. Then you're ready to try the same movements with three balls. Now you must keep two balls in the air at once. When you master your technique with three balls, you can try juggling additional balls or other objects.

ALSO READ: CIRCUS.

JULY　July is a popular time for vacations. It is one of the best months for swimming, camping, and hiking. July can be a very hot month in the northern part of the world. Flowers and crops grow in the warm sunshine. But in the southern half of the world (below the equator), July is the middle of winter.

Independence Day, or the Fourth of July, is an American holiday. On July 4, 1776, the Declaration of Independence was announced by the members of the Continental Congress. Most people do not have to work on this holiday. Celebrations are held with parades, speeches, and fireworks.

July is the seventh month of the year and has 31 days. In the old Roman calendar, July had about 36 days and was called *Quintilis*, meaning *fifth* in Latin. Julius Caesar or-

▶ *These Chinese performers are acrobatic jugglers. They are spinning plates on stocks while mounted in a pyramid formation.*

dered the Roman calendar to be changed, and *Quintilis* became the seventh month. After the calendar was changed, the month was still called *Quintilis* for a while. Many people believe that Julius Caesar renamed the month after himself.

July's flower is the larkspur. Its birthstone is the ruby.

ALSO READ: CALENDAR, HOLIDAY, INDEPENDENCE DAY, MONTH, SEASON, SUMMER.

JUMPING BEAN Can you imagine a small seed that seems to jump around nervously? That's exactly what a jumping bean is. The "bean" is really a small nut-like seed from trees of the *spurge* family, which grow in Mexico, South America, and Africa.

A small moth commonly lays its eggs inside the seeds of this tree. When the eggs hatch, the larvae of the moth, which look like tiny white worms, grow inside the seeds. These seeds are less than half an inch in length, but the larvae are even tinier. A larva takes up very little space in the seed, using the rest of the seed as food. When the seed is placed on a flat surface, the movements of the larva cause the seed to "jump." In the United States, these seeds are commonly called "Mexican jumping beans," and are fun to watch.

JUNE "And what is so rare as a day in June?" These words, written by the American poet, James Russell Lowell, express the way many people feel about June. For many children, June is the month when school ends and summer vacation begins.

In the northern part of the world, the first day of summer (the summer solstice) falls on June 21 or 22. It is the longest day of the year. The weather is warm, and flowers, trees, and shrubs are in bloom. But in the southern part of the world (below the equator), winter begins during this month.

DATES OF SPECIAL EVENTS IN JULY

1 • First circulating library was opened in Philadelphia (1731).
 • Battle of Gettysburg began (1863).
 • Battle of the Somme began during World War I. It is the bloodiest battle of recorded history (1916).
 • Dominion Day, a national holiday in Canada.
2 • President James Garfield was shot. He died September 19 (1881).
3 • Samuel de Champlain founded Quebec (1608).
4 • Independence Day to celebrate the adoption of the Declaration of Independence by the Continental Congress in 1776.
 • First rodeo competition (1888).
5 • Venezuela became the first South American country to gain independence from Spain (1811).
6 • John Paul Jones, an American hero of the seas, was born (1747).
 • First "talkie" movie, *The Lights of New York*, was shown in New York City (1928).
7 • First American is made a saint: Frances Xavier Cabrini (1946).
11 • Robert Bruce, Scottish patriot who freed Scotland from English rule, was born (1274).
 • President John Quincy Adams was born (1767).
 • United States Marine Corps was founded (1798).
 • Alexander Hamilton was killed in a duel with Aaron Burr (1804).
12 • Henry David Thoreau, American author, was born (1817).
 • Orange Day in Northern Ireland (Ulster). Protestants celebrate victory over the Catholics in the Battle of the Boyne in 1690.
14 • Storming of the Bastille, a Paris prison, touched off the French Revolution (1789).
15 • Rembrandt, Dutch painter and etcher, was born (1606).
16 • District of Columbia was established (1790).
 • World's longest road tunnel was opened to traffic (1965). It stretches for just over seven miles, goes under Mont Blanc (15,781 ft.), and is located between Italy and France.
17 • Spain officially gave up Florida to the United States (1821).
 • Spanish Civil War began (1936).
18 • Disneyland, then the world's largest amusement resort, was opened (1955).
19 • First meeting organized in United States to press for women's rights took place in New York (1848).
20 • First manned landing on the moon (1969).
21 • Ernest Hemingway, American author, was born (1899).
22 • Battle of Atlanta took place during the Civil War (1864).
24 • Simon Bolivar, Venezuelan freedom fighter, was born (1783).
25 • George Stephenson first demonstrated a successful steam locomotive (1814).
26 • George Bernard Shaw, Irish playwright, was born (1856).
27 • Korean Conflict ended (1953).
 • United States State Department was formed (1789).
29 • Benito Mussolini, Italian dictator, was born (1883).
30 • English attacked the Spanish Armada, defeating Spain (1588).
 • First representative assembly in American colonies met in Jamestown, Virginia (1619).

June is the sixth month of the year. It has 30 days. In the old Roman calendar, it was the fourth month, and it had only 29 days. The extra day was added when Julius Caesar had the calendar changed. June's flower is the rose. The birthstone for June is pearl or alexandrite. Father's Day is celebrated on the third Sunday of June.

No one knows for sure where the name June comes from. It might

DATES OF SPECIAL EVENTS IN JUNE

3 • Jefferson Davis, president of the Confederacy during the Civil War, was born (1808).

5 • First public balloon flight took place in France (1783).

6 • Nathan Hale, American patriot, was born (1755).
  • YMCA (Young Men's Christian Association) organized in London (1844).
  • D-Day, the invasion of Europe by Allied troops. They landed on the coast of Normandy in the heart of German-occupied territory (1944).

8 • Frank Lloyd Wright, American architect, was born (1869).

9 • Peter the Great, Czar of Russia, was born (1672).
  • George Stephenson, known as the inventor of the railroads, was born (1781).
  • Cole Porter, American writer of songs popular the world over, was born (1893).

11 • John Constable, English painter famous for his beautiful landscapes, was born (1776).
  • Continental Congress appointed a committee to draw up a declaration of independence (1776).

14 • Continental Congress adopted the U.S. flag (1777).
  • Harriet Beecher Stowe, author of Uncle Tom's Cabin, was born (1811).
  • First non-stop flight across the Atlantic Ocean, from Newfoundland to Ireland, made by Alcock and Brown (1919).

15 • King John of England signed Magna Carta (1215).
  • George Washington was made Commander in Chief of the Continental Army (1775).
  • Edvard Grieg, Norwegian composer, was born (1843).

16 • Ford Motor Company was founded (1903).

17 • Mississippi River was discovered by Father Jacques Marquette and Louis Joliet (1673).
  • Battle of Bunker Hill, first big battle of the American Revolution (1775).

18 • United States declared war on Britain (1812).
  • Battle of Waterloo in which Napoleon was defeated (1815).

20 • Congress adopted the design for the Great Seal of the United States (1782).
  • Queen Victoria of England was crowned (1837).
  • President Andrew Johnson announced the purchase of Alaska from Russia (1867).

21 • U.S. forces captured Okinawa from Japan after one of the bloodiest battles of World War II in the Pacific (1945).

22 • France surrendered to Germany (1940).

23 • William Penn signed famous treaty with Indians (1683).

25 • George Custer and his troops were killed by the Sioux Indians at the Little Bighorn in Montana (1876).
  • North Korea attacked South Korea, beginning the Korean Conflict (1950).

26 • United Nations Charter signed by 50 nations in San Francisco (1945).

27 • Helen Keller, deaf and blind American who grew up to be an author and lecturer, was born (1880).

28 • Archduke Franz Ferdinand of Austria was assassinated. His death was used as an excuse to start World War 1 (1914).
  • Treaty of Versailles was signed officially ending World War I (1919).

have been named for Juno, the Roman goddess of marriage. June is still a popular month for weddings. It may have been named after an important Roman family, Junius. The month of June was originally dedicated to youth, so it may have received its name from the Roman word *juniores*, which means "young people."

ALSO READ: CALENDAR, MONTH, SEASON, SUMMER.

JUNGLE A jungle is a forest that grows in a hot, wet climate near the equator. Jungles are different from the forests of temperate (medium-temperature) climates. Jungles can grow up only in areas that get over 80 inches of rain a year and have an average temperature of about 80 degrees. Most jungles have wet and dry seasons, but they are hot all year round. A jungle is a thick, tangled growth of trees, vines, and grasses. Vines and creepers wind around the trees, which are often covered with parasitic plants and animals. People cannot walk through a jungle without cutting their way through the undergrowth.

Jungles are found in South America, Central America, Africa, Southeast Asia, India, Australia, and on other islands in the South Pacific. The kinds of plants and animals that live in a jungle depend on its location. Plants in Asian jungles are completely different from those in African and South American jungles. Many plants that never get very large in temperate climates grow to giant sizes in the jungle.

A jungle contains at least three distinct levels of plant and animal life. Each level is an ecosystem—a group of plants and animals that live with and feed off each other. The animals of one level may never see or have anything to do with animals on the other levels.

The first level starts on the ground and goes up to about 25 feet. Short palm trees, ferns, and many beautiful plants, such as the philodendron, which people enjoy as house plants in colder places, grow on this level. Most of the large jungle mammals are also found on the jungle floor. Tapirs, anteaters, jaguars, and wild pigs live in South American jungles.

Tigers and leopards live in Asian and African jungles. Some kinds of birds—and the insects they live on—live at ground level. Crocodiles live in jungle rivers. Rhinoceroses and hippopotamuses make their homes near the rivers in jungles. Giant butterflies and moths also live on the first level. Many kinds of snakes—some of them poisonous—live here. Even certain crabs that normally live only near water can exist comfortably on the damp jungle ground.

The second level covers the area from 25 to 50 feet above the ground. The animals that live in the tops of the taller trees can be found here. The pottos of African jungles and other small mammals live on this level. The tadpoles of tree frogs swim in puddles of water held up by giant leaves. These tadpoles become frogs, but they never go down to the ground. They gobble up insects that live on this level. The plant life here includes mosses and pink, red, and purple orchids. Their roots are not buried in soil—they cling to the branches of trees. The air in a jungle is so humid (damp) that the roots can get the moisture they need from the air. Giant ferns also grow up to this level.

The top level of the jungle is called the *canopy*. This area includes the tops of the very tallest trees, 100 feet high or more. Vines and the foliage at the tops of trees meet and intertwine here, forming a kind of roof over the jungle. Many kinds of monkeys live here. They travel along—and swing from—branches and vines. In South American jungles, the sloth spends its whole life hanging from high branches and spends most of its time eating. It never even cleans its fur, which looks green because of the algae (tiny plants) that grow in it. At the top of the canopy—in the sunlight —are the huge, brightly colored flowers and fruits of trees and vines whose roots are planted in the ground

100 feet below. Butterflies, bees, grasshoppers, other insects, parrots (and hummingbirds, in South America) flit back and forth in the canopy.

Many well-known and widely used products come from jungles. The rattan palm and bamboo of Asia are used to make porch furniture. Teak trees grow in Asian jungles, and mahogany trees grow in Central and South America. Both trees furnish wood prized by furniture makers. Cashew trees grow in Asian and Central and South American jungles. The chicle tree, from which chewing gum is made, grows in Central America. Balsa trees, used to make model airplanes, boats, and buoys, grow in American jungles.

People of the Jungle

The jungle is a very hot and steamy place for people to live. Much of a person's energy is used up surviving the high temperature and the humidity. Little sun reaches the dark jungle floor, so farming is impossible unless a clearing is made. Even then, farming is difficult because of the thick roots remaining in the soil. The few people who live in the jungle live in small villages in the clearings or at the edge of the jungle. Some villages are surrounded by high wooden fences to keep wild animals out. The people hunt, fish, and gather fruit. They build houses out of bamboo, wood, and leaves from the jungle. They make rafts,

▲ *Jungle vegetation covers vast areas of India. In these areas the rivers are often the only possible means of transportation.*

▲ *A group of Explorer Scouts on the trail in a tropical rain forest preserve in the Panama Canal Zone.*

▼ *A doctor counsels a delinquent girl. He helps his patient to become more aware of the problems that caused her to act as she did.*

weapons, and tools from bamboo and other jungle materials.

Other Tropical Forests

Seasonal forests grow up each year in areas that have a rainy season followed by an extremely dry season. During the dry season, leaves fall and ferns die. Then the rain falls and everything sprouts again or becomes green.

Cloud forests grow on tropical mountainsides. They are called "cloud forests" because they are always misty and rainy. Mosses and lichens grow over all the other plants. In some places they form a layer thicker than the tree trunks.

Tropical rain forests are "grown-up" jungles. Over long periods of time, the canopy of a jungle becomes so thick that it blocks all the sunlight from the plants and animals living below. Many plants on the lower levels then die. Because of the darkness, the trunks of the tall trees have no leaves. Therefore, there is much less undergrowth in a tropical rain forest than in other jungles.

ALSO READ: ALGAE, ANIMAL, CLIMATE, LICHEN, MAMMAL, MONKEY, MOSSES AND LIVERWORTS, ORCHID, PALM, PLANT.

JUVENILE DELINQUENCY A boy or a girl under a certain legal age—usually 17 or 18—who breaks laws continually is called a juvenile delinquent. A juvenile delinquent often does things such as using harmful drugs, destroying property, or hurting other people or themselves. A young person's delinquent behavior in some cases is just a stage on the way to becoming a normal adult. The way his delinquency is treated by his community may turn him toward, or away from, an adult life of crime.

What makes a young person break laws? Often he feels anger towards the adult world. His parents may be divorced or separated. Or

they may fight often, may not love him, or may not discipline him (make him behave). If the parents do not show respect for the community and its laws, the child may not either.

Poverty may also cause a youth to break laws. He may begin to steal things that others have but that he cannot afford. If he lives in a slum, he may hate the run-down houses and poor schools there, and may destroy property out of anger.

When there are no activities for young people in a community, they are more likely to get into trouble. Bored teenagers may roam the neighborhoods in gangs, breaking windows or stealing cars. Young people may also commit crimes just to be accepted by other young people who do these things.

What happens to a young person who breaks laws? Sometimes the police talk to the youth's parents, or send him to an agency for help. Often, however, the young person must go to juvenile court. The court may send him to a *probation officer*, a person who will try to help the youth solve his problems, and will check on him to make sure he stays out of trouble. The court can also send the delinquent to a *psychiatrist*, a doctor who helps people who have mental or emotional problems. If the youth lives in an unhappy family, the court may place him in a *foster* home. Foster parents are volunteers who try to give these young people happy homes. Sometimes, juvenile delinquents are sent to live in state institutions.

Young people who become juvenile delinquents often hurt themselves more than their communities. Their offenses sometimes keep them from going to school and getting good jobs. They lose self respect, and the respect of others.

ALSO READ: ADDAMS, JANE; CITY; CRIME; DRUGS AND DRUG MAKING; MOOD MODIFIER; PARK; SANITATION; SOCIAL WORK; SOCIOLOGY.

KALEIDOSCOPE Beautiful patterns like multi-colored snowflakes can be seen in a kaleidoscope. These patterns are made by reflections of reflections. The kaleidoscope was invented in 1816 by Sir David Brewster.

You can easily make a kaleidoscope with two long mirrors, tape, black construction paper, wax paper, and pieces of colored paper, glass, or beads. Fasten the mirrors together along one long edge of each so that they are shaped like a V, with their shiny sides facing each other. Tape a piece of black con-struction paper across the top of the V. Use the black construction paper to make a triangle the same size as the end of the kaleidoscope. Cut a round peephole in it. Tape the triangle to one end of the kaleido-scope. Cover the open end with wax paper. Drop in several pieces of col-ored paper, glass, beads. Look in the peephole and you will see a perfect pattern. Each time you shake the kaleidoscope, you will get a new pattern. No matter how often you shake it, you will never get two pat-terns exactly alike.

ALSO READ: LIGHT, MIRROR.

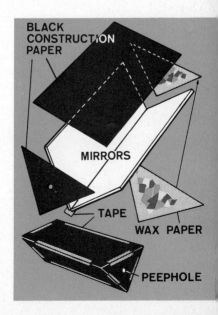

BLACK CONSTRUCTION PAPER

MIRRORS

TAPE

WAX PAPER

PEEPHOLE

▲ A bronze statue of Kamehameha I stands before the Judiciary building in Honolulu's civic center. Thousands of flowers are draped around the statue every June 11, Kamehameha Day.

▼ Rock wallabies, sometimes called rock kangaroos or wallaroos, have gray fur. They are found in mountainous areas of Australia.

KAMEHAMEHA I (1758-1819)

The first king of all the Hawaiian Islands was Kamehameha. At first, Kamehameha ruled only one "big island" of Hawaii. He wanted to rule all five of the major Hawaiian Islands. So in 1795 he gathered an army of about 16,000 men, bought guns from white traders, and brought together enough war canoes to line the beach for four miles.

His invasion force conquered the island of Maui, then attacked the second largest island, Oahu (where Honolulu is today). The climax of the bloody battle came high in the central mountains. Legend says that several hundred defenders were driven off the high cliffs to their death. Kamehameha later gained control of the two remaining islands, unifying all Hawaii into one kingdom in 1810.

King Kamehameha encouraged trade. Hawaii sold sandalwood to ship captains who sold it in China to make incense and fine furniture. Kamehameha encouraged fishing, farming, and industry. He sometimes caught his own fish, built boats, and farmed a small vegetable patch. But he kept a stern hand on island war lords to keep his kingdom unified.

ALSO READ: HAWAII.

KANGAROO

Kangaroos live only in Australia and the nearby island of Tasmania. They are the Australian national animal. Kangaroos come in all sizes. The largest kangaroo is the red kangaroo, which is sometimes seven feet tall and weighs 200 pounds. The smallest is the rat kangaroo, which is about the size of a rabbit. Medium-size kangaroos are also called *wallabies*. Another kind of kangaroo is the tree kangaroo. It has strong claws that help it hold on to branches as it jumps from tree to tree. It even sleeps in trees.

The red kangaroo is a shy, nervous animal that eats grass and leaves. If a kangaroo sees a wild dog

▲ The great gray kangaroo is found in the eastern and western parts of Australia. Like all kangaroos, it loves to gaze and stare—in this case, at the photographer.

or another enemy approaching, it hops away on its giant hind legs. A red kangaroo usually hops five to ten feet in a single jump. The red kangaroo can travel 25 miles an hour. A kangaroo will defend itself by kicking with its powerful hind legs. A kangaroo can kill another animal by kicking it.

Kangaroos belong to a branch of the animal kingdom called the *marsupials*. Each female marsupial has a pouch, or furry pocket, under the skin of its belly. A female kangaroo usually has only one baby at a time. The newborn kangaroo is only about an inch long. As soon as the baby is born, it makes its way to its mother's pouch. Inside the mother's pouch is a nipple. Milk comes from the end of the nipple. The newborn kangaroo fastens its mouth to the nipple. It lies cozily in its mother's pouch for about two months, while it develops enough to begin to explore the outside world.

A young kangaroo is called a "joey." The joey learns to eat grass and take care of itself. But the joey hurries back to its mother's pouch whenever there is danger about.

ALSO READ: ANIMAL KINGDOM; AUSTRALIA; AUSTRALIAN ANIMALS; COOK, CAPTAIN JAMES; MAMMAL.

KANSAS

You have probably watched many gunfights in the dusty streets of Dodge City—in movies or on television. Have you ever wondered where Dodge City is? It is in southwestern Kansas. The town was founded in 1872 on the Arkansas River near Fort Dodge. Railroads reached it three years later, and Dodge City became a cattle town. Herds of Texas cattle were driven there to be loaded aboard trains. The cowboys who brought the cattle were paid in Dodge City. Their rip-roaring celebrations on payday made Dodge City a wild place. Famous lawmen, such as Wild Bill Hickok and Wyatt Earp, struggled to bring order to Dodge City.

The town is very different today. Cattle are now sold by the thousands at its big stockyards. It is no longer a wild, noisy town, but people still remember Dodge City's colorful past. Some of the wooden shops and saloons that lined old Front Street in the 1870s have been rebuilt. Shots ring out every summer evening as actors stage gunfights for tourists in front of the Long Branch Saloon.

History was made in Kansas, largely because the state lies at the nation's crossroads. It is at the very center of the 48 states that make up the main part of the United States. Long wagon trains traveling west passed through Kansas on the Santa Fe and Oregon trails. Some of the old forts, which were built along the wagon trails to protect travelers from Indian attacks, can still be seen.

The Land

Kansas is almost a perfect rectangle. Only the northeast corner of the boundary line is crooked. The Missouri River forms the boundary there. Nebraska is north of Kansas, and Oklahoma is south of it. Colorado lies to the west, and Missouri to the east.

Nature has divided Kansas into two very different parts—western Kansas and eastern Kansas. The two areas differ in surface, soil, and climate, and have different kinds of agriculture.

Western Kansas is in the Great Plains. The land is highest near the Colorado border, and it slopes toward the east. Most of the land has gentle hills, but some of the slopes are very steep. In places, flat-topped hills with rocky sides rise above the plain. Much of the soil is sandy, but all of it is fertile and good for farming. Rainfall is light in western Kansas, too light for raising corn. Short buffalo grass grows wild here. The bison that once roamed the plains fed on it, and so do cattle today. Certain kinds of wheat need only light rainfall. The big crop of western Kansas is winter wheat. It is planted in October and is ready to harvest by late spring.

Eastern Kansas is prairie land. Rain is much more plentiful here. Tall grass once covered the fertile valleys. Its long roots, decaying year after year, made the soil richer and richer. Good rainfall, fertile soil, and hot summers are just right for corn. It is the main crop of eastern Kansas. Before the land of eastern Kansas was planted over with corn, the prairie was covered with waving grass. This prairie grass can be seen in the area called the Flint Hills. This upland section stretches from north to south. Grass is kept growing there for feeding cattle.

KANSAS

State flower
Sunflower

State bird
Western meadowlark

State tree
Cottonwood

Capital
Topeka (125,011 people)

Area
82,264 square miles
(ranks 14th)

Population
2,249,071 people
(ranks 28th)

Statehood
January 29, 1861
(34th state admitted)

Principal rivers
Kansas, or Kaw, River
Arkansas River

Highest Point
4,135 feet, on the
Colorado border

Largest city
Wichita (276,554 people)

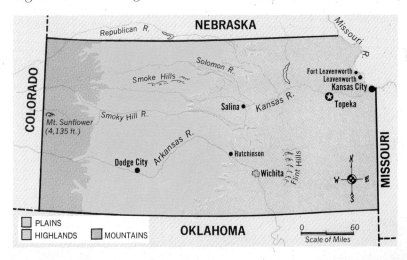

▲Boot Hill Cemetery in Dodge City, the resting place of outlaws who died in the days of the violent West.

History

The story of Kansas begins with the three main Indian tribes—the Pawnee, the Osage, and the Kaw. The Kaw Indians were also called the Kansas, which means "people of the South wind." The state got its name from them.

The Indians lived in villages of earthen huts. The women raised corn, beans, and squash. Their men went out in bands to hunt bison. They hunted on foot, because Indians had no horses until the white men came.

Spaniards were the first Europeans to come to this region. A small army from New Spain (Mexico) arrived in 1541. Its commander was a nobleman named Francisco Coronado. He was looking for a land rich in gold and silver. French explorers claimed the region in the late 1600s, but very few settlers went there during the next 100 years.

Spaniards had started ranches in New Mexico. Indians found that ranch horses were easy to steal, and some horses simply wandered away from the ranches. Herds of wild horses roamed the Great Plains. In-

▼Skyscrapers soar on the Kansas City skyline. Kansas City is an important livestock marketing center.

dians all the way to Kansas—and beyond—soon had their own herds.

The United States bought France's large territory of Louisiana in 1803. All of what is now Kansas, except the southwestern corner, was part of that Louisiana Purchase. Americans began exploring the new territory.

The first new settlers in Kansas were Indians from farther east. The U.S. government moved them there from their eastern lands to make room for white farmers. Many of the Indian newcomers were farmers themselves. They cleared land and built cabins in eastern Kansas.

▲A reminder of the old West—a parade of covered wagons bring out residents and visitors in a Kansas town.

More white settlers began to move to Kansas after Congress passed the Kansas-Nebraska Act in 1854. This law created the territories of Kansas and Nebraska. Americans at this time were quarreling over whether to allow slavery in new states and territories. The Kansas-Nebraska Act permitted the people of the Kansas and Nebraska territories to decide the issue for themselves. Northerners and southerners both came to live in Kansas. The southerners wanted to use slave labor on their farms. The northerners wanted to keep slavery out of Kansas. Many violent battles were fought. John Brown, the famous anti-slavery leader, led a raid at Pottowatomie Creek in 1856, killing five pro-slavery men. The northerners of Kansas finally became stronger in numbers, so they had their way. Kansas entered the Union as a free, non-slave state in 1861. The Civil War began that same year, and fighting again broke out in what was called "Bleeding Kansas."

New railroads brought thousands of settlers to Kansas during the late 1860s and the 1870s. Many freed slaves and Union veterans of the Civil War were among the new settlers. The Mennonites, a religious group from Russia, settled in western Kansas in 1874. These people brought wheat seed to plant. The wheat, called Turkey Red, was a kind that needed only a little rain. The Mennonites started the wheat farming that now brings much wealth to Kansas.

Kansans at Work

Manufacturing earns more money than agriculture does in Kansas today. Most factories are in the three largest cities, Wichita, Kansas City, and Topeka. Aircraft, motor vehicles, and other transportation equipment are the state's leading manufactured products. Food products and chemicals are next in manufacturing importance.

Agriculture is not far behind manufacturing in money value. Kansas produces more than a billion dollars' worth of livestock a year. Wheat is the most valuable crop. Kansas leads the entire United States in wheat production. Three other grains—sorghum, corn, and rye—are also important crops. Much grain is fed to livestock instead of being sold.

Kansas has resources under its soil, too. Petroleum brings the most money. Natural gas is next.

ALSO READ: BROWN, JOHN; CORONADO, FRANCISCO; EARP, WYATT; GREAT PLAINS; HICKOK, WILD BILL; LOUISIANA PURCHASE; PRAIRIE; WESTWARD MOVEMENT.

▲ *A karate instructor uses a training staff for the purpose of sharpening a student's reflexes.*

KARATE An expert in the ancient Oriental art of karate could split a brick or board in two with one blow of his bare hand—or foot! Karate is a way of fighting developed in China thousands of years ago. In the 1600s, karate was used by Japanese peasants as a method of self-defense against armed warriors. The word "karate" is Japanese for "empty fist," showing that the fighter has no weapons but his hands and feet.

In karate a fighter uses his hands, elbows, knees, and feet to strike blows to vital points, such as the stomach or throat, of his opponent's body. Since a karate expert can kill with a single blow, he will only use it as a form of self-defense. Today karate is a sport, requiring intense training and discipline. A student trained in karate is taught to avoid striking his opponent. Contests are usually judged according to the skill shown in performing movements.

There are various levels of achievement and skill in karate. The student must earn the right to advance. As his technique improves, the student's instructor awards him different colored belts. Karate clothing consists of loose-fitting, white trousers and a jacket without buttons. A belt is worn around the outside of the jacket. Usually, the beginner wears a white belt. As he progresses, he will successively wear a purple, then a brown belt. If he becomes skillful enough, he will earn the right to wear a black belt.

Karate should never be attempted without an instructor. Before he matches his skill against an opponent, the karate student must spend many hours in training and conditioning. The important requirements of karate training are balance, coordination, breath control, and timing.

KELLER, HELEN (1880–1968) A baby girl born in Tuscumbia, Alabama, was a normal, healthy, happy baby until she was 18 months old. Then she became very sick. Her illness left her both blind and deaf. Soon she forgot all the sights and sounds of her babyhood, and the few words she had learned.

She was examined by many doctors, but there seemed no hope that the girl, Helen Adams Keller, would ever be able to understand or communicate with others. When she was nearly seven, Helen's parents asked the Perkins Institute for the Blind and Deaf in Boston to send a teacher to help the child. Anne Sullivan, a young teacher, came to the Keller home to do what she could for Helen.

Anne Sullivan became Helen's constant companion and began to teach her about the world that Helen could not see or hear. Miss Sullivan used the manual alphabet to "spell" the names of objects that Helen could feel with her fingers. Miss Sullivan would place her fingers in Helen's palm and spell the name of an object by changing the position of her fingers. The first word Helen learned was *water*. Over and over again Miss Sullivan would pump water over Helen's hand and then spell the word for water. One day Helen suddenly got the idea—the movement of fingers in her hand meant the same thing as

▲*Helen Keller, a courageous American.*

the wet stuff that she felt. For the first time, Helen realized she could communicate with someone.

Helen began to learn rapidly. Within two years, she had learned to read and write well in Braille, the method used by blind people. Later, she learned to speak by putting her fingers against Miss Sullivan's throat and feeling the vibrations of Miss Sullivan's speech. Helen would then put her fingers against her own throat and try to make the same kinds of vibrations. Miss Sullivan taught Helen the subjects that other children study in school and prepared her for college. Helen graduated with honors from Radcliffe College, where for four years Miss Sullivan "spelled" all the lectures into her hand.

Helen Keller devoted the rest of her long life to helping the blind and the deaf. She and Miss Sullivan traveled throughout the world, making appearances to raise money for this cause. After Miss Sullivan's death, Polly Thompson became Miss Keller's companion. Helen Keller wrote many articles and books to help people understand their responsibilities toward the handicapped. She was active in her work until her death.

When you have finished reading this sentence, shut your eyes tightly, hold your hands firmly over your ears, and think what it would be like if your world were totally dark and without sound—all the time. Now, perhaps, you can imagine a little bit what life was like for Helen Keller, who became one of the most educated and active women who ever lived in spite of those handicaps.

ALSO READ: BRAILLE, HEARING, SIGHT, SPECIAL EDUCATION.

KENNEDY, JOHN FITZGERALD (1917–1963) "My fellow Americans," said John F. Kennedy in his address when he was inaugurated President of the United States, "ask not what your country can do for

THIRTY-FIFTH PRESIDENT   JANUARY 21, 1961—NOVEMBER 22, 1963

JOHN FITZGERALD KENNEDY

Born: May 29, 1917, Brookline, Massachusetts
Parents: Joseph Patrick and Rose Fitzgerald Kennedy
Education: Harvard University, Cambridge, Massachusetts
Religion: Roman Catholic
Occupation: Author and legislator
Political Party: Democratic
State Represented: Massachusetts
Married: 1953 to Jacqueline Lee Bouvier Kennedy (born 1929)
Children: 1 daughter; 2 sons (one died in infancy)
Died: November 22, 1963, Dallas, Texas
Buried: Arlington National Cemetery, Arlington, Virginia

you; ask what you can do for your country." All that needed to be done could not be accomplished in a hundred days, not even in a thousand, he said, "But let us begin."

John F. Kennedy was born in Brookline, Massachusetts, on May 29, 1917. He was one of four boys in a family of nine children. His father, Joseph Kennedy, was a wealthy businessman who later served as ambassador to Great Britain.

During World War II John, the second son, joined the United States Navy. He was commander of a motor torpedo boat in the South Pacific. One night, his boat was rammed by a Japanese destroyer. Lieutenant Kennedy was later awarded various medals for the courage he showed in saving the lives of some members of his crew. Kennedy had injured his back several years before. His efforts to save his crew and ship brought back this old injury. He was ordered back to an American naval hospital for surgery. He was discharged (given permission to leave) from the Navy for medical reasons.

A year after his discharge from the Navy, he went into politics. At the age of 29, he was elected to the United States House of Representatives as a congressman from Massachusetts. In 1952 he was elected to the Senate, but while serving as a Senator, he had to have another

operation on his back. He lived through the operation, but he was never again completely free of pain. While recovering, he wrote *Profiles in Courage,* a collection of biographies about earlier lawmakers who had shown great courage. This book won the Pulitzer Prize in 1956.

Senator Kennedy was nominated for President by the Democratic Party in 1960. During the campaign, he showed outstanding qualities of leadership and intelligence, and he became a popular candidate. Millions of Americans watched a series of televised debates between Kennedy and his Republican opponent, Richard Milhous Nixon. In his campaign, Kennedy promised to open up for America a "New Frontier"—a program of new ideas to improve the lives of all Americans. He defeated Nixon in a close election.

In his first year as President, he worked for laws to help the poor people of America with better housing, more relief (money for people unable to work), and a higher minimum hourly wage (the smallest amount of money a company is allowed to pay a worker). Kennedy founded the United States Peace Corps. The Peace Corps sends many young Americans to work with the people of underdeveloped countries. Kennedy also encouraged the development of the U.S. space program. During the early 1960s, the civil

President Kennedy's book, *Profiles in Courage,* is published in an edition especially for young readers. Your school or city library will probably have a copy.

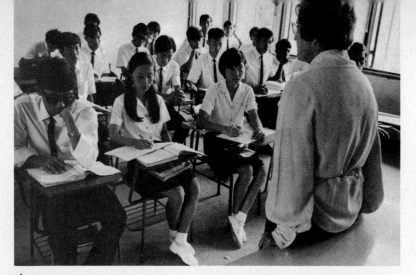

▲*The Peace Corps was started during President Kennedy's administration. Peace Corps workers, such as this woman, went all over the world to teach and help people.*

rights movement was organizing to protest discrimination against black people in the United States. Kennedy tried to persuade Congress to pass a civil rights law, to give black people equal rights. But he was unable to get support in Congress.

Kennedy, his wife Jacqueline, and their two children, Caroline and John Jr., brought the life and gaiety of a young family to the White House. Jacqueline Kennedy had many of the rooms in the White House furnished with historical furniture of the 1700s and 1800s. The Kennedys invited famous artists, musicians, and writers to the White House and encouraged their work.

Kennedy worked for a more friendly relationship between the U.S. and the Soviet Union. An attitude of suspicion and hostility, called the "cold war," had existed between the two countries since the end of World War II. Kennedy and the Soviet premier, Nikita Khrushchev, met to discuss common problems. But in 1961, the U.S. backed an invasion of the island of Cuba, which had recently been taken over by a Communist government. The invasion was a failure. The following year, the Russians began to build missile bases in Cuba. The United States told the Soviet Union to remove the missile bases or risk starting a war. The Russians finally removed the weapons. In 1963, the United States, the Soviet Union, and Great Britain signed a treaty saying that they would not test nuclear weapons in air or under water.

On November 22, 1963, President Kennedy was assassinated in Dallas, Texas. The whole world mourned for the young President who was killed before his work was completed. Events surrounding the assassination were so confused that no one knew how many people were involved in the killing of the President. A commission (a group of people organized to carry out certain legal duties) was set up to investigate the assassination. The commission concluded that Kennedy had been shot by a man named Lee Harvey Oswald. The commission decided that Oswald had acted alone and was not part of any conspiracy (a group of people who plot to do something evil). Oswald had been shot by a man named Jack Ruby before he could be tried. Kennedy was succeeded by his Vice President, Lyndon Baines Johnson. Johnson persuaded Congress to pass several laws that Kennedy had failed to get passed, including the Civil Rights Bill.

No one will ever know how much Kennedy would have accomplished if he had lived. His ideas and words continue to inspire people throughout the world. Millions have visited his grave in Arlington National Cemetery. In 1971, the John F. Kennedy Center for the Performing Arts was opened in Washington, D.C., as an active memorial to him.
ALSO READ: ASSASSINATION; CIVIL RIGHTS MOVEMENT; CUBA; JOHNSON, LYNDON BAINES; KHRUSHCHEV, NIKITA; NIXON, RICHARD MILHOUS; PEACE CORPS; SPACE TRAVEL; WHITE HOUSE.

KENTUCKY The heartland of Kentucky is known for thoroughbred race horses. It is the famous bluegrass region. Only in spring—usually in May—does the grass have a bluish tint. But blue or green, Kentucky bluegrass is excellent food for horses. Horse farms lie all around the city of Lexington. Race

▲*Kentucky has long been noted for its champion race horses. Some of the finest horse farms in the country are in the bluegrass region around Lexington.*

KENTUCKY

State flower
Goldenrod

State bird
Kentucky cardinal

State tree
Tulip poplar

Capital
Frankfort (21,356 people)

Area
40,395 square miles
(ranks 37th)

Population
3,219,311 people
(ranks 23rd)

Statehood
June 1, 1792
(15th state admitted)

Principal river
Ohio River

Highest point
Big Black Mountain,
4,150 feet

Largest city
Louisville (361,472 people)

horses are given the best of care in clean, white stables. Many horse farms are open to visitors and do not charge an admission fee.

The Land

Kentucky lies north of Tennessee. It is west of Virginia and West Virginia. Its northern boundary is formed by the Ohio River, which separates Kentucky from Ohio, Indiana, and Illinois. The Ohio River meets the Mississippi River near the western end of Kentucky. The Mississippi River separates Kentucky from Missouri. The Mississippi makes a sharp double curve along this border. It cuts off an area of about ten square miles from the rest of Kentucky. To reach this area from the main part of Kentucky, you must go through a bit of either Missouri or Tennessee!

Kentucky is divided into three land regions—all very different. The first is the southeastern third of the state. It belongs to the Cumberland Plateau. Streams have cut narrow valleys through this highland. Steep, narrow hills separate the valleys. There are many coal mines here.

The second part stretches westward from the first. It covers all the rest of the state's southern part. Here is the Pennyroyal, or Pennyrile, Plateau. Its name comes from that of a fragrant wild plant found there. Parts of the plateau are hilly, but other parts are almost level. The

plateau is good farming country. North of it is another big coal field.

The third part of Kentucky is separated from the second by the Knobs, a curving knob-like range of hills. This third part is the bluegrass region. The best farmland is here. Crops, as well as horses, are raised.

Kentucky has a good climate for farming. Summers are long and hot. There is usually enough rain. Winters are short. They are just cold enough for occasional snow.

History

Many ancient Indian tribes lived in Kentucky. Graves, stone tools, and bits of pottery found here show us where their villages once stood. Some of these Indians lived in caves.

White men were rather late in settling Kentucky. The Appalachian Mountains formed a natural barrier between this land and the colonies on the East Coast. Only a few French and English explorers entered it before 1750. In that year, five Virginians, led by Dr. Thomas Walker, reached it. They followed an Indian trail which took them through a pass through the Appalachians into Kentucky. Dr. Walker named the pass Cumberland Gap in honor of the Duke of Cumberland.

The British government did not want American colonists to move west. It wanted the land beyond the Appalachian Mountains left to the Shawnees, Wyandottes, Cherokees,

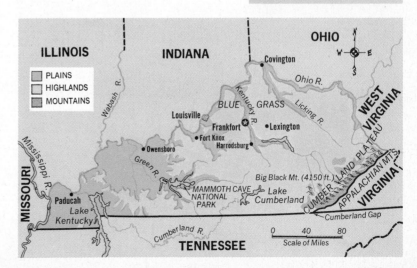

and other Indians. They hoped this would prevent more Indian wars. And Indian hunters would always be able to get the furs that the English wanted. But it was impossible to hold back the frontiersmen. James Harrod, Daniel Boone, and other frontiersmen hunted and explored in Kentucky. They liked the bluegrass region especially. Boone called it "a second paradise." Harrod led a group of pioneers to central Kentucky in 1774. They founded Harrodsburg. In Pioneer Memorial State Park, you can see a reconstruction of the log fort they built. The next year Daniel Boone and his friends

the Union, but soldiers from Kentucky joined both the northern and southern armies.

The state's biggest crop has always been tobacco. For a time, most of Kentucky's money came from this one crop. When tobacco didn't sell very well, farmers had little money. The whole state suffered.

The state was helped by the growth of manufacturing. Kentucky is rich in bituminous (soft) coal. Sixty or seventy years ago, coal was the fuel used for almost all manufacturing, transportation, and heating. Kentucky mine owners grew rich, but many Kentuckians who worked

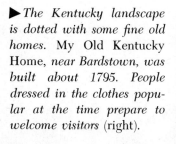

▶ *The Kentucky landscape is dotted with some fine old homes.* My Old Kentucky Home, *near Bardstown, was built about 1795. People dressed in the clothes popular at the time prepare to welcome visitors (right).*

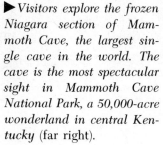

▶ *Visitors explore the frozen Niagara section of Mammoth Cave, the largest single cave in the world. The cave is the most spectacular sight in Mammoth Cave National Park, a 50,000-acre wonderland in central Kentucky (far right).*

began work on Boonesborough. These were the first two settlements in Kentucky.

During the American Revolution, Kentucky settlers fought Indians who were on the British side. Sometimes British soldiers helped the tribes in battle. The last big Indian fight on Kentucky soil took place in 1782. Kentucky became a state ten years later. It was the first state west of the Appalachians. Thousands of settlers came there by wagon on the Wilderness Road which led through the Cumberland Gap. Others floated down the Ohio River in clumsy flatboats. The population of Kentucky grew quickly.

Slavery was legal in Kentucky. But many of the state's people believed it was wrong. When the Civil War began, the state did not leave

as miners were very poorly paid. By the 1940s, however, their wages were much higher. But two new fuels—oil and natural gas—were taking business away from the coal miners. Some mines closed because they couldn't sell enough coal. The mines that stayed open began using machines. With machines, a few miners could do the work of many. Thousands of miners lost their jobs. Today, unemployment and poverty are still serious problems in the coal fields of Kentucky.

Kentuckians at Work

Manufacturing is the leading industry in Kentucky today. Most of it is done along the Ohio River. The largest factory center is the city of Louisville. Things to eat and drink head the list of products manufactured in Kentucky. Whiskey is an important product. Machinery is second among factory products. Chemicals are third.

Agriculture, the second biggest business in the state, brings in less than a third of the income manufacturing does. Farming is divided about equally between livestock and crops. Tobacco brings in more money today than all of the other crops put together. Kentucky ranks second to North Carolina among the tobacco-raising states.

Mining is the third-biggest business. In spite of the economic problems, coal is still the state's leading underground resource. Only West Virginia and Pennsylvania mine more coal than Kentucky.

The fourth-largest business in the state is tourism. Millions of tourists come to Kentucky each year. Horse racing draws crowds from outside, as well as inside, the state. The Kentucky Derby is one of the world's great racing events. It is held near Louisville each May.

Among Kentucky's natural wonders is Mammoth Cave. It is one of the largest caves on earth. About 150 miles of its underground passages have been explored. Visitors can take guided trips through the cave. Historical places attract thousands of tourists to Kentucky. They can see, among other things, the birthplaces of Abraham Lincoln and Jefferson Davis, presidents of the North and the South during the Civil War. Both men were born in Kentucky log cabins.

ALSO READ: APPALACHIAN MOUNTAINS; BOONE, DANIEL; HORSE RACING; WILDERNESS ROAD.

KENYA The Republic of Kenya is one of the busiest tourist centers of East Africa. Many wild animals of Africa can be seen in Kenya in protected areas called game preserves. Every year, tourists from all over the world travel on *safari* into these vast wildlife reserves to photograph elephants, lions, giraffes, and many other animals.

Kenya is about the size of the state of Texas. The Somali Republic and the Indian Ocean form the country's eastern boundary. Tanzania lies to the south, and Uganda forms the western boundary. The Sudan and Ethiopia are its northern neighbors. (See the map with the article on AFRICA.)

In Kenya, the land rises gently inland from the palm-fringed beaches and the bustling port of Mombasa. The modern capital of Nairobi is a mile above sea level in the green, rolling highlands of central Kenya. The climate in the highlands is cool and temperate compared to the tropical heat of the coast. The snowcapped peak of Mount Kenya, the highest mountain in the country, is located about 100 miles northeast of Nairobi. Cutting

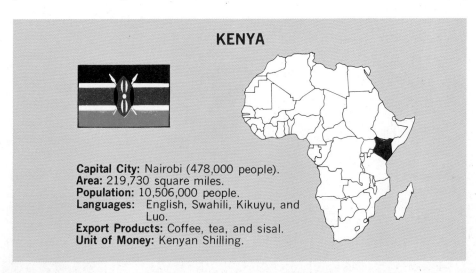

KENYA

Capital City: Nairobi (478,000 people).
Area: 219,730 square miles.
Population: 10,506,000 people.
Languages: English, Swahili, Kikuyu, and Luo.
Export Products: Coffee, tea, and sisal.
Unit of Money: Kenyan Shilling.

▲ *The Kisii people perform one of their traditional dances to the rhythm of the drums. The peoples of Kenya are proud of their heritage.*

▼ *Nikita Khrushchev, the Russian premier in the late 1950s, meets with President Eisenhower.*

through the highlands from north to south is the Great Rift Valley. This huge valley stretches from Syria in the north through the Red Sea and East Africa to Mozambique. In northern Kenya, Lake Rudolf lies in the valley. To the east of the valley is a hot, dry region of barren mountains and scrub-covered plains.

Among the tribes in Kenya are the Kikuyu, Luo, Baluhya, Kamba, and Masai. The tall, thin Masai people dress in blankets and skins and wear colorful jewelry. They tend herds of cows. Kikuyu people and most other Kenyans make their living by farming. Coffee, corn, wheat, and tea are the principal crops grown in the highlands. Sugar, cashew nuts, and cotton are grown on the coastal plains. Kenya is one of the most industrialized countries in East Africa. Agricultural products are processed for export and goods are manufactured for the Kenyan people. Tourism is a major source of income.

Arabian merchants set up trading posts on what is now the Kenyan coast in the 600s. They traded in slaves and ivory. Hundreds of years later, Portuguese, Indian, and British traders also settled in the region. In 1895, the British took over the coast and began to develop the interior. The whole region became a colony of Great Britain. White settlers began to take over farmland which belonged to the Kikuyu tribe. Some Kikuyus, led by Jomo Kenyatta, began a movement during the 1950s to drive white people out of Kenya, and to win independence from the British. These Kikuyus called themselves the *Mau Mau.*

Kenya finally won its independence in 1963. It became a republic, with Kenyatta as its first president. An elected assembly helps Kenyatta to govern the country.

ALSO READ: AFRICA.

KEPLER, JOHANNES see ORBIT.
KEY, FRANCIS SCOTT see STAR-SPANGLED BANNER.

KHMER REPUBLIC see CAMBODIA.

KHRUSHCHEV, NIKITA (1894–1971) The man who was premier and head of the Communist Party of the Soviet Union from 1958 to 1964 was the son of a poor coal miner. Throughout his career, Nikita Sergeyevich Khrushchev worked to give the Russian people an easier and more prosperous way of life. He always believed that Communism should be the most important political force in the world. He often urged that Communist ideals should be spread by peaceful means and nations should try to live together in peace.

Nikita Khrushchev was born in the village of Kalinovka, in southwest Russia. At the age of 15, he went to work in the coal mines. He fought in the Russian civil war (1918–1920), in which the Bolsheviks (Communists) established themselves as rulers of the new Soviet Union. Khrushchev went to Communist Party schools after the war and then rose rapidly in party ranks. He had become head of the Communist Party in Moscow by 1935. Four years later, he was named a member of the Politburo, the top committee in the Communist Party.

The Soviet dictator, Joseph Stalin, died in 1953. Georgi Malenkov succeeded him as premier. Malenkov was replaced by Nikolai Bulganin in 1955. Khrushchev became premier after a fierce struggle for power among the top men in the government. The Russian people had suffered terrible restrictions under Stalin's dictatorship. Khrushchev gave the people more freedom and set up programs to give them a better standard of living. He made this change in policy more dramatic by openly accusing Stalin of having committed crimes against the Russian people. Khrushchev encouraged the growth of industry and technology in the Soviet Union. While he was premier, the Russian pilot Yuri Gagarin became the first man to orbit the Earth.

Under Khrushchev's rule, the terror of Stalin's government was relaxed. The people in countries under Soviet domination began to demand greater freedom. Khrushchev at first gave in to their demands, but a major revolt that broke out in Hungary was repressed with merciless force.

A "cold war" had existed between the Soviet Union and the United States since World War II. Khrushchev now spoke of the need for peace and friendship between the two powers. But in 1962, he brought the two countries to the brink of war by setting up missile bases on the island of Cuba, close to U.S. borders. War was averted only when President John F. Kennedy forced Khrushchev to withdraw the missiles. A quarrel also developed between Russia and China.

By the 1960s, other top members of the Soviet government were seriously concerned about the quarrel with China. They felt that Khrushchev had been weak in his dealings with the West. Khrushchev's development programs in the Soviet Union had not been highly successful, and he was losing popularity with the people. On October 14, 1964, the Soviet Communist Party removed Khrushchev as leader of the Soviet government. He lived in retirement until his death in 1971.
ALSO READ: KENNEDY, JOHN FITZGERALD; SOVIET UNION.

KICK THE CAN Kick the Can is an outdoor game that can be played with any number of people. Everyone gathers at home base—a tree, a porch, or any place. One player is chosen as It. Another player kicks a can as far as possible from home base. As It goes to get the can and bring it back to home base, the other players run and hide. When It reaches home with the can, the game becomes Hide and Seek.
ALSO READ: HIDE AND SEEK.

KIDD, CAPTAIN see PIRATES AND PRIVATEERS.

KIDNEY The kidneys are two purplish-red, bean-shaped organs, which rid the body of liquid waste called *urine*.

There is one kidney on each side of your backbone, just above the small of your back. A human kidney is about four and one-half inches long, two inches wide, and one and one-half inches thick.

A kidney has two main parts, an outer *cortex* and an inner *medulla*. Blood enters a kidney through an artery which divides into branches within the medulla. These branches go to the cortex, where they further divide into tiny knots of capillaries called *glomeruli*. Surrounding the glomeruli are tiny kidney *tubules*. Each tubule, along with a single glomerulus, forms what is called a *nephron*. Each kidney contains thousands of nephrons. The nephrons separate waste matter from plasma, the liquid part of the blood. The wastes, together with a small amount of water in which they are dissolved, make up urine. The blood, cleaned of wastes, goes out of the kidney through a vein.

Urine goes from a nephron to a tube called a *collecting tubule*. Urine from many collecting tubules flows down from each kidney through a tube called a ureter. The two ureters empty into the *urinary bladder*.

A kidney may become diseased and fail to work. If this happens to both kidneys, wastes collect in the blood, and this eventually causes death. It is now possible to help a person whose kidneys do not function. A healthy kidney, from another person, may be *transplanted*, or surgically attached in place of a diseased kidney. This can be done successfully only when the transplanted kidney comes from a very close relative of the sick person.

If there is no one from whom to get a kidney, a person with kidney failure can be kept alive by use of a *hemodialysis machine*, which is also

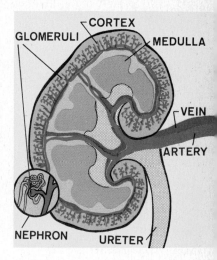

GLOMERULI CORTEX MEDULLA VEIN ARTERY NEPHRON URETER

called an artificial kidney. A tube is put into an artery in the sick person's arm, and another tube is put into a vein in his arm. His blood flows from the artery into the machine and is cleaned of wastes. The purified blood then returns to his body through the vein. This treatment usually is needed twice a week.

ALSO READ: BLOOD, DIGESTION.

KING, MARTIN LUTHER, JR. **(1929-1968)** "I have a dream that one day this nation will rise up and live out the true meaning of its creed: 'We hold these truths to be self-evident, that all men are created equal.'" These words were spoken by Martin Luther King, Jr. in 1963. He was speaking to a crowd of more than 200,000 people who had come to Washington, D.C. to march for civil rights for all people. Dr. King believed in equal and fair laws and opportunities for all people, no matter what their race, their religion, or what country they come from. Dr. King worked all his life to make this dream of equality and

brotherhood among men come true.

Martin Luther King, Jr., was born in Atlanta, Georgia. He was the son of a Baptist minister, and became a Baptist minister himself in 1947. He graduated from Morehouse College in 1948, received his Bachelor of Divinity degree (B.D.) from Crozer Theological Seminary in 1951, and his Doctor of Philosophy degree (Ph.D.) from Boston University in 1955. In 1954, he became pastor of a church in Montgomery, Alabama.

Dr. King first became known in the civil rights movement during the 1950s. In 1955, he led the black citizens of Montgomery in a peaceful *boycott* of the city buses. During a boycott, people refuse to use certain things, buy certain products, or deal with certain companies. The black people of Montgomery refused to ride the city's buses because blacks were always made to sit in the back. The boycott succeeded. The bus company finally agreed to let the blacks sit in any seats on a Montgomery bus.

Dr. King helped organize the Southern Christian Leadership

▶*Martin Luther King, Jr., (center) leads the March on Washington on August 28, 1963.*

Conference (SCLC) in 1957. The purpose of this organization was to fight for civil rights and against racial discrimination. As president of the SCLC, Dr. King led many marches against racial discrimination. These marches made people see the injustice of discrimination, and encouraged lawmakers and government officials to do something to correct it.

Dr. King preached *non-violence* throughout his life. His idea of non-violence was simple—changes must be made without fighting and without damaging other people's rights. With non-violence he gained many victories in the struggle for equal rights for blacks. King's work was largely responsible for the passage of the Civil Rights Act of 1964 and the Voting Rights Act of 1965. In 1964, Dr. King received the Nobel peace prize. He gave this prize of over 70,000 dollars to the civil rights movement.

Dr. King worked hard for equal school opportunities for both black and white children. In most areas of the country, black people could not buy or rent homes in certain white neighborhoods. Dr. King led marches in Chicago and other cities to protest racial discrimination in housing. Dr. King also fought against job discrimination. Companies often would not hire a black person—even if he were qualified for the job—simply because he was black. And even if the black person were hired, he would not receive the same benefits and promotions as white workers. Many businesses now advertise that they are "equal opportunity employers." This means that they no longer pay attention to a person's race, but hire people on the basis of their qualifications, and promote people on the basis of their abilities. These and many more are changes that have taken place through the efforts and bravery of Dr. King and other workers for civil rights.

Although Dr. King advocated non-violence, he died a violent death. In 1968, in Memphis, Tennessee, Dr. King was shot and killed by James Earl Ray. In memory of Dr. King, many people now celebrate his birthday, January 15, as a special holiday.

ALSO READ: CIVIL RIGHTS, CIVIL RIGHTS MOVEMENT, NEGRO HISTORY.

KING, W. L. MACKENZIE (1874-1950) William Lyon Mackenzie King was Prime Minister of Canada for a longer period than anyone else in Canadian history. Born in Ontario in 1874, he was named after his grandfather, who had led an unsuccessful rebellion against the British in Canada in 1837.

Mackenzie King studied at the University of Toronto, the University of Chicago, and Harvard University. The social work he did in Chicago inspired him to investigate and expose unhealthy and unfair working conditions in Toronto. He helped to establish a Department of Labour in Canada and later served as Minister of Labour.

Mackenzie King was chosen as the leader of the Liberal Party in 1919. His party won the election of 1921, and he became prime minister. Except for a brief period in 1926 and the five years from 1930–1935, Mackenzie King served in that office until his retirement in 1948.

He began a national social security program in Canada by establishing old age pensions (salaries for retired people). Mackenzie King helped to unify his country by treating both English- and French-speaking Canadians fairly.

ALSO READ: CANADA, COMMONWEALTH OF NATIONS.

▲*Mackenzie King, Canadian prime minister, votes in an election.*

KINGS AND QUEENS A king is a man who rules a country for life, usually by inheriting the position. A queen is either the wife of a king or a woman who rules a country herself. Such a ruler—male or female—is

▲Queen Elizabeth II in her coronation robes. Her robe is lined with ermine and she wears the crown used on important state occasions. She holds the scepter and the orb that represent her authority.

▼A Venetian throne made of carved wood in the 1700s. The throne symbolized the king's authority.

called a *monarch.* The monarch's wife or husband is called a *consort.* Monarchs and their families are called *royalty.* The royal family includes not only a monarch's immediate family but his cousins, uncles, aunts, nieces, nephews, and grandparents. The monarch rules until he or she dies, or steps down, or abdicates, rather than for a fixed number of years.

A monarch usually takes office in an elaborate ceremony called a *coronation.* At this ceremony the crown—the symbol of his power—is placed upon the monarch's head.

The eldest son of a king usually becomes king when his father dies. If the king has no sons, his oldest daughter becomes queen after his death. Queen Elizabeth II became the monarch of Great Britain after her father, King George VI, died. When a monarch has no children, a brother or another close relation may succeed to the throne.

Long ago, a chief or king would rule a tribe that moved from place to place. When a tribe settled permanently in an area of land, the king ruled this area, called a *kingdom.* Forty-five centuries ago in the land called Mesopotamia (now Iraq), Sumerian kings ruled city-states. To lead an attack against another city-state, the king would put on his golden helmet, climb into his war chariot, and order his soldiers, who were armed with lances and bows and arrows, to follow him into battle.

The ancient Babylonians, who came to power in Mesopotamia after the Sumerians, had an odd custom. At the time of the New Year, the real king would "retire" for a day to get out of the sight of gods who might be angry with him. The Babylonians then chose a prisoner or a slave to be "king-for-a-day." A festival was held, with music, games, and food for all. When the day ended, the real king returned, and the substitute king was killed.

The ancient Egyptian kings were called *pharaohs.* The Egyptians believed that their pharaohs were gods. The pharaohs ordered great pyramids built as burial places for themselves. The pharaoh was almost always a man. But Hatshepsut broke this tradition in about 1500 B.C., when she proclaimed herself pharaoh. She assumed all the titles and badges of office and even wore a false beard. She ruled for 14 years.

Alexander the Great was an important king during the time when ancient Greece was powerful. He became King of Macedonia, a land to the north of Greece, when he was 20 years old. Before he died at the age of 33, he had conquered much of the land surrounding the eastern end of the Mediterranean Sea, as well as the vast Persian Empire. Alexander brought Greek civilization to all these regions. He was one of the most successful military commanders of all times.

Julius Caesar was a Roman statesman and general. Although he ruled the Roman Empire like a king, Caesar took the title of *dictator* instead. Julius Caesar was so powerful that the Roman emperors who followed him all took the title "Caesar." The leader of the Russian Empire before World War I was called a *czar,* from the word *Caesar.* And the Emperors of the Holy Roman Empire, Austria, and Germany were called *kaisers.*

Kings of the Middle Ages

Many stories are told of the great King Arthur. A king named Arthurius did rule in western England in the Middle Ages. But storytellers made up the fascinating tales of the adventures of Arthur and his Knights of the Round Table.

A famous real king of the Middle Ages was Charlemagne. He extended his empire from what is now France to include most of western Europe. Charlemagne was a wise and hard-working king. He wanted his people to become educated, so he established schools where both rich and poor boys could study.

In 1215, England began to limit the power of kings. A group of noblemen forced King John to sign a document that promised the noblemen certain rights. This document was called *Magna Carta.* The king at the same time agreed that all free-

▲*An Assyrian king gives an audience to some of his subjects. Giving audiences helped the king understand the needs of his people.*

▼*King Darius III of Persia, in a chariot, leads his army in the Battle of Issus in 333 B.C. Alexander the Great led the Greek forces.*

men had definite legal rights that no king could take away from them. Some ideas from Magna Carta are found in democratic constitutions to this day.

Modern Kings

Over the centuries, the power of kings has declined. Republics have taken the place of many kingdoms. The people elect legislatures to make laws. Today, almost no king can do just as he wishes. Most modern kings *reign* (hold office), but they do not rule over the people.

In England, Queen Elizabeth II reigns, but Parliament and the prime minister govern. The English people feel that their king or queen gives them an important symbol of unity. And they enjoy the ceremonies associated with the royal family. In Europe, the countries of Norway, Sweden, and the Netherlands each have a king or a queen. But a prime minister and a legislature make the laws that govern each country.

In Morocco, a country in Africa, King Hassan II is trying to use his power to build up his nation. Japan adopted a democratic constitution

▼*King George III of England wearing his coronation robes trimmed with valuable ermine. This fur was a symbol of the king's power.*

▲*Emperor Hirohito of Japan and the empress enjoy a moment of family life with their children and grandchildren.*

after being defeated in World War II, but it kept its emperor. Today, the Emperor of Japan attends ceremonial functions and lives in the Imperial Palace in Tokyo.

At least one storybook kingdom still remains. It is Sikkim, a small country tucked in the Himalayas between India and Burma. In 1963, an American college girl named Hope Cooke married Maharajah (king) Namgyal of Sikkim. India controls the international relations of Sikkim. But within their country, the maharajah and his maharani (queen) rule their kingdom in much the way kings of the Middle Ages did.

For further information on:

Rulers, *see* DICTATOR, GOVERNMENT, MAGNA CARTA.

Ancient Kings, *see* ALARIC; ALEXANDER THE GREAT; CAESAR, JULIUS; NERO; TUTANKHAMEN.

Kings, *see* ALFRED THE GREAT; ARTHUR, KING; BRUCE, ROBERT; CANUTE; CHARLEMAGNE; CHARLES, KINGS OF ENGLAND; CHARLES, KINGS OF FRANCE; CHARLES, HOLY ROMAN EMPERORS; CHARLES MARTEL; EDWARD, KINGS OF ENGLAND; EDWARD THE CONFESSOR; FRANCIS, KINGS OF FRANCE; GENGHIS KHAN; HENRY, HOLY ROMAN EMPERORS; HENRY, KINGS OF ENGLAND; HENRY, KINGS OF FRANCE; ISABELLA

AND FERDINAND; JAMES, KINGS OF ENGLAND; JOHN, KING OF ENGLAND; LOUIS, KINGS OF FRANCE; NICHOLAS, CZARS; PHILIP, KINGS OF FRANCE; PHILIP, KINGS OF SPAIN; WILLIAM, KINGS OF ENGLAND; WILLIAM AND MARY.

Queens, *see* ANNE; CLEOPATRA; ELEANOR OF AQUITAINE; ELIZABETH I; ELIZABETH II; GREY, LADY JANE; LILIUOKALANI; MARY, QUEEN OF SCOTS; MARY, QUEENS OF ENGLAND.

KIPLING, RUDYARD (1865–1936)

The British writer Rudyard Kipling was born in Bombay, India. India was part of the British Empire at the time. Kipling glorified the empire in many of his works, but he also wrote with sympathetic understanding about the people and stories of India.

Kipling was sent to England to be educated when he was only six. At the age of 17, he returned to India and went to work as a newspaper reporter. He began to write the short stories that made him famous. Kipling was a brilliant, imaginative storyteller. He vividly described the excitement and atmosphere of the places in his stories. His first two collections of stories, *Soldiers Three* and *Plain Tales from the Hills*, were very successful. Kipling returned to England in 1889. He wrote more stories and a popular series of verses, *Barrack Room Ballads*, about the life of British soldiers in India. In 1892, he married an American girl and went to live in Vermont. But he later returned to England and settled.

He wrote several successful novels, including *Kim*, about the adventures of an orphan boy in India, and *Captains Courageous*, about a spoiled rich boy who changes his ways after spending some time with deep-sea fishermen on a ship. The adventures of Mowgli, a boy brought up by animals, are described in Kipling's two *Jungle Books*. Other books which he wrote for children are *Puck of Pook's Hill* and the *Just So Stories*.

▼*Rudyard Kipling, English author.*

KITCHEN The kitchen is the food workshop of the home. All the family's meals are prepared there, and the family may also eat there. The kitchen is often a gathering place, too. Many people feel most comfortable talking with their friends and neighbors in a warm, cozy kitchen. In the early colonial days in America, kitchens were usually large rooms in the house. On plantations, the kitchen was often in a separate building. Cooking in early kitchens was done over an open fire. The warmth of the fire also heated the house. People would often gather around the fire to talk, tell stories, and sing songs.

It includes cupboards, drawers, shelves, and closets where pots and pans, dishes and utensils, cleaning supplies and foods are stored. In some kitchens, pots and pans, dishes, and some foods, such as spices, are hung from pegs or placed in racks on the walls. The refrigerator and freezer make up part of the storage area, too.

Many other features of the modern kitchen also help the cook. Mixers, blenders, toasters, and portable broilers speed meal preparation. Drawers and cupboards revolve, glide out, or tilt, to bring supplies into easy reach. Exhaust fans clear the kitchen of fumes and odors.

▼*A colonial American kitchen* (left). *The cooking was done in the huge fireplace behind the table.*

▲*A modern kitchen* (above) *is usually equipped to make work easier for whoever does the cooking and cleaning up.*

In those days, kitchen tasks were difficult. Water and firewood had to be brought in from outside, and kitchen utensils (tools) were heavy.

Modern kitchens are designed to save time and steps. They are often divided into three areas. The first is the cleaning and preparation area, which includes the sink for washing and draining, and counter space for mixing and chopping. Garbage disposals and dishwashers save time here. The second area is the cooking area. Foods are cooked on burners or in an oven. These can be combined in a range, or separated, and installed in countertops and walls. Ranges and built-in burners and ovens use gas or electricity for fuel. The third area is the storage area.

Timers "watch" a meal as it cooks. Gay curtains and wallpaper, bright floors and tiles, and shiny stoves and refrigerators make the kitchen colorful and attractive. All these things, combined with tempting smells, warmth, and happy talk, help to make the kitchen a pleasant place to work.

ALSO READ: COOKING, FOOD, INTERIOR DECORATION.

KITE For thousands of years, kites have been made and flown by people of all ages living in most parts of the world. Kites have been especially popular in Asian countries. In Korea, people fly kites on the first few days of the new year as a kind of celebration. In Japan, kite flying is

▲*This tiny Japanese kite, perhaps the world's smallest, measures only 1½ by 2¼ inches. It can fit in a matchbox—and may actually be flown!*

▲*A giant box kite and a simple flat kite being flown in a contest.*

an important part of the boys' festival that is held each May. In China, one day out of every year is celebrated as Kites' Day. At these special "kite celebrations," hundreds and thousands of kites are flown. They are made in all shapes, colors, and sizes. Some are shaped like fish, dragons, butterflies, or birds. All of them are very bright and colorful.

A simple kite can be made with two crossed pieces of light wood glued to a sheet of paper or plastic. Then, all that's needed is a cloth tail, for balance, and a ball of cord—and, of course, a good wind.

Most kite fans fly their kites just for fun, but serious kitefliers enter contests and tournaments. These events are conducted under the rules of the International Kitefliers Association.

Kites are used for practical purposes, too. The U.S. Weather Bureau used kites to gather information about winds and weather. Some of the kites used in this work carry scientific instruments, and fly higher than 20,000 feet.

The *flat kite* is the simplest and most popular kite. The *box kite* is another popular type. Both flat kites and box kites are sold in many stores. Another favorite kite looks something like a bird.

To launch a kite, it's usually necessary to run into the wind for a few feet. As the kite begins to rise, let out more line and give it some short tugs.

Do not fly a kite near trees or power lines. Also, you should not fly a kite in an area where there are low-flying aircraft.

KLONDIKE see YUKON TERRITORY.

KNIGHTHOOD In early medieval times in Europe, military battles were fought between soldiers on horseback. These mounted warriors fought each other with swords and lances. They carried shields and wore armor to protect themselves. These warriors were called *knights*

in English, *chevaliers* in French, *ritters* in German, and *caballeros* in Spanish. The French *chevalier* Bayard, who lived from 1474 to 1524, was one of the most famous knights of all time. Known as "the brave and virtuous knight," he was fearless in battle and generous to all men.

In the early days, knights were landowners who owed allegiance (pledged loyalty) to a lord—a king, a prince, or a nobleman. The lord protected the landowner from bandits and robbers. In return, the landowner agreed to fight against his lord's enemies. This arrangement was part of the organization of society known as the feudal system.

The landowners could not stay away at war for a very long time, since they had to look after their lands and families. But the nobleman who was fighting a long war needed soldiers he could depend upon. Gradually the custom developed that a landowner's youngest son would serve in his father's place in the nobleman's army.

A young man first had to prove that he knew how to ride a horse and use a sword. Contests were held in which young men fought against each other in a mock battle. These contests were called *tournaments*. If a young man proved he was a good fighter, he was knighted by the nobleman. In this ceremony, the young man would kneel before the nobleman. The nobleman would touch him on the shoulder with a sword and say, "I dub thee Sir John," or whatever the young man's first name was. "Sir" was the English title of knighthood.

After a great many years, a complicated system developed for training young men to be knights. A young boy of seven or eight would leave his family. He would become a *page* at a nobleman's castle. He waited on table, ran errands, and was brought up by the nobleman and his wife as if he were part of their family. He also began to learn the things a knight had to know to be a good and brave warrior.

When the boy was a teenager, he became a *squire,* or servant, to a knight. The knight taught him how to ride a horse and how to fight with weapons. The squire took part in tournaments. Whenever the knight rode through the countryside, the squire rode with him and carried the knight's sword and armor. The squire helped the knight put on his armor before a battle. He followed the knight into battle carrying his banner. If the squire proved himself brave and faithful, he was knighted at a special ceremony. He spent the whole night before the ceremony in prayer before the altar of a church. This was called a *vigil.* In the morning, he was dressed in a white robe and knightly armor. His lord then touched him with a sword and dubbed him knight.

The knights were expected to be more than just warriors. When they were knighted, they swore to obey certain rules of behavior called the code of *chivalry.* Bayard's father taught his sons to "serve God. Be kindly and courteous to all men of gentle breeding. Be honorable and serviceable to all people. Be neither a flatterer nor a teller of tales. Be faithful in deed and word." Knights were expected to be courteous and helpful to women. A knight would wear his lady's scarf into battle. The greatest honor for a knight was to be sent on a dangerous *quest,* or mission. The legends of King Arthur and the Knights of the Round Table give a vivid picture of chivalry.

During the holy wars known as the Crusades, religious orders of knights were formed. The knights who joined these orders took an oath of poverty and obedience, as if they were monks. They also swore they would fight to free the Holy Land from the Muslims. The most famous among these religious orders were the Knights Templar and the Knights of Malta.

▲*Two mounted knights about to duel with swords. They fought and lived according to special rules of chivalry.*

When methods of warfare began to change about 500 years ago, the warrior knights were no longer needed. The order of knighthood has now become an honor that is given for outstanding accomplishment in some type of work. The king or queen of Great Britain still creates knights by dubbing them with a sword.

ALSO READ: ARMOR; ARTHUR, KING; CRUSADES; FEUDALISM; MIDDLE AGES; NOBILITY; WAR.

KNITTING Knitting is the art of weaving yarn with needles to form fabric. People first began to knit by hand in Scotland in the 1400s. Today, knitting is a well-developed machine industry.

A hand-knitter usually works with a single length of yarn, looping it with long "sticks" called needles to form interlocking chains. He shapes the piece as he works. If he adds loops, the piece grows wider. If he takes some loops off, the piece becomes narrower. He can make patterns by using different combinations of two basic stitches, called *knit* and *purl.* He makes different textures by using different types of yarns.

A knitting machine was invented by William Lee of England in 1589. But Queen Elizabeth I would not grant him a patent because she thought the machine would put hand-knitters out of work. Knitting machines finally became widely

HOW TO KNIT

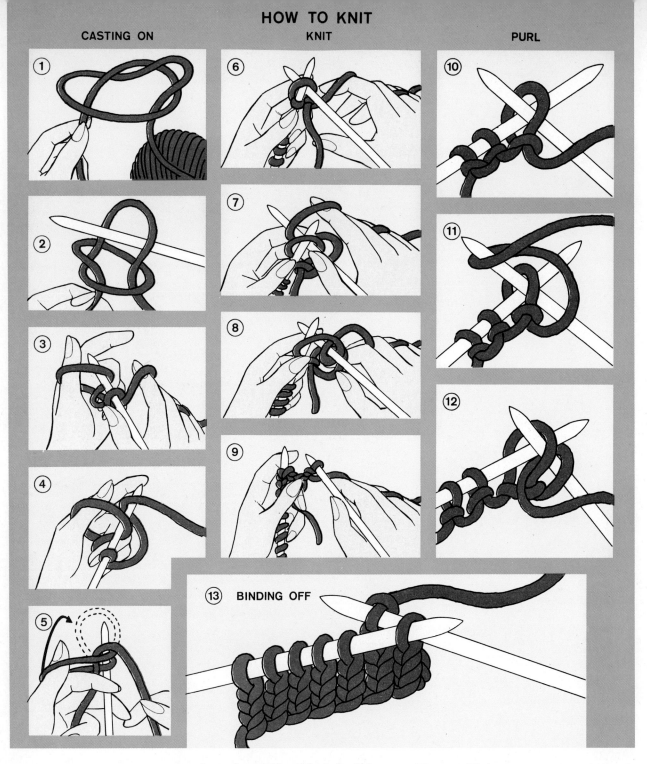

CASTING ON   **KNIT**   **PURL**

① ② ③ ④ ⑤ ⑥ ⑦ ⑧ ⑨ ⑩ ⑪ ⑫

⑬ **BINDING OFF**

used in the 1700s. They had hundreds of needles, instead of the two, or four, that hand-knitters use. Machines today make sweaters, mittens, hats, stockings, dresses, and knit fabrics that can be cut and sewn like cloth. Wool, cotton, silk, and synthetic yarns are used.

Hand-knitting has almost disappeared as an industry, although some people in villages in Scotland and Ireland still support themselves by hand-knitting. But many people enjoy knitting by hand as a hobby.

How to Knit

If you are a beginner at knitting, you can start by making a scarf. You will need a pair of size 11 knitting needles and one 4-ounce *skein* (coil) of 4-ply wool or synthetic yarn. Ask the salesperson whether the yarn must be wound into a ball.

CASTING ON. This is a process in which stitches are put onto the needle. Pull out of the skein yarn equal to three lengths of the needle. Make a loop (a slip knot) as in Diagram 1. Slide the needle into the loop. Pull the loop around the needle (Diagram 2), and tighten the stitch. To add stitches to the needle, wrap the yarn around your left thumb. Slide the needle in your right hand between your thumb and the yarn around it. Look at Diagram 3. Move the yarn in the right hand over the point of the needle from the back (Diagram 4). Put the loop on your left thumb over the needle point. Look at Diagram 5. Fit the stitch snugly on the needle. Continue casting on stitches.

KNIT. Place the needle with the stitches on it in your left hand. Insert the right needle through the first stitch on the left needle. Make sure that the right needle is behind the left needle. See Diagram 6. Using the right hand, put the yarn around the back side of the right needle. Look at Diagram 7. Slide the yarn through the loop, as shown in Diagram 8. Remove the stitch from the left needle, as shown in Diagram 9.

PURL. Insert the right needle in front of the left needle containing the stitches. Look at Diagram 10. Place the yarn around the right needle from the right side, as shown in Diagram 11. Bring the right needle through the stitch, as shown in Diagram 12. Remove the old stitch from the left needle.

BINDING OFF. When you have completed something, you must remove the stitches from the needles and finish off your work so that it will not come apart. Slip the first stitch from the left needle onto the right needle. Knit the second stitch on the left needle. Put the left needle into the first stitch. Slide the first stitch over the second stitch. Look at Diagram 13. Keep sliding the first stitch so that it comes off the needle. Continue this procedure until one stitch remains on the right needle. Cut the yarn so that a piece four inches long remains. Bring the loose end through the loop and pull tightly.

Using size 11 needles, cast on 30 stitches. Knit two rows, Purl two rows. Continue this pattern until the scarf is as long as you want it to be. Bind off all 30 stitches.

ALSO READ: NEEDLEWORK.

KNIVES, FORKS, AND SPOONS

All our tableware is called *cutlery*, which means cutting instruments, because knives were the first articles of tableware to be used. When spoons and forks developed, they were included in the term.

The knife has been found in every part of the world. It is mentioned in the oldest known laws, the Code of Hammurabi, dating from 2100 B.C. Bronze-age knives have been found in places where people lived in ancient times. Men used knives for hunting, self-defense, and for spearing or cutting food. Knives were made in many shapes and sizes. Roman invaders of Europe carried pocket knives that opened and shut. Rounded kinds of knives came to be used as table knives.

Seashells may have been the first spoons. Egyptians used small spoons carved from bone or ivory. By the time of the Roman Empire, spoons were made of brass, copper, and other metals. Spoons were made by pouring hot, liquid metal into molds. When the metal cooled and hardened, the molds were removed and the spoon was polished. American pioneers made pewter tableware in the same way. Pewter is an *alloy* (mixture) of tin, copper, lead, and antimony. Forks came much later. For many centuries food was eaten with the fingers. Forks were first mentioned as table implements in 1611, although an ancient tool with prongs, found in England, dates from about 800 A.D.

Sheffield, England, has been the cutlery center of the world since the 1100s. Cutlers worked in shops called *hulls*. Most of the tools used in the settlement of America came from Sheffield. Even the famous

▲*This machine stamps out the basic shape of spoons from metal blanks.*

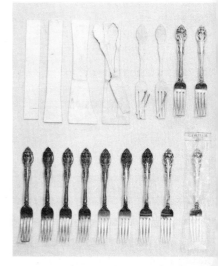

▼*The various steps in the manufacture of a fork. The strip of metal* (top left) *becomes the shining piece of silverware* (lower right).

Bowie knife! Even though it was a true American design, it was manufactured in England. The first American cutlery works opened in Meriden, Connecticut, in 1835, with a work force hired from Sheffield.

Stainless steel has become a popular alloy for cutlery in recent years. Silver plate and sterling silver have been used for many years.

ALSO READ: TOOLS.

KNOT Every civilization has used knots. Early hunters and fishermen made traps by knotting ropes made from vines or animal muscle and hair. Museums exhibit Egyptian knotted ropes that are 3,500 years old. Peruvian Incas used *quipus,* or knotted strings, to keep records and lists. An ancient Greek legend tells of Gordius, king of Phrygia, who tied his cart reins in a complicated knot. A prophet said that whoever opened the Gordian knot would be ruler of Asia. Alexander the Great slashed the knot open with his sword, and later conquered Asia.

People used to think knots had magical powers. The Romans believed that a wound would heal faster if the bandage were tied in a "Hercules knot." A Hercules knot is now called a *square* or *reef knot*. In parts of northern Europe, people believed that wizards could catch the wind in knots tied in rope. Sailors would buy rope tied in three knots from these wizards. If a sailor were at sea and needed a wind to move his ship, he untied the first knot which was supposed to contain a gentle breeze. The second knot was supposed to contain a stronger wind, and the third knot, a wind of hurricane force.

Knots are used for many kinds of jobs. They can be used to lift, pull, or support anything from very heavy to very light loads. A knot can fasten things together, or it can join two ropes to make one long one. Knots have been most widely used by sailors for tying ships' rigging and for lifting and hauling loads of various kinds.

In tying knots, there are some important things to consider. Do you want the knot to stay put for a long time, or will you be untying it very soon? Will your knot be used for heavy or light loads? The knot you use should be right for the job, and it should be easy to untie.

Types of Knots

Knots are divided into groups according to how they are used. These groups are stoppers, bends, hitches, binding knots, and loop knots.

Stoppers are used to keep a rope from slipping out of a hole or out of the loop of another knot. The knot tied to the end of thread to keep it from slipping out of the needle is a stopper. The *overhand knot,* shown in the diagram, is a kind of stopper. It is easy to tie, but it can jam easily, which makes it hard to untie.

Loop knots are tied to form a loop that is then slipped around something and tightened. The *honda* knot, shown in the diagram, is a loop knot that is used to tie a bowstring to a bow or to make a cowboy's lasso. First tie a loose overhand knot, draw the rope around in a short loop, and bring the rope through the overhand knot. Tie a stopper to the end of your rope to keep it from slipping out.

Binding knots are used to fasten things tightly together or to hold something in place. A binding knot will hold a bundle of things together. It is also used by surgeons for stitching wounds. The *bowknot* that you tie shoes with is a binding knot. The *square,* or *reef knot,* shown in the diagram, is used for many jobs. It will stand a lot of weight, but it can jam and become hard to untie if too much weight is put on it. To make a reef knot, wrap a rope around an object. Take one end of the rope and bend it so that it forms a kind of loop. Take the other end of the rope, draw it through the

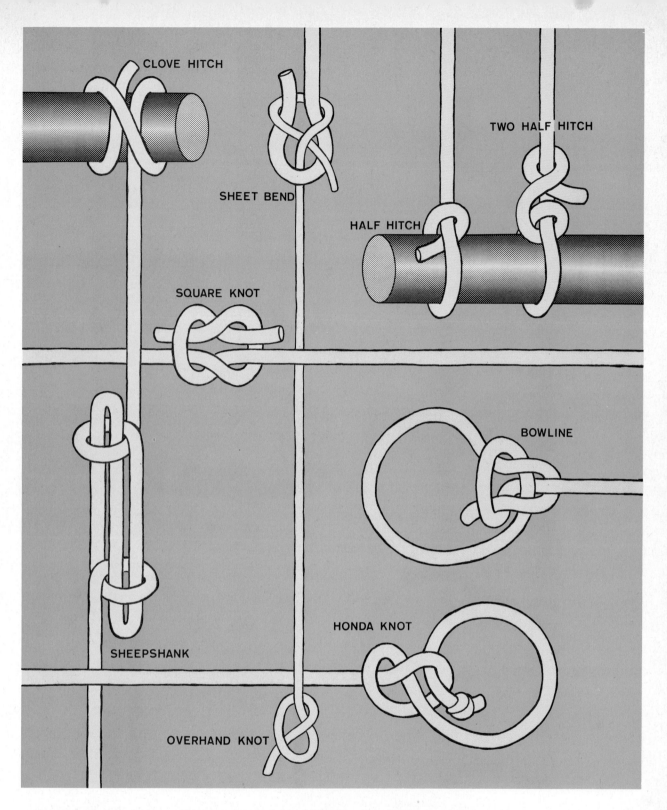

CLOVE HITCH

SHEET BEND

TWO HALF HITCH

HALF HITCH

SQUARE KNOT

BOWLINE

HONDA KNOT

SHEEPSHANK

OVERHAND KNOT

loop, and over the bottom part of the loop, then bring it back under and through the loop again and pull the knot tight.

Bends are usually used to tie two ropes together to make one long rope. A bend knot does not slip. The *sheet bend*, shown in the diagram, is a strong knot that does not slip and is easy to untie. Take two ends of rope, and form one end into a loop as you did for the reef knot. Draw the other end through the loop, bring it around the back of the loop to the front, and then draw it between the two pieces of rope on the right side of the loop. Then pull the knot tight. To make a *double sheet bend*, wrap the rope around the loop twice, and draw it under the length of rope that you first put through the loop. This is a complicated knot, but with a little practice, you will be able to tie it easily.

Hitches are used to tie a rope onto something. Horsemen use them to tie horses' reins to posts. They are very easy to untie. The *half hitch*, shown in the diagram, is a knot used when you are in a hurry. It is a loose knot that comes untied easily. Throw the rope over something and wrap one end around the other. The *two half hitch*, shown in the diagram, is stronger. Start by making a half hitch and wrap the rope around a second time.

These are just a few simple, basic knots. There are many more that you can learn after you have mastered these.

ALSO READ: EGYPT, ANCIENT; HERCULES; ROMAN EMPIRE; SAILING.

KOALA The stuffed animal toy called the "teddy bear" is modeled after the koala. The koala is not really a bear. Koalas live only in Australia, and the females have pouches, like female kangaroos. When a koala is born, it is only three-fourths of an inch long. The newborn koala lives in its mother's pouch until it is six months old and measures about six inches long. The young koala then begins to ride around on its mother's back until it learns to find its own food. Animals that carry their young in pouches this way are called *marsupials*.

The koala has a chubby body cov-

▼*A koala in a eucalyptus tree.*

ered with gray fur, and it has no tail. Its eyes are small and bright, and its ears are large and bushy. It has a little black, rubbery nose. A full-grown koala weighs about 30 pounds and is about the size of a two-year-old child.

Koalas are *nocturnal* animals. (They are awake and active mainly at night.) The koala, a skilled climber, lives in only one kind of tree—the eucalyptus. This is because eucalyptus leaves are all the koala ever eats. A koala never drinks water, because it gets all the liquid it needs from the eucalyptus leaves.

Koalas are very shy animals and hardly ever leave their trees. This makes them easy to catch. At one time, koalas almost became extinct (disappeared) because hunters were killing them to sell their fur. Now there are strict laws to protect the koalas from such danger.

ALSO READ: AUSTRALIA, AUSTRALIAN MAMMALS, MAMMAL.

KON-TIKI see HEYERDAHL, THOR.

KORAN The Koran is the book of holy writings, or scripture, of the faith of *Islam*. People who believe in Islam are known as *Muslims*. According to their beliefs, an Arabian named Muhammad was chosen to be God's messenger to the world. The word of God was told to Muhammad by the angel Gabriel in the year 610 A.D. Muhammad could not read or write, but he repeated what the angel had told him to his followers, who memorized it and wrote it down. These collected writings are called the *Koran*, which means "reading" in Arabic. The Koran is divided into 114 chapters, called *surahs*. It contains rules for almost every part of a Muslim's life. It teaches that there is only one God, or *Allah*, who created the universe. The Koran says that God sent many prophets, or messengers, to Earth to help man live a better life, and that Muhammad was the last and greatest of these. Some earlier prophets were Abraham, Moses, and Jesus Christ. The Koran tells that everyone will be judged for his actions by Allah on the last day. The book includes stories and history that are also found in the Bible. The Koran is read every day in all Muslim schools and *mosques* (temples). One of the holiest things a Muslim can do is to memorize the entire Koran.

ALSO READ: ARABIC, ISLAM, MOSQUE, MUHAMMAD.

KOREA Koreans call their homeland Chosen, "the land of the morning calm." Their country has been divided into two parts since the end of World War II. North Korea is a Communist country called the People's Democratic Republic of Korea. Its capital is Pyongyang. South Korea is known as the Republic of Korea. Its capital is Seoul. Korea occupies a peninsula about the size of the state of Kansas. It is in eastern Asia with water on three sides—the Sea of Japan, the Korea Strait, and the Yellow Sea. The Yalu River forms Korea's northern boundary with China. (See the map with the article on ASIA.)

Much of Korea is very mountainous. Mount Kwanmo (8,337 feet) is the highest peak. Most of the rivers are short, swiftly flowing mountain streams. There are no large lakes.

The climate of Korea has sharp regional and seasonal variations. In the northern part of the country, long, cold winters are common and summers are fairly warm. But in central and southern Korea, winters are brief, and summers are longer and warmer. Most rain falls between April and November in both the north and south.

Nearly 70 per cent of all Koreans earn their living by farming. Chief crops are rice, barley, wheat, sweet potatoes, yams, and soybeans. The rest of the people work in manufacturing, especially in the north, where there are steel and textile mills, as well as cement and chemical plants. Other factories in the north turn out rubber products, glass, pottery, and porcelain. Textiles, chemicals, glass, cement, and steel are manufactured in the south. Fishing is an important industry in the coastal areas of the country. The forests of North Korea are also a source of income to that region.

The Korean people are similar in appearance to Japanese and Chinese, but they are usually taller. The Korean language is similar to Japanese in its grammar, but the vocabulary is different. The Koreans have their own alphabet, but they often use Chinese writing in their literature. Many different religions are practiced in Korea. The oldest religion is *shamanism*, which teaches that there are good spirits and evil spirits in such things as rivers, trees, animals, winds, and fire.

▲*Part of a page from the Koran. It is written in Kufic, an early form of the Arabic alphabet used especially for making fine copies of the Koran.*

NORTH KOREA

Capital City: Pyongyang (653,000 people).
Area: 49,096 square miles.
Population: 13,300,000 people.
Language: Korean.
Export Products: Iron, steel, and minerals.
Unit of Money: Won.

SOUTH KOREA

Capital City: Seoul (3,795,000 people).
Area: 36,152 square miles.
Population: 31,139,000 people.
Language: Korean.
Export Products: Plywood, fish, seaweed products, and tungsten.
Unit of Money: Won.

▲A Korean father, dressed in traditional white robe, takes his daughter for a seaside stroll.

▼A helicopter is used to fly a wounded American soldier away from the battlefield in the Korean Conflict.

Other religions in Korea are Confucianism and Buddhism. They were introduced into the country from China over 500 years ago. Christianity was brought to Korea about 200 years ago.

Korea's powerful neighbors, Japan, China, and Russia, have battled for control of the peninsula. In 1910, Japan established Korea as a colony. After World War II, Korea became independent, and Syngman Rhee became president in 1948. Later that year, people living in the northern part of the country formed a Communist government. In 1950, Communist troops from the north invaded the southern part of the country. The fighting that followed became known as the Korean Conflict. After the fighting stopped in 1953, Korea remained a divided country.

ALSO READ: ASIA, KOREAN CONFLICT.

KOREAN CONFLICT The main events leading up to the Korean Conflict began at the end of World War II. Korea had been occupied by Japan since 1910. When the war was over, Korea was freed from Japan. Soviet troops occupied North Korea. U.S. troops occupied South Korea. The United Nations said it would be glad to supervise elections throughout Korea in order to establish a single government for the entire country. The Soviet Union refused. So separate elections were held in the north and the south, and two countries were established. Both U.S. troops and Soviet troops withdrew.

On June 25, 1950, the Soviet-trained army of North Korea invaded South Korea by surprise. The South Korean army fell back. The United Nations tried to stop this aggression. The UN called on its members to send troops to help South Korea. President Harry S. Truman of the United States immediately ordered land, naval, and air forces into Korea. Other countries later helped, but the U.S. and South Korea bore most of the burden. U.S. General Douglas MacArthur became the UN supreme commander in Korea.

By the end of July, the North Koreans had pushed the UN forces into a small area at the southeastern tip of Korea. But within this area was the important port of Pusan. Meanwhile, UN aircraft bombed North Korean tanks and supplies. U.S. troops began arriving at the port. Trying for a quick victory, the North Koreans attacked the area with thousands of soldiers. The defenders held.

On September 15, U.S. Marines came ashore from landing craft at Inchon, farther north on the west coast of Korea, in the same way they had invaded islands held by the Japanese in World War II. The Marines overcame the North Korean resistance, moved inland, and soon captured the South Korean capital, Seoul. The UN troops defending Pusan now broke out. North Koreans surrendered by the thousands. Thousands of others were killed. The rest of them fled to the north.

On October 1, three months after the war began, South Korean troops crossed the thirty-eighth parallel dividing North and South Korea. The UN force under MacArthur's command pushed into North Korea in an effort to unify the entire country.

North Korea undoubtedly would have fallen, but the Chinese entered the war on North Korea's side. On October 26, a strong Chinese army attacked UN forces. Attack followed counterattack in freezing winter weather. By January 1, 1951, the Chinese had pushed UN troops back south of the thirty-eighth parallel. Seoul fell to the Communists.

Now it was the UN's turn. General Matthew Ridgway launched a counteroffensive that by April had pushed the Chinese north of the parallel once again. The Chinese had been hurt badly enough to want a cease-fire. Truce talks began on July 10—a little bit more than one year after the North Koreans had invaded South Korea.

The truce talks went on for two years. The fighting continued, but the battle line moved little. On July 27, 1953, an agreement was reached to end the Korean Conflict. A buffer zone 2½ miles wide was laid out between North Korea and South Korea. No troops from either side could go into this buffer zone.

ALSO READ: KOREA; MAC ARTHUR, DOUGLAS.

KRAKATOA see VOLCANO.

KREMLIN In the center of Moscow stands a magnificent group of brightly colored buildings topped with tall spires and golden domes and surrounded by a high stone wall. This is the Kremlin. Many Russian cities are built around kremlins, or fortresses, but the 500-year-old Moscow Kremlin is famous throughout the world.

The wall surrounding it is over a mile long and as tall as 70 feet in some places. Nineteen towers rise high above the wall. Many of the buildings inside the wall are joined by underground passageways. The buildings were constructed at various times over several centuries,

dating back to the Middle Ages.

The Grand Kremlin Palace, completed in 1849, has the most imposing buildings within the Kremlin. It was the home of the Russian *czars* (kings) until the last one, Nicholas II, was put to death by revolutionaries in 1918. The throne room of the palace is now the meeting place of the Supreme Soviet (legislative assembly of the Soviet Union).

Several magnificent, golden-domed cathedrals are also in the Kremlin. Like many other churches in Russia, they have been turned into museums. They contain priceless paintings, jewels, and czarist crowns. Another Kremlin landmark is the Tower of Ivan the Great, a belltower 320 feet high. Near the Tower is the Czar's Bell, the largest bell in the world. It weighs nearly 200 tons!

The Soviet Palace of Congresses is the newest building in the Kremlin. The modern glass and steel structure is often the site of concerts, operas, and ballets.

When the Communists gained control of the Russian government in 1917, the Kremlin was closed to the public. Many government offices were located in the Kremlin, and it was the home of the dictator Joseph Stalin. After Stalin's death in 1953, many offices were moved outside the walls. The Kremlin was opened to the public as a national museum in 1955.

ALSO READ: MOSCOW, RUSSIAN HISTORY, SOVIET UNION.

KUWAIT see ARABIA.

▲*The Kremlin is brilliantly lit during a Soviet celebration. Floating above the building is a huge balloon bearing the portrait of Lenin, the first Soviet leader.*

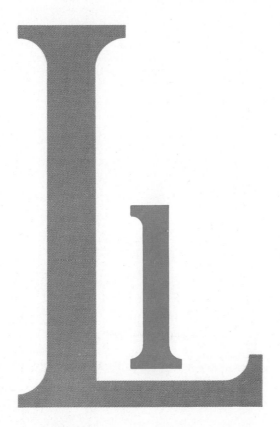

LABOR UNION   One worker alone often finds it very difficult to obtain better working conditions. But when many workers join together in a group to ask their employer for the same thing, they can more easily get what they want. "Labor" is a word for working people as a group. When working people join together to form an organized group to obtain better working conditions, the group is called a labor union.

The idea of labor unions began in Europe in the Middle Ages. Men skilled in a particular kind of work formed organizations called *guilds*, in order to obtain aid and protection. Great changes occurred in England and the United States in the 1700s and 1800s, during the Industrial Revolution. Time-saving machinery was invented and large factories were built. Manufacturing and mining industries were developed. Great numbers of people went to work in the factories and the mines. They were forced to live in crowded, unsanitary housing near their jobs. They were paid low wages, and working conditions were often harsh and dangerous. Workers rebelled against this unjust treatment, and formed the first labor unions to obtain improved working conditions.

The first labor unions in the United States were started by shoemakers and carpenters in Philadelphia about 1790. Soon workers in other trades also formed unions. There are two kinds of labor unions. People doing the same kind of work, such as carpenters, belong to *craft unions.* All the people working in the same industry, no matter what their job is, belong to an *industrial union.* For example, members of the United Auto Workers of America might be welders, painters, or electricians, but they all work in the auto industry.

Single, or local, unions often join together to form national unions. In 1866, the craft unions throughout the United States joined together to become the American Federation of Labor (AFL), the first successful collection of different unions. In 1938, the industrial unions became the Congress of Industrial Organizations (CIO). These two groups merged in 1955 to form the AFL-CIO.

The growth of labor unions was marked by much violence and bloodshed. In the early days, workers' demonstrations were often cruelly suppressed. The workers themselves often used violence when nobody would listen to their requests. Today, labor and management (company owners) try to talk to one another in a process called *collective bargaining.* Both unions and management have representatives who meet to discuss the workers' demands. They try to understand each other's point of view, and reach a fair and peaceful decision. Sometimes a third party, not involved in the argument, tries to help them come to an agreement. If this does not work, unions often go on strike, or stop working. When thousands of workers throughout the country go on strike to aid each other, entire industries can be stopped.

When a group of workers whose services are considered to be needed for the public's safety, such as firemen, go on strike, the employer can obtain a court *injunction.* This forces the workers to return to their jobs. If they don't, they or their leaders may be fined or jailed.

Early labor unions had simple demands. They wanted shorter work weeks, higher wages, and safer working conditions. Now unions ask for health and welfare benefits, paid holidays, insurance, and many other side, or *fringe,* benefits. Labor unions in the United States have become very important in politics. Millions of workers can have tremendous influence on an election, because many of them will vote for the candidate who promises to do the most for workers. Also, labor

▲*Samuel Gompers, first president of the American Federation of Labor.*

▼*A certificate of membership in the Brotherhood of Locomotive Engineers.*

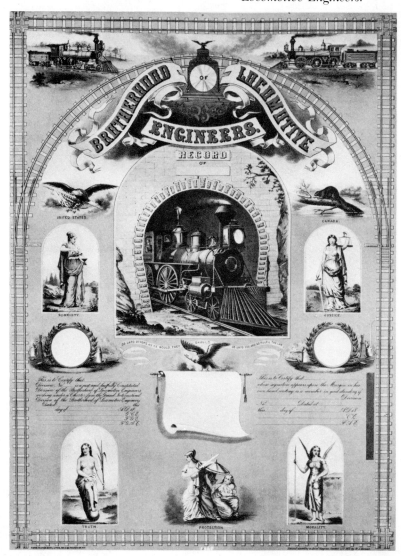

unions have political action funds —often large sums of money they give to the campaign funds of candidates they back. Many of the original aims of labor unions have already been achieved, and today Americans are among the world's highest paid workers.

ALSO READ: GUILD.

LABRADOR see NEWFOUNDLAND-LABRADOR.

▲*The finest lace is still made by hand. The work requires skill and patience.*

LACE Lace is a delicate open fabric, woven of silk, cotton, linen, nylon, or other thread. Clothing decorated with lace was very fashionable in Europe among wealthy people during the 1500s, 1600s, and 1700s. Both men and women of the nobility wore lace collars, lace sleeves, and even shoe decorations made of lace. Women often wore lace scarves. In Spain, where these scarves are still worn, they are called *mantillas*. European men often had lace cuffs on their trousers, and some wealthy women even wore dresses made entirely of lace.

Today, lace is not quite so popular as it once was. Men rarely wear it at all. But lace is still widely used for women's underclothing, formal dresses, handkerchiefs, scarves, tablecloths, and curtains.

The two main types of handmade lace are *needlepoint* lace and *bobbin*, or *pillow* lace. Needlepoint lace is made with a needle and thread and a piece of parchment or paper backed with cloth. The design for the lace is first drawn on the parchment, and heavy stitches are made in the parchment around the border of the design. These border stitches are used as the base for the design stitches. The lace-maker never sews through the parchment. She attaches the design stitches to the border stitches. When the lace is done, the parchment is removed by cutting the border stitches.

Bobbin lace is made with several spools, or bobbins, of thread and a long stuffed pad, or pillow. The design is drawn on parchment, and pins are stuck through the parchment, along the lines of the design, into the pillow. The threads of the bobbins are looped around the pins and then passed under, over, or around each other, so that the threads are woven into delicate designs. When the lace is done, it is removed by pulling out the pins.

Lace, as we know it today, was first made in Italy in the 1400s. Other countries later developed their own styles of lace-making. Belgium, Italy, France, Spain, Ireland, England, and Flanders all became centers of fine lace-making. Laces became fancier and more costly as years passed. Some laces were made of gold and silver threads.

Most lace today is made by machine. An English manufacturer made the first machine lace in the late 1700s. The bobbin net machine, invented by John Heathcoat of England in 1809, was able to make patterned net that looked very much like handmade Brussels lace. Heathcoat's invention was the model for today's lace-making machines. Machine-made lace can be produced much more quickly and more cheaply than handmade lace, but fine handmade lace is still made all over the world.

ALSO READ: NEEDLEWORK, SEWING.

LACROSSE

LACROSSE   When the French pioneers first settled in eastern Canada, they saw the Indians playing a strange game. The Indians tossed a small ball of stuffed leather back and forth with long-handled sticks. The sticks were crooked and had nets at the top. To the French, the sticks resembled a cross, so they called the game *la crosse*.

Lacrosse is now an international game and an Olympic sport. It is played mostly by men, but there are also women's lacrosse teams. For many years, lacrosse in the United States was played only on the East Coast. Now, the game is spreading to other parts of the country. Lacrosse players must be fast runners and must be able to throw and catch the ball skillfully with their lacrosse sticks. A lacrosse stick is made either of hickory wood or fiberglass, and is from four to six feet in length. A triangular net made of strings of leather is attached to the end of the stick. The lacrosse ball is made of hard rubber.

A lacrosse team has 10 players—a *goalkeeper*, three *defensemen*, three *attackmen*, and three *midfielders*. The field is 110 yards long and 60 yards wide. It is divided in half by a *center lane*. Six-foot square nets are placed at opposite ends of the field. The midfielders can play all over the field, but the defensemen must stay on their own side of the field, and the attackmen must stay on the opponent's side.

The object of a lacrosse game is for one team to score more goals than the other. A goal, which counts one point, is scored when a player throws or kicks the ball past the other team's goalkeeper and into the nets. A game is usually divided into four 15-minute quarters.

Men lacrosse players use both their sticks and bodies to prevent the other team's players from running onto their half of the field and coming within close shooting range of their goalkeeper. A player may hit the stick of a ball-carrier, in order to knock the ball loose. But he cannot hit the ball-carrier on his head, arms, or body. Players, except for the goalkeeper, cannot touch the ball with their hands. In many ways, lacrosse is like ice hockey. Because men's lacrosse is a rough game, the players wear thick, padded gloves. They also wear protective helmets and face guards.

ALSO READ: ICE HOCKEY.

LAFAYETTE, MARQUIS DE

LAFAYETTE, MARQUIS DE (1757-1834) A 20-year-old, wealthy French nobleman became one of the greatest heroes of the American Revolution. The Marquis de Lafayette was born in Chavaniac, France. He entered the French army at 14, and rose to the rank of captain by the time he was 19 years old!

When the American colonies declared their independence, Lafayette went to America and offered to serve in the colonial army without pay. By a special resolution of the Continental Congress, Lafayette was commissioned as a major general in the Continental Army. He was then 20 years old.

Lafayette was placed on General Washington's staff, and served with distinction in several battles. He also gave much of his own fortune to help the colonies. In 1825, Congress granted him almost 12,000 acres of land in Louisiana.

Upon his return to France, Lafayette played a leading role in the French Revolution. He became a member of the French National Assembly, commander of the French National Guard, and helped to write the French Bill of Rights. When he opposed the violence of the French rebels, he was declared a traitor, his property was taken by the government, and he was exiled. Lafayette fled from France. But he was arrested abroad as a leader of the Revolution and was held in Prussian and Austrian prisons for five years.

▲*The action in a lacrosse game sometimes gets a little rough as the players hit each other with their sticks.*

▼*The Marquis de Lafayette, French soldier and statesman and hero of the American Revolution.*

In 1799, Lafayette returned to France. He had little to do with politics because he disapproved of the policies of Napoleon Bonaparte, who was by that time leader of the French government. But for the rest of his life, Lafayette fought for social equality, religious tolerance, and freedom of the press in France.

ALSO READ: AMERICAN REVOLUTION, FRENCH REVOLUTION.

LAFFITTE, JEAN see PIRATES AND PRIVATEERS.

LA FONTAINE, JEAN DE (1621–1695) The famous French poet Jean de La Fontaine is best known for his imaginary stories, or fables. La Fontaine was born in Chateau-Thierry, France. He was educated as a priest and as a lawyer. But he later decided to devote his life to writing. His first literary work was the *Contes et Nouvelles en Vers*, a book of stories told in verse.

His *Fables* were written later, in three groups, between 1668 and 1695. They were based mainly on the fables of the ancient Greek writer, Aesop. The fables are stories about animals that speak and behave like people. Each story has a moral, or teaches a lesson about life. La Fontaine retold Aesop's fables in verse and added wise and amusing comments of his own. "The Fox and the Grapes," "The Grasshopper and the Ant," and "The Lion and the Mouse" are a few of these tales.

The fable of "The Fox and the Crow" tells how unwise it is to listen to flatterers. The crow found a large piece of cheese one day, and flew up into a tree to eat it. The fox, who wanted the cheese, sat under the tree and told the crow what a beautiful voice she had. "Let me hear you sing but one song," he said. When the crow opened her beak to caw, the piece of cheese fell to the ground and was gobbled up by the fox. Although La Fontaine wrote his *Fables* for adults, children everywhere have enjoyed them ever

▲ *Jean de La Fontaine, French author.*

since. His works brought him great fame during his lifetime, and he enjoyed the financial help and encouragement of several noble and wealthy patrons.

ALSO READ: AESOP, FABLE.

LAKE Have you ever watched puddles form in the street when it rains? The rain water collects in low places in the pavement. Lakes are formed in a similar way. Water collects in large *depressions* (hollows or low places) on the surface of the Earth. The depressions fill either with rainwater or with the water that flows from rivers, mountain streams, or underground springs.

Most of the world's lakes lie in regions where huge *glaciers* (masses of slowly moving ice) moved across the land during the Ice Age, about 10,000 years ago. The glaciers carved hollows in the land as they traveled. These hollows filled with water as the glaciers melted, and lakes formed. If you fly in an airplane over Minnesota, you can see many lakes formed in this way.

Lakes are formed in other ways, too. Crater Lake in southwestern Oregon lies in the *crater* (bowl-shaped opening) of an *extinct* volcano. (An extinct volcano is one that no longer erupts.) Crater Lake is not connected with any rivers or streams. Melting snow keeps it full. Lakes are also formed when the Earth's *crust* (outer layer) shifts and cracks. Water fills the crack. Lake Baikal in the Soviet Union began in this way. It is the world's deepest lake. Another kind of lake is the *sinkhole lake*, which is found in limestone regions. Limestone is a kind of soft rock that dissolves easily. Rain water slowly wears a depression in the rock, and the depression fills with water. Northern Florida has many sinkhole lakes.

Some lakes are called "seas," although they are not connected with the oceans. The Caspian Sea, in the Soviet Union, and the Dead Sea, between Israel and Jordan, are salt-water lakes. Saltwater lakes are fed by rivers and streams, but they have no outlets. Water can leave these lakes only by evaporation. The Sea of Galilee, in Israel, is a freshwater lake. The Jordan River passes through it, bringing water in at one end and carrying it out at the other.

Man can make artificial lakes by building dams across rivers. The river water backs up behind the dam, and a lake is formed. A new lake, called Lake Powell, was created in Arizona in 1963. It formed behind Glen Canyon Dam, which blocks the Colorado River. Both natural and man-made lakes are useful to man. Canals can be built to bring water from lakes to irrigate farmlands. Lakes can also be used as *reservoirs* (areas for storing drinking water). And lakes provide fun for people—fishing, boating, swimming, and water skiing.

In the future, new lakes will form, and the lakes that exist today will disappear. Some will be filled in little by little with bits of sand or earth carried by rivers and streams. Others may slowly dry up because of a change in climate or because the streams that feed them dry up.

ALSO READ: ARAL SEA; CASPIAN SEA; DAM; DEAD SEA; FOOD WEB; GALILEE, SEA OF; GLACIER; GREAT LAKES; GREAT SALT LAKE; VOLCANO.

LAKE DWELLERS In very ancient times many people began to build their houses over water. They did this in order to escape their enemies—wild animals or other people. Lake dwellers seem to have existed as long as 1½ million years ago, when the Stone Age began. Two kinds of lake dwellings were built. People made mounds of stone, brush, or mud, in the water. They drove short *pilings* (heavy pieces of wood) into the mounds and built houses on the pilings. On stormier lakes, they made stronger bases for the pilings by placing square log frames on the lake bottom. They would drive long poles into the lake bottom within these frames, and then build their houses on these long

▲*Lakes are not only beautiful, they are also good places for recreation. Water skiing is one of the most popular lake sports.*

SOME INTERESTING LAKES

LAKE COMO, a lake formed by the action of glaciers, is one of the most beautiful lakes in the world. It is located in northern Italy at the foot of the Alps, the largest mountain system in Europe. Its shores are lined with magnificent homes and gardens.

LOCH NESS is thought by some people to be the home of a giant sea monster over 30 feet long. This lake is in Scotland.

LAKE SUPERIOR, one of the five Great Lakes of North America, is the largest freshwater lake in the world. It covers 31,800 square miles.

THE CASPIAN SEA is the largest saltwater lake in the world. It covers 143,630 square miles and is located in the Soviet Union and Iran.

LAKE TITICACA lies at the highest level above the sea of any large lake in the world. It is located 12,507 feet above sea level on the border between Peru and Bolivia.

LAKE MOERIS was one of the first lakes used to irrigate the land. The ancient Egyptians harnessed this natural reservoir, which was fed by the waters of the Nile River.

BRATSK LAKE, located in the Soviet Union, is the largest man-made lake in the world.

poles. The lake dwellers had to climb ladders to get into their houses. They would pull the ladders up after them, so that no enemy could follow. By living on the water, the lake dwellers were able to use more of the good land around a lake for farming. A person could even go fishing without leaving his home!

When people began to use bronze and iron tools, they were able to build larger, stronger houses. In Switzerland's lakes, people have found ruins of large, well-built lake communities. Even today, some groups of people—such as those in the Philippine Islands and along the Amazon River in South America—still live in houses built over the waters of lakes.

ALSO READ: ANTHROPOLOGY, STONE AGE.

▲*Charles Lamb, English writer.*

LAMB, CHARLES (1775–1834) Charles Lamb was a popular British writer of essays and poetry. He is also known for the book, *Tales from Shakespeare*, in which the stories of Shakespeare's plays are rewritten in simple language for children. Lamb was born in London, England. When he was 17 years old, he went to work as a clerk in the East India House of London. He stayed there until he retired in 1825. Lamb's life was a tragic one, but he was helped by his many friends and admirers. His sister Mary Ann suffered from fits of insanity all her life. Lamb took care of her when she was not in an institution. He never married. He and Mary worked together on *Tales from Shakespeare*. She rewrote the comedies, and he the tragedies.

Lamb's writings included many poems, articles, and criticisms of plays, but his witty, amusing essays brought him his greatest fame. Most were written under his pen name, *Elia*. One of his best-liked and funniest essays was the "Dissertation on Roast Pig." This essay tells how a farm caught fire one day and all the farmer's pigs were burned. The farmer touched one of the pigs and burned his fingers. He put his sore fingers in his mouth and became the first man to discover the sweet taste of roast pork.

LAMP see LIGHTING.

LAMPREY see FISH.

LANGLEY, SAMUEL see SMITH- SONIAN INSTITUTION.

LANGUAGE ARTS Man's entire civilization is built on language—on man's ability to communicate and understand. For this reason, and others, language is one of the most important skills people develop. Language arts is the study of how to use language effectively. In the language arts, you learn how to express your ideas so that others will understand you. And you also learn how to listen and read so that you will understand other people's ideas.

The language arts include listening, speaking, reading, and writing. All of these are skills that you learn by practice. You learn them by *doing* them. When you were a baby, you first learned to talk by listening carefully to the words used by people around you. Then you tried to imitate (copy) those words yourself. You repeated the words over and over until you got them right.

Listening and speaking skills go together. When a person speaks, there must be someone to listen; otherwise there is no communication. A good listener must be able to concentrate on (pay attention to) the speaker's words. He must be able to follow the speaker's ideas and sort out the important parts of the message from the unimportant parts. A listener must also pay attention to the speaker's "tone of voice." The tone of voice tells you the speaker's feelings or the mood of his message. A speaker might say, "I really like Mrs. Crumbubble." But his tone of voice might show that he really doesn't like her. A good listener, by understanding more, gets more enjoyment from what he hears. A good listener will enjoy a movie more than a bad listener, who may miss half the dialogue and not understand what is happening on the screen.

Speaking well means sending messages so that listeners will understand them. You may have a brilliant idea in your mind, but if you jumble up the message, people will have a hard time understanding what your brilliant idea was. Good speaking also means being sure you don't bore your listeners. Bored people don't listen—and if they don't listen, there is no communication. A good speaker must consider his listener. For example, a baby or younger child will not understand you if you use big words when talking to him. A speaker should be able to give information clearly, accurately, and without wasting words. For example, if you give your classmates directions for a science experiment, they will need to know each step in order, stated clearly so they will know exactly what to do.

Reading and writing skills go together, just as listening and speaking skills do. The writer sends a message for the reader to receive. Communication takes place in written language, which you read, rather than in spoken language, which you listen to.

The reader must do what the listener does. A reader must learn to follow the writer's ideas and sort out the important ideas from the less important ones. He must also pay attention to the "tone of voice," or the mood, of the written message. An important part of the reading skill is learning to enjoy reading. Good readers learn to read not only for information, but for the pleasure they can get from imaginative writing (literature), such as short stories, poems, novels, and plays.

Writing means sending messages in written form so that readers will understand them. You begin to write by learning how to form the alphabet letters and arranging them to spell words. As you learn to spell words, you practice arranging them on paper so that they form messages that others can read and understand. Writing and speaking are very much alike. A writer must present his ideas clearly and accurately, and he must try not to bore his readers. A writer must also consider who his readers will be. You probably wouldn't write a story or article the same way for adult readers and for small children.

By learning to communicate well through listening, speaking, reading, and writing, you can understand others better and help them to understand you. You also learn about the world by communicating with language. If people send and receive unclear, jumbled-up messages, no one will learn very much and civilization will not progress very far. This is why the language arts of listening, speaking, reading, and writing are taught all through school.

High-speed communications systems have made good listening and reading very important. Television, telephones, and computers provide gigantic amounts of information that must be listened to or read. The language arts teach you to read and listen for important information, and then take care of it fast before more information piles up. Thousands of books, magazines, and newspapers are published every year. You also gain skills that help you understand a good novel or poem and help you enjoy a play.

Through language arts, you learn to develop and improve your writing and speaking skills. You learn to give speeches, argue in debates, and participate in panel discussions. You learn to create stories, poetry, advertisements, reports, letters, and all other forms of writing. You even study the English language itself. You learn about its history and about the way it works. Language arts involves dramatics, too—everything from easy pantomimes to big stage plays. In the language arts, you learn skills that help you find information and judge the value of the material you find.

For further information on:

Listening, *see* HEARING.

Speaking, *see* DEBATING, DRAMA, PRONUNCIATION, PUBLIC SPEAKING, SPEECH, VOCABULARY.

Reading, *see* AUTOBIOGRAPHY, BIOGRAPHY, CHILDREN'S LITERATURE, FAIRY TALE, LEGEND, LITERATURE, NOVEL, POETRY, READING, SCIENCE FICTION, SHORT STORY.

Writing, *see* ALPHABET, CAPITALIZATION, FIGURES OF SPEECH, HANDWRITING, JOURNALISM, LETTER WRITING, PICTURE WRITING, PUNCTUATION, SPELLING, WRITTEN LANGUAGE.

General *see* ADVERTISING, BOOK, COMMUNICATION, ENGLISH LANGUAGE, GRAMMAR, LANGUAGES, MAGAZINE, NEWSPAPER, PARTS OF SPEECH, RADIO BROADCASTING, TELEVISION BROADCASTING, WORD GAMES.

LANGUAGES   Suppose a baby shipwrecked alone on a desert island was able to live and grow. Would he be able to speak in a language that another person could understand? Most people would agree that this is unlikely. He would have *ideas,* such as the fact that a particular bird bone would make a good hook for fishing. But he would be unlikely to have words to express these ideas. If he remained alone on his desert island, he would probably never feel the need to express them.

But suppose one day another person appeared on the beach. The boy would certainly then feel the need for expressing his thoughts, for being understood, and for understanding the other person. The two could probably communicate through grunts or signs. But this would not get them very far. Through grunts they could express friendship, and by making signs toward their mouths they could show hunger. But how could one ask the other, "How long have you been here?" They would need a common language.

What is a language? It is a system used by human beings for communicating through words. Animals are known to communicate with one another, in various ways, but not through words. Scientists are studying the different types of communication between animals. But for the time being, we can say that language is a characteristic only of human beings.

Development of Language

A language can be spoken or written. In most cases, spoken language develops before written language. People will make up a system of talking to one another through words. They will agree upon different names for different things and ways of expressing different actions. A very long time may then pass before they invent a way of writing their system down. To make up even the simplest language is not easy. For instance, how would you express the fact that something is big? The Araucanian Indians of Chile solved this problem by doubling the name of something big. They call one of their rivers the "Calle Calle River." Its name is Calle, and because it is very wide and long, they say the name twice!

Some languages never cross the gap from spoken to written language. The Maya Indians, who built a powerful civilization in Central America, had their own language, Maya. They also developed their own kind of writing. The Inca Indians, who established a vast empire high up in the Andean mountains of South America, spoke their own language, *Quechua.* But, as far as we know, they never invented a way of writing it.

If you study any language, you will see in it a clear reflection of the people who speak it, their surroundings, and their history. For instance, the Arabic language has many different ways of saying the word for "camel." This is because the life of the Arabs has always been closely connected to this animal. They eat its meat, drink its milk, use it for transportation and as an article of trade. A similar point might be made with the word automobile in the English language today. Including brand names and slang, how many words can you find in English to mean automobile?

Whenever a language is preserved, even if it is only a few words, future generations can find out something about the people who spoke it. Wherever man goes, across continents or up into space, he takes his language with him. Scholars can trace the movements of peoples in the past by words that have passed from one language into another. As people change and develop, so do languages. Think of man's recent trips to the moon. Were there names in the English language for all the different kinds of inventions and mechanisms that came into existence so that man could make this momentous journey? Obviously not. An official in the space program says that many technical words were coined (made up) from Greek or Latin roots (words), but quite a lot of others have come from slang and engineering jargon (specialized language). *Exosphere, parametric receiver,* and *photosphere* are some examples of words made up from Greek and Latin. *Bird* (for rocket), *brain* (for guidance system), and *scrub* (for cancellation of mission) are examples of slang or jargon. These words are now part of the English language. This is just *one* example of how a language expands, borrowing words and making up others as new needs arise.

Languages also die. Civilizations break up, nations are conquered by others, and in many cases people pick up the language of the conquering nation and stop using their own in daily conversation. Classical

Greek and Latin, once major European languages, are now written and spoken by few people. Other languages are not used at all.

▲*Israel is a nation in which more than one language is commonly spoken. This sign is in English and Hebrew.*

Today's Languages

How many languages exist today? It is extremely difficult to pinpoint the exact number, but some scholars have counted around 3,000. The languages of the world have been divided into several families by scholars of linguistics, which is the study of language—its sounds and its changes.

The main language families are Indo-European; Semito-Hamitic (these include languages of the Middle East such as Arabic, Hebrew, and Aramaic); Uralic-Altaic (mainly Finnish and Turkish); Japanese and Korean; Sino-Tibetan (Chinese, Thai, and Burmese); Dravidian (languages of southern India); Malayo-Polynesian (spoken in the extensive area of the South Pacific). There are three African language families: Sudanese-Guinean, Bantu, and Hottentot-Bushman. American Indian languages can be roughly divided into more than 100 families.

Scholars believe that the languages of the Indo-European family have all come from one common and very ancient "mother" language spoken in Central Europe around 4000 B.C. Certain words, such as those for mother and father, are similar in all the Indo-European languages. Branches of this extensive family range from the Hindustani language of India to the languages spoken in Russia. They include almost all the languages of Europe and, naturally, the European languages spoken in the Americas.

Two branches of the Indo-European language family are of particular interest—the Romance and the Germanic languages of Europe. Latin has been the most important influence on the Romance languages, which are Italian, French, Spanish, Portuguese, and Rumanian. Languages grouped in the Germanic branch include English, German, and Dutch-Flemish. Related to the Germanic branch are the Scandinavian languages, Danish, Norwegian, Icelandic, and Swedish. All these languages are spoken in a densely populated region of the world. They have been greatly influenced by wars of conquest, shifts of population, inventions, and changing fashions. Linguists trace the passage of thousands of words from one language to another, particularly in the Germanic and Romance branches. The word "ele-

phant" is an example of the way in which a word can travel through many languages, changing on the way. Linguists believe the word was originally "elpend" and was an Egyptian word. In ancient times, it traveled from Egyptian to Greek ("elephas"), and then to Latin ("elephantus"). From Latin, it went into the French language ("olifant"), and was then borrowed by Old English ("elifaunt"). Over the centuries, the English spelling has changed to become the word we know today—elephant.

A person must know two or more languages well to *translate* (say the same thing in another language) written or spoken words. A translator must have a thorough knowledge of the grammar, vocabulary, and syntax (word order) of the languages he uses. He should also know their *idioms* (characteristic expressions peculiar to a language) in order to translate *meaning* rather than just *words*. For example, the American expression "no skin off my nose" makes no sense to a Frenchman when translated word for word.

Expert interpreters can become *simultaneous translators*. They translate words as soon as they are spoken. The United Nations uses simultaneous translators to make speeches understandable to all its members. Many other experts translate books and periodicals.

Several "universal languages" have recently been invented, so that people all over the world might understand one another. Some of these invented languages are Esperanto, Interlingua, and Novial. But none of these languages has been completely successful. Some people think that a simple form of our language, called Basic English, may prove to be an international language. Certain major languages, such as French and English, are taught as a "second language" in many countries. But a person should still try to learn as many different

▼ *Because President Johnson and Premier Kosygin of the Soviet Union speak different languages, a translator sat between them when the two leaders met at Glassboro, New Jersey, in 1967.*

INDO-EUROPEAN				
	GERMANIC or TEUTONIC		**WESTERN GERMANIC**	ENGLISH FRISIAN (N. Sea) DUTCH AFRIKAANS (S. Afr.) FLEMISH (Belg.) GERMAN YIDDISH PA. DUTCH (USA)
			NORTHERN GERMANIC	SWEDISH DANISH NORWEGIAN ICELANDIC
	GREEK	**BALTO-SLAVIC**	**NORTHERN SLAVIC**	LETTISH (Latvia) LITHUANIAN
			EASTERN SLAVIC	RUSSIAN UKRAINIAN WHITE RUSSIAN
			NORTHWEST SLAVIC	POLISH CZECH SLOVAK
	ARMENIAN		**SOUTHERN SLAVIC**	SERBIAN CROATIAN (Yug.) SLOVENIAN BULGARIAN
	ALBANIAN GHEG (North) TOSK (South) **LATIN**		**ROMANCE**	PORTUGUESE SPANISH CATALAN FRENCH PROVENCAL SARDINIAN ROMANSH (Swit.) ITALIAN RUMANIAN
	CELTIC		**GOIDELIC**	IRISH (Erse) SCOTS GAELIC MANX
			BRYTHONIC	WELSH BRETON CORNISH
INDO-IRANIAN	**SANSKRIT**	**PALI PRAKRIT**	HINDUSTANI	FARSI (Persian) PASHTO GUJARATHI MARATHI PUNJABI RAJASTHANI ORIYA BENGALI BIHARI HINDI URDU PAKISTANI SINGHALESE (Ceylon)

languages as possible if he wants to know other peoples of the world.

For further information on:

Ancient Languages, *see* GREEK, LATIN.

How Languages are Spoken, *see* HEARING, PRONUNCIATION, SPEECH, VOCABULARY.

How Languages are Written, *see* ALPHABET, DICTIONARY, FIGURES OF SPEECH, GRAMMAR, SPELLING.

Languages Spoken Today, *see* ARABIC; CHINESE; ENGLISH LANGUAGE; GERMAN LANGUAGE; HEBREW; INDIANS, AMERICAN; ROMANCE LANGUAGES; RUSSIAN; SCANDINAVIAN LANGUAGES; YIDDISH.

The Study of Languages, *see* LANGUAGE ARTS, READING.

What Languages are Used for, *see* COMMUNICATION, LITERATURE.

▲ *A Laotian farmer plowing the fields in much the way his ancestors have done for centuries. Almost all Laotians work the land using very primitive farming methods.*

LAOS Elephants walking along a city street are a common sight in Laos, known as the "Land of a Million Elephants." This kingdom in Southeast Asia is about the same size as the state of Kansas. Its northern boundaries are formed by Burma, China, and North Vietnam. South Vietnam lies to the east, and Cambodia lies to the south. Thailand is its western neighbor. Laos has two capital cities. Vientiane, the largest city in the country, is the administrative capital, while Luang Prabang, where the king lives, is the royal capital. (See the map with the article on ASIA.)

About nine-tenths of Laos is covered with mountains. The Mekong River is the most important river. It flows through the western part of the country. Laos has no outlet to the sea, so the river is a major transportation route.

The climate is affected by the tropical monsoons. These winds bring warm rains from May to October. Between November and February, Laos is cool and dry. During the rest of the year, it is hot and dry.

Most Laotians earn their living by farming. Rice is the most important crop. Other agricultural products are cotton, tobacco, fruits and vegetables, poppies for opium production, sugar cane, and coffee. The forests contain many valuable trees, including teak. The country's most important manufacturing industry is wood-processing. Laos has no railroad and few good roads.

Most Laotian people practice the Buddhist religion. Life in the villages often centers around the temples where many festivals are held.

At one time, much of Laos was part of Thailand, but the French gained control of it in the late 1800s. The country was part of French Indochina until 1949, when it gained independence. Since then, Laotian Communists have tried to get control of the country. They have been helped in their fight against the government of Laos by North Vietnamese Communists. The

LAOS

Capital City: Vientiane (162,000 people).
Area: 89,343 square miles.
Population: 2,893,000 people.
Languages: Lao and French.
Export Products: Tin, timber, and coffee.
Unit of Money: Kip.

United States has helped the Laotian government to defend itself against the Communists.

ALSO READ: ASIA, BUDDHISM, INDO-CHINA, MONSOON.

LAPLAND Lapland, the home of the Lapps, is a bleak, barren region of Europe north of the Arctic Circle. Lapland is not a nation but a region covering the northern parts of Norway, Sweden, Finland, and the northeastern Soviet Union.

The Lapps are a short, fair-skinned people. They speak a language similar to Finnish and Hungarian. Only about 35,000 Lapps live in Lapland today. Some herd reindeer, just as their ancestors have done for centuries. These herders follow their reindeer through valleys, swamps, and mountains in search of pastures. Reindeer feed on moss and lichens. Very little else grows in this region above the Arctic Circle. The herders get meat, milk, and cheese from the reindeer. The hides are used to make clothes and tents. Reindeer also pull sleds over snow and ice, and serve as pack animals. Commercial slaughterhouses in northern Sweden help control the increasing herds and provide a livelihood for the Lapps.

Herders who move from place to place are called *nomads*. All Lapp families were once nomads. Now most Lapps have settled in small fishing and farming villages, or work in Lapland's rich iron mines. Even the wives and children of nomadic herders today stay in villages so that the children can go to school.

ALSO READ: FINLAND, LICHEN, NORWAY, SOVIET UNION, SWEDEN.

LA SALLE, SIEUR DE (1643-1687) The first European to sail down the Mississippi River to the Gulf of Mexico was a French explorer, Robert Cavelier, later called La Salle. Born in Rouen, France, he was trained to be a Jesuit missionary. But in 1666, La Salle emi-grated to Canada, where he became a fur trader. La Salle made many explorations across the northeastern wilderness of North America and became familiar with the languages and customs of the Indians. La Salle claimed to have discovered the Ohio River in 1671.

In 1674, La Salle was sent to France as a representative of the French colonial governor to get permission to build Fort Frontenac, a trading station at the mouth of the St. Lawrence River. His mission was successful. He not only received command of the fort, but also a title, Sieur de (Lord of) La Salle.

In 1682, La Salle sailed up the St. Lawrence to near where the city of Buffalo, New York, now stands. There his men built a ship called the *Griffin* to sail on the Great Lakes to Lake Michigan. He built Fort Crève-coeur on the Illinois River, near present-day Peoria. Two years later he led a group of men down the Mississippi River to its mouth, claiming all the lands through which the river flowed for King Louis XIV of France. He named the land "Louisiana" in the king's honor.

La Salle then hoped to create a French empire stretching from the St. Lawrence River to the Gulf of Mexico. In 1684, he sailed from France with a fleet of four ships to

▲*The Lapps wear colorful and comfortable clothing. They manage to use their bleak environment to their advantage.*

▼*La Salle claims the Mississippi River for France.*

establish a colony at the mouth of the Mississippi. He landed by mistake on the shore of Matagorda Bay, in Texas. La Salle set out for Canada with 17 men to get supplies and help. On the way, his men mutinied, and La Salle was killed.

ALSO READ: EXPLORATION.

LATIN Latin is a riddle. It was once one of the most important languages in the world. Today, few people speak it, and even fewer read or write it. And yet, almost everybody in Europe and America uses Latin in his speech every day. How can this be?

Latin was the language spoken by the ancient Romans, who lived in the country known today as Italy. The Romans built up an empire so powerful that its armies were sent to every corner of the known world. The people conquered by the Roman armies learned Latin. In a short time it became the language of trade, schools, churches, and government throughout the Roman Empire. Great works of literature, such as the poems of Virgil and Ovid, were written in Latin. In some areas conquered by the Romans, people almost completely forgot their own languages. The Latin they spoke developed into what are now called the *Romance languages*. Spanish and French are two of these.

After the Roman Empire broke up, scholars and churchmen throughout Europe continued to speak and write Latin. Many Latin words and forms of grammar became part of the English language. Most European languages used the Latin alphabet. The Roman Catholic Church still uses Latin in some ceremonies and services. Many Latin words and names are used in biology and zoology and by members of the medical and legal professions. Latin is still used in many mottoes. United States coins, for instance, carry the Latin saying *E Pluribus*

Unum which means "Out of many, one." Latin words are also used as a foundation for forming new words. As an example, in English, every word that starts with "aqua" is using the Latin word for water. A glance at the dictionary shows us such words as aquamarine, aquaplane, aquarium, and aquarius. Latin is still studied in some European and American schools. Some scholars think that mastering the logical and orderly rules of Latin grammar is good preparation for learning other subjects.

ALSO READ: ALPHABET, ENGLISH LANGUAGE, LANGUAGES, ROMAN CATHOLIC CHURCH, ROMANCE LANGUAGES, ROMAN EMPIRE, VATICAN CITY.

LATIN AMERICA see CENTRAL AMERICA, SOUTH AMERICA.

LATITUDE AND LONGITUDE Latitude is a measure of the distance of any point on the Earth's surface north or south of the equator. Longitude is the measure of any point east or west of an imaginary line that runs from the North Pole through Greenwich, a town near London, England, and then to the South Pole.

To measure latitude, the Earth is divided into circles parallel to the equator. Each circle is called a *parallel of latitude*. Latitude is measured in degrees. The equator has a latitude of zero degrees (0°). The North Pole has a latitude of 90° north, and the South Pole, a latitude of 90° south. Thus, there are 90 degrees (90°) of latitude between the equator and either of the poles. Each degree is divided into 60 parts, called *minutes*. This is written as: 60'. Each minute is divided into 60 *seconds*. This is written as: 60". The distance between two parallels of latitude that are one degree apart is 60 nautical (sea) miles. This means that one minute of latitude equals about one nautical mile. A nautical mile is 796 feet longer than a land mile.

To measure longitude, the Earth is divided into equally spaced circles running through both the North and South Poles. These circles are *meridians of longitude*. Unlike parallels of latitude, meridians are not everywhere at equal distance from each other. The distance between two meridians is widest at the equator and narrows toward the poles, where the distance between them becomes zero as the meridians meet.

The meridian running through Greenwich is at zero degrees (0°) longitude. Any place half way around the world from the Greenwich meridian has a longitude of 180 degrees (180°). This meridian divides the Earth into two halves, or *hemispheres*, each having 180 degrees of longitude. Any place west of Greenwich has west longitude, and any place east of Greenwich has east longitude. For example, St. Paul, Minnesota, is at 90° west longitude, and Helsinki, Finland, is at 25° east longitude.

If you know the latitude and longitude of any place, you can locate it on a map or globe of the earth. Let's say an airplane pilot radios this message: "I am at 22° north latitude and 157° west longitude." Look on a map, and you will find the point where that parallel and meridian cross. A clue is that you will find it near a well known Pacific island. Did you locate the plane on a map?

ALSO READ: EARTH, EQUATOR, GEOGRAPHY, INTERNATIONAL DATE LINE, MAP.

LATTER-DAY SAINTS The people who belong to the Church of Jesus Christ of Latter-Day Saints are usually called *Mormons*. Joseph Smith founded the church in 1830. Smith said he had a revelation, or vision, in which God told him to start a new faith. In another vision, an angel showed Smith where to find a set of golden plates, or tablets, with Egyptian writing on them. Smith translated these writings,

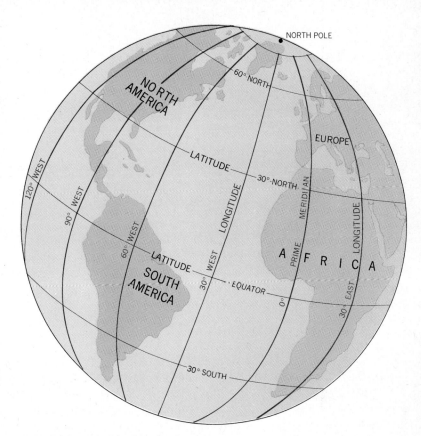

which have come to be known as *The Book of Mormon*. The Mormons consider the writings to be their holy scripture.

The new religion grew, and Smith moved his followers to Kirtland, Ohio. Many people in Kirtland did not want the Mormons to live there, and forced them to move away. They went to Missouri and then to Illinois, where they founded the city of Nauvoo. After a few years there, Joseph Smith was killed by an angry mob. Brigham Young became the new leader, and the Mormons moved once again, this time to the Great Salt Lake Valley, in Utah. Today there are over two million members of the church, and more than half of them live in the state of Utah.

At one time, the Mormons were strongly criticized because some of their men practiced *polygamy*—the practice of having more than one wife. This practice was stopped in the U.S. in 1890 when the Federal Government passed a law against it.

ALSO READ: SMITH, JOSEPH; UTAH; YOUNG, BRIGHAM.

▼*The sunstone, one of the few remaining items left from the fire that destroyed the Mormon Temple in Nauvoo, Illinois, in 1846.*

LATVIA

Capital City: Riga (733,000 people).
Area: 24,600 square miles.
Population: 2,299,000 people
Languages: Lettish and Russian.
Export Products: Ships, machinery, electronic equipment, and processed food products.
Unit of Money: Soviet Ruble.

LATVIA Latvia, a land of rolling hills and fertile soil, is one of the three Soviet republics on the Baltic Sea. The other two are Estonia to the north and Lithuania to the south. Two Russian republics of the Soviet Union are eastern neighbors. (See the map with the article on EUROPE.) To the west, Latvia has 300 miles of coast along the Baltic Sea and the Gulf of Riga. This gulf freezes solid in winter. In summer, the weather is mild in Latvia. Riga, a Baltic port city, is the capital of the country.

The Latvians, also known as Letts, are an ancient people with a rich culture. They have lived along the Gulf of Riga for almost 2,000 years. Their language is one of the oldest now spoken in Europe. Their land has been under foreign rule many times. From the middle 1200s to the middle 1500s, the Latvians had to work the land for German noblemen. But they kept their own traditions and never became German. The Poles gained control of Latvia in the 1500s, and the Swedes ruled part of Latvia during the 1600s. Russia began to dominate the country in the 1700s and ruled until Latvia won independence in 1918. The Latvians divided the land among the peasants and elected a democratic government. But the Russians conquered them again in 1940. The Germans occupied Latvia during World War II from 1941 to 1944. The Soviet Union won the land back and named it the Latvian Soviet Socialist Republic.

Under Soviet rule, all land in Latvia has become government property. The government tells the farmers what to plant and how much each farm must produce. There are many dairy farms. Other farms breed sheep, hogs, poultry, and horses. The main crops are barley, oats, and rye. Latvian factories produce textiles, machinery, motors, electronic equipment, ships, and processed foods.

The United States and a few other countries do not recognize the Soviet Union's control of Latvia. These countries continue to regard Latvia as an independent nation.

ALSO READ: RUSSIAN HISTORY, WORLD WAR I, WORLD WAR II.

LAUNDRIES AND DRY CLEANERS No one knows where or when the very first laundry began. Perhaps it began two thousand years ago in ancient Rome, where laundrymen were paid to wash clothes.

In 1849 and 1850, the thousands of men who rushed to California to dig for gold had to launder their own clothes. But everybody was too busy looking for gold to do much laundering. One day a man named Davis, who hadn't been able to find much gold, decided to open a laundry to earn money for food. He started the Contra Costa Laundry in

▼*The church of Saint Peter towers above the skyline of Riga, the Latvian capital.*

1851 in Oakland, California. After a while, he put in a washing machine operated by a 10-horsepower steam engine. Soon his laundry was more valuable than some gold mines.

Today, thousands of commercial laundries have big, automatic washing machines and dryers. Some laundries specialize in tablecloths, work uniforms, and similar materials for hotels, restaurants, and business firms. Other laundries wash only babies' diapers. Many cities have self-service "laundromats," where people do their laundry in machines that operate when coins are put into them. Large apartment houses also have this kind of equipment.

In commercial laundries, the things to be washed are sorted according to colors and fabrics. Bed linens, towels, and other strong fabrics or white things are washed in water hot enough to scald your hands. Darker colors are washed at lower temperatures, and *synthetic* (man-made) fabrics are washed at medium-warm temperatures. The wash that belongs to one family is put into numbered net bags to keep the clothes all together while they are in the washing machine. Most laundries stamp numbers or letters inside shirt collars with ink that will not wash out. These numbers are used to identify the owners.

Before clothes are dried, the wash is put into *extractors*. Extractors are large tubs with holes in the sides. They spin the clothes around at very high speeds to remove most of the water from the wash. Then some of the clothes are ironed while they are still damp. Other clothes are dried in machines that tumble them around, while air—at any temperature from room temperature to very hot—is blown through them.

Some materials, such as linen, silk, and wool may shrink or fade if washed in soap and water. So these fabrics are often *dry-cleaned* instead of laundered. Dry-cleaning is done with special kinds of chemicals. Sol-*vents* used in dry-cleaning dissolve and remove grease and dirt. The process is called "dry" cleaning, because no water is used.

Some kind of dry-cleaning was used several thousand years ago in Greece and Rome. Men called *fullers* made cloth and yarn thicker by wetting and pressing it, but first they cleaned the cloth and yarn with *fuller's earth*. Fuller's earth is a kind of soft clay that removes grease spots. It was probably the first dry-cleaning substance.

Modern dry-cleaning was invented in Paris in 1849 by a French tailor, Jolly Belin. In those days, dry-cleaning was done by hand. Now it is done by automatic machinery.

ALSO READ: SOAPS AND DETERGENTS.

LAURIER, SIR WILFRID (1841-1919)

Sir Wilfrid Laurier, a Canadian statesman, became the first French-Canadian prime minister of Canada. Sir Wilfrid was born in St. Lin, Quebec, just north of Montreal. Laurier's family spoke only French, so they sent him as a boy to live for two years with an English-speaking family, and to attend an English school. He graduated from both a French college and an English university. Therefore, he knew and understood the English and French languages and the English and French peoples of Canada.

Laurier found the influence of the church in Quebec too old-fashioned. He joined a political party that was working to modernize French Canada. Later, he joined the Liberal Party in the Canadian federal government and was soon chosen to be the party's leader. He was elected prime minister in 1896. As prime minister, he worked to bring about cooperation between the French-speaking and English-speaking groups of Canada. He encouraged people to settle in western Canada, and had miles of railroad tracks and roads built.

▲*In poor countries where there is no supply of running water in the home, women often go down to a stream to do their laundry.*

▼*An attendant puts the finishing touches on a pair of trousers that have been dry cleaned.*

▼*Sir Wilfrid Laurier, Canadian statesman.*

Laurier also worked hard to make trade easier between Canada and other countries. His government was finally defeated in 1911. He was voted out of office when he tried to persuade Canadians to make an agreement with the United States, in which neither country would tax imported goods from the other.

ALSO READ: CANADA.

LAVA see VOLCANO.

LAVOISIER, ANTOINE LAURENT (1743-1794) Antoine Lavoisier, a French scientist, was one of the founders of modern chemistry. He was the first to explain what burning is—the rapid combining of a material with oxygen. He also explained that respiration, the breathing of animals and plants, is a kind of slow burning process. In a famous series of experiments, Lavoisier proved that in chemical changes, such as burning, matter is never created nor destroyed. It is only changed in form.

▲ *Antoine Lavoisier, French chemist.*

Lavoisier made his discoveries mainly by extending and improving the work of other scientists, and then proving his new ideas by brilliant experiments. He was one of the first to use careful measurement as a tool.

Lavoisier was born in Paris, France, to a wealthy family. In school, he showed great interest in science. His wealth made it possible for him to spend most of his life in scientific work. The high quality of his work was recognized. He was appointed to a number of government offices, including one dealing with weights and measures.

Lavoisier was a member of a group that collected taxes for King Louis XVI. In 1789, the French Revolution broke out, and the king was dethroned. Lavoisier was executed, along with the other members of the group in 1794.

ALSO READ: CHEMISTRY; ELEMENT; FRENCH REVOLUTION; LOUIS, KINGS OF FRANCE; RESPIRATION.

LAW Small children are told they must not cross the street by themselves. Teenagers may be told not to play music so loudly that they disturb other members of the family. Parents set up rules, or laws, to protect children and to make it easier for members of a household to live together.

Law is a set of rules which regulates the actions of each member of a group of people, for the good of the entire group. The group may be as small as a family or as large as a nation, but it must have some kind of law to help people to get along with each other. Law, whether written or unwritten, is based on man's past experiences in living. One of the oldest sets of laws known to man is the Ten Commandments. These are laws of proper behavior that men followed thousands of years ago and still follow today. Law should be a "living" thing. This means that as social habits and customs change, the law should be *flexible*, or able to change with them. Two basic systems of law used in the world today are the English common law system and the Napoleonic Code.

English Common Law

English common law began about a thousand years ago. Under the Saxons (early tribesmen who lived in England), laws were called "dooms" or "ordinances." People with complaints would go before the local lord who would decide what should be done. After the Normans (French warriors) conquered the Saxons in 1066, local decisions were handled by "king's courts." The king sent his royal judges to all parts of the kingdom to listen to arguments and make decisions in his name. These decisions became *precedents*, or examples to be followed.

The early American colonists brought their knowledge of English common law to the New World. United States law is based on the English common law. Law students today study common law based on the study of precedents.

CIVIL LAW. There are many "branches" of common law. Civil law deals with decisions that affect man's daily life. It handles such things as accidents, damages, contracts, and property arguments. If somebody owes you money and refuses to pay it back, you may take the case to a civil law court.

CRIMINAL LAW. Whenever a society has law, it also has ways of dealing with lawbreakers. Criminal law handles acts such as burglary, kidnapping, and murder, that harm individuals or the community. Penalties for criminal acts are also based on precedents. The lawbreaker is punished in the name of the rest of society.

STATUTE LAW. Laws made by kings or legislative bodies such as parliaments or congresses are called statute law. Statute law can explain things that are unclear in civil law, and can *overrule* (change) the decisions made in civil law courts.

The Napoleonic Code

So many different laws existed in France in the 1700s that the philosopher Voltaire said: "A traveler in France has to change laws as frequently as he changes horses." Napoleon I appointed a group of judges to figure out a system of law for all of France in 1804. They wrote down a detailed system of law, which came to be called the Napoleonic Code. It was a combination of Germanic law and Roman law. An up-to-date version of the Napoleonic Code is still used in France today. Many other nations also use the Code as a model for their own legal systems. The legal system of the state of Louisiana is based on the Napoleonic Code.

Other Forms of Law

Constitutional law deals with the rights and powers of persons and governments under rules set down in their constitutions. The job of the Supreme Court is to explain the laws contained in the United States Constitution. The court can rule that some decision or law is *unconstitutional* (against the Constitution). It can also overrule the findings of a lower court. State supreme courts explain the laws contained in state constitutions.

Military law applies to any person in the army, navy, or other branch of the military. The United States military has its own courts and system of punishment. In 1951, the U.S. Congress passed laws changing some of the military codes. They decided that the same code should be used for all branches of military service. This was done to make sure that enlisted men (those who are not officers) get fair treatment, and to allow civilian (non-military) lawyers to appear at military trials.

International law applies to conduct between nations. International law is difficult to apply or enforce, because it is not backed by one nation or legal system. If a country or group of countries "breaks" an international law, there is really no way to punish them. The United Nations is working on a solution to this problem.

▲*The power of the Law is represented here by a majestic figure. The Law is supported on either side by men representing the various kinds of law.*

For further information on:

Careers in Law, *see* FEDERAL BUREAU OF INVESTIGATION; GOVERNMENT CAREERS; HOLMES FAMILY; LAWYERS AND JUDGES; MARSHALL, JOHN; MARSHALL, THURGOOD.

History of Law, *see* CONSTITUTION, UNITED STATES; ENGLISH HISTORY; FRENCH HISTORY; GERMAN HISTORY; MAGNA CARTA; TALMUD.

Kinds of Law, *see* CHILD LABOR, CIVIL RIGHTS, INTERNATIONAL LAW, LEAGUE OF NATIONS, MARRIAGE, PASSPORTS AND VISAS, PATENTS AND COPYRIGHTS, PROHIBITION, STATES' RIGHTS, UNITED NATIONS.

Legal Systems, *see* CRIME; CONGRESS, UNITED STATES; COURT SYSTEM; JUVENILE DELINQUENCY; LEGISLATURE; SUPREME COURT; TRIAL.

▲*Lawrence of Arabia.*

Charlotte E. Ray, first American Negro woman lawyer, was admitted to the Supreme Court of the District of Columbia on April 23, 1872. She received the LL.B. degree from the School of Law, Howard University, Washington, D.C.

▲ *A Salvation Army officer acts as a lawyer for a friendless man appearing in court. The judge listens to both the defendant's and the police's cases.*

LAWRENCE OF ARABIA (1888–1935) Thomas Edward Lawrence was a scholar and a writer. He was the author of a well-known book about the Middle East called *The Seven Pillars of Wisdom.* It tells about his adventures in the Arab world. He also translated Homer's *Odyssey.* As Lawrence of Arabia, he is remembered as a romantic adventurer and soldier. Lawrence was born in Wales and later educated at Oxford University.

During World War I, Lawrence joined the British Intelligence Service in Egypt. At that time, the British were encouraging the Arab subjects of the Ottoman Empire to revolt against their Turkish rulers. Lawrence organized and led the Arab armies.

After the war, Lawrence felt that Britain had been unfair to the Arabs. He argued that Britain had promised to help the Jews make Palestine a Jewish state, taking it away from the Arabs.

He resigned from his job in the British Colonial Office in 1922 and enlisted as a private in the Royal Air Force. He did not enjoy being treated like a famous person. To escape the publicity attached to his name, Lawrence changed it first to Ross and then to Shaw. He later died in a motorcycle accident in England.

ALSO READ: MIDDLE EAST, OTTOMAN EMPIRE.

LAWYERS AND JUDGES People who live in a simple society do not need lawyers. In frontier days, for example, few lawyers were needed in the little settlements of the West. A circuit judge (a traveling judge who covered an area) would ride into town now and then to hear the few cases that had arisen. In modern times, the laws are so many and so complicated that the ordinary person cannot possibly know them all. When someone has a special need to know about certain laws, he must get the services of a lawyer.

An *attorney,* or lawyer, is the legal representative of people, or groups, or governments, in their disputes or relations with each other. He may represent a government (and its citizens), or a business. Some lawyers only deal with cases of a certain kind, such as corporate law (business affairs), maritime law (law dealing with ships), or criminal law. Lawyers spend much of their time advising their *clients* (customers) about what they legally can or cannot do. In this way, lawyers often keep people out of trouble.

Many lawyers today are working with poor people in cities. They help and advise them when they run into problems with their jobs, landlords, or government officials. Such lawyers often do not charge fees.

▼*A group of law students get practical training by interviewing a defendant and his mother before the trial of his case.*

A lawyer may be *retained,* or hired, for many reasons. A lawyer may draw up a *contract* (agreement) between a person who has something to sell and a person who wants to buy it. There are many state and federal laws about handling the *estate* (money and property) of someone who has died. A person who wants his money and property handled in a certain way will get a lawyer to draw up a *will.* The will states exactly what will be done with the person's estate after that person dies.

The *defendant* (accused person) has the right to be represented by a lawyer in any criminal trial held in the United States. If the defendant cannot afford to pay a lawyer, the court will appoint one and pay his fee. The lawyer is required to use all his knowledge of the law to help his client. Even though a man may be guilty, he has the right to have his case presented in the best possible way.

To become a lawyer, a person must study the laws of his state and country. He must learn about past legal cases and decisions. He attends law school for three years after he has graduated from college. He must then pass an examination in the state where he wants to work and be interviewed by a committee of lawyers. If he passes the examination and is considered to be of good character, he is sworn in before a judge. He can then practice law in that state.

In the United States, the people who become judges are most often lawyers, although they do not have to be. A judge presides over a trial in a court of law. He may explain legal points, instruct the jury, and pass a sentence after the jury has delivered the *verdict* (decision). Judges are either appointed (by the governor or President) or elected to their posts. This usually depends on the state law or the kind of court the judge will preside over. Members of the Supreme Court are appointed by the President. They must be approved by the Senate.

ALSO READ: COURT SYSTEM, LAW, SUPREME COURT, TRIAL.

LEAF A leaf is a flat or slightly curved green structure that grows from the stem of a plant. Leaves do not grow on every kind of plant. Simple plants, such as algae, do not have leaves. Mosses and some other plants have structures that look much like leaves, but under a microscope, differences can be seen.

Shapes and Parts of Leaves

Leaves have an amazing variety of shapes. Oak and pine trees, rose bushes, corn plants, and grass all have leaves—as do thousands of other kinds of plants—and all these leaves have different shapes. In fact, if you carefully study every single leaf on one large tree, you will discover that no two of them are alike!

Some leaves are round and some are long and thin. Some leaves have smooth edges, but others have edges that look like saw teeth. Evergreen leaves look like needles or tiny lances. Leaves of maple, oak, elm, and fruit trees are called *simple leaves*. They are all in one part. The leaves of clover, rose bushes, and walnut and butternut trees are *compound leaves*. Each of these leaves is made up of several *leaflets* (little leaves). Many different kinds of leaves are shown on the next page.

The broad, flat part of a leaf is the *blade*. Many kinds of leaves are attached to the plant stem by a thin stalk. This stalk is the *petiole*. If you look closely at the undersides of most leaves, you will see *veins*, a network of tiny tubes that carry water, food, and minerals into and out of the leaf. The veins also act as a kind of skeleton, keeping the leaf from collapsing.

A Tiny Food Factory

The most amazing feature of leaves is that each one is a tiny "food factory." Only green plants—those that contain the substance *chlorophyll* —can make their own food.

A leaf uses two raw materials— water and carbon dioxide—to make food. It gets energy from sunlight to combine these two materials. A leaf combines the water and carbon dioxide to make its "food," *glucose*, which is a kind of sugar. The leaf then changes the glucose to starch. The chlorophyll helps the leaf combine the water and carbon dioxide, but the chlorophyll is not a part of glucose or starch. The process of

▲ *It's lots of fun to play in a pile of autumn leaves. New leaves will grow on the nearby trees in spring.*

Some leaves have special jobs. The *tendrils* of peas and melons look like tiny wire coils. They hold the plants up by gripping a pole or fence. Cactus *spines* are sharp needles that guard the plant and prevent water loss.

RED MAPLE
(Palmate veins)

AMERICAN (Pinnate veins)
ELM

BEECH

WHITE
BIRCH

HINDS   WALNUT

BLADE

MIDRIB

LARGE
VEIN

HORSE
CHESTNUT
(Palmate
compound)

WHITE
OAK

PETIOLE

TULIP

BASSWOOD

WHITE ASH
(Pinnate compound)

SYCAMORE

RED
OAK

BALSAM FIR
(Needle-like)

WHITE PINE

making starch is called *photosynthesis*, which comes from the Greek words that mean "to put together with light." All life depends on the process.

An Important Part of Life

One result of photosynthesis is that when the leaf takes in carbon dioxide from the air, oxygen is produced. All other living things stay alive only because of this. Plants are the first step in the food web. For example, cattle and sheep eat plants. Other animals—including people—eat the cattle and sheep. People also eat leaves, such as lettuce and cabbage. Can you think of some other leaves people eat?

Leaves are important for other reasons, too. Some leaves, such as mint, flavor your food. Tea is made from the leaves of the tea plant. Drugs are made from the leaves of many kinds of plants. Many dyes, such as indigo (dark blue), are also made from leaves. In some tropical areas, large leaves are even used to construct the ceilings and walls of houses.

Watching Photosynthesis Take Place

You can easily study the process of photosynthesis. Pin strips of tinfoil or black paper across the upper sides of one or two leaves on a living plant. Do not cover the whole leaf. Leave the plant in a sunny place for two or three days. At the end of a sunny day, cut the partly covered leaves from the plant. Remove the covering strips, and soak the leaves in alcohol overnight.

Take the leaves out of the alcohol. Using a medicine dropper, put drops of iodine all over the tops of each leaf. Iodine turns blue when starch is present. What does your test show? Photosynthesis cannot occur without sunlight.

ALSO READ: CHEMISTRY, CONIFER, DRUGS AND DRUG MAKING, FOOD WEB, PHOTOSYNTHESIS, PLANT, PLANT KINGDOM, TREE.

LEAGUE OF NATIONS At the end of World War I, the victorious nations, including Great Britain, France, Italy, and the United States, decided that there must never be another war. They felt that the way to prevent war was to form an organization of nations that would work for world peace and international cooperation. The League of Nations was established in 1920, with its headquarters at Geneva, Switzerland. Forty-seven nations were members at the beginning, and several others joined later.

The member nations of the League agreed to bring their disagreements to the League Council for advice, instead of immediately going to war. If the League ruled that a country should not go to war, and that country began fighting anyway, other members would refuse to trade with that nation. They could also use military force against the nation if the League Council recommended it. The League also set up agencies to help nations improve health, education, trade, industry, and transportation.

Woodrow Wilson, who was President of the United States at the time, was one of the main organizers of the League. The United States never joined the League, because the Senate refused to approve the League's constitution. At this time, many Americans—perhaps a majority—believed that the U.S. should not become deeply involved in

▲*The first session of the League of Nations took place on November 15, 1920. The delegates of the member countries assembled at the Palace of Nations in Geneva, Switzerland.*

world affairs. People with this view were known as *isolationists*, because they felt that the U.S. should remain isolated, or apart, from the problems and quarrels of other nations.

Without the United States as a member, the League was weakened from the start. It was further weakened when Japan and Germany withdrew in 1933. Italy, the Soviet Union, and many other members also dropped out later.

In its short life, the League of Nations settled a number of small disputes and helped improve conditions in many countries. But it failed to stop Japan's invasion of Manchuria in 1931 and Italy's attack on Ethiopia in 1935. It also failed to prevent World War II. The League was ended in 1946, but it served as a model for the United Nations, which replaced it.

ALSO READ: INTERNATIONAL RELATIONS; WILSON, WOODROW; UNITED NATIONS.

LEAKEY, LOUIS S. B. see MAN.

LEANING TOWER OF PISA Have you ever seen a building that seemed to be leaning to one side? Most buildings that look as if they are falling over soon do, but the famous Leaning Tower of Pisa in Italy has been leaning for over 600 years! The tower is the campanile (bell tower) of the cathedral in Pisa.

Builders began work on the bell tower in 1173. The stone foundation they built was not strong enough to support the heavy tower, and it began to sink unevenly in the soft soil. The tower was already leaning when it was finished in the second half of the 1300s. It now leans 14 feet to one side, and the tilt increases a little each year. Some architects say the tower will fall down within the next 100 years. The Italian government is now running a contest hoping to get some new ideas for supporting the famous old tower.

The round tower is made of white

▼*The Leaning Tower of Pisa draws tourists from all over the world.*

marble and is about 180 feet high. Each of its eight stories is surrounded by a series of arches supported by columns. If you have enough energy to climb almost 300 steps on a circular stairway, you can look out from the top and see the entire city of Pisa.

LEAP YEAR see TIME.

LEAR, EDWARD (1812–1888) The British writer Edward Lear described himself in one of his own poems.

"How pleasant to know Mr. Lear! Who has written such volumes of stuff! Some think him ill-tempered and queer, But a few think him pleasant enough."

Lear was born in London, England. He became a commercial artist at the age of 15. Water-color paintings were his specialty. He worked for the London Zoological Society, making highly accurate, beautiful paintings of birds, particularly parrots. Lear's bird pictures won him a job with the Earl of Derby, sketching the animals in the earl's private zoo. Lear often entertained the earl's grandchildren with his comic poems and drawings. His delightful first *Book of Nonsense* was dedicated to them. Four more nonsense books were published later. One of his best-known nonsense poems is about "The Owl and the Pussycat," who went to sea

"In a beautiful pea-green boat; They took some honey, and plenty of money Wrapped up in a five-pound note." Other strange characters in Lear's nonsense books are "The Pobble who has no Toes," who swam across the Bristol Channel, and "The Dong with the Luminous Nose." The Dong wanders about

"When awful darkness and silence reign Over the great Gromboolian plain."

Lear traveled a great deal, visiting Italy, Greece, Albania, and the Near East. He painted water-color scenes and landscapes wherever he went, and published several illustrated travel books. His travel books are probably his best works. But his nonsense verses made him more famous. He also wrote many amusing five-line poems called *limericks*, and soon people all over the country were reciting his limericks and making up their own. This is one of Lear's limericks,

"There was an old man with a
  beard,
Who said, 'It is just as I feared!'
Two Owls and a Hen, four Larks
  and a Wren,
Have all built their nests in my
  beard."

ALSO READ: LIMERICK.

LEARNING Do you remember the first time you tried to roller skate or ride a bicycle? You are probably able to skate or ride much better now than you could then. This skill is the result of the process of learning.

When you look up something in this encyclopedia, you are usually interested in learning something. Many other people have already learned what is written here, and because you have already learned to read, you can share their knowledge. What is learning? Scientists have been working many years to find the answer to this question. The most accepted answer is that learning is a process by which people use their past experiences to determine their behavior, classify information, and form habits.

Learning takes place every day of your life from the time you are born. As a baby you discovered that if you cried when you were hungry you would be fed. You also learned to cry when you were uncomfortable or lonely. You learned from past experiences that crying would cause a certain response.

Learning How to Learn
The most important learning that takes place is "learning how to learn." We talk about "learning" the multiplication tables or "learning" the correct spelling of words. These are learned *facts*. But only the person who knows *how* to learn can take these facts or information and question them, connect them to what he already knows, and reach conclusions.

HOW YOU "CONNECT" INFORMATION. Suppose you read that Abraham Lincoln was the sixteenth President of the United States. You will not have too much trouble learning this information if you already know what a President is, what the United States is, or something about Abraham Lincoln. You can easily make some connection between this new fact and something you have already learned.

Suppose you learn how to throw a baseball. You learned how to stand, balance yourself, swing your arm, and aim the ball exactly where you want it to go. If you remember what you have learned, you will not have much trouble learning to throw a basketball. The balance, swing, and timing might be different, but the basic elements have already been learned and can now be used in the new situation.

How Does Learning Take Place?
There are no easy ways to explain just how people learn. It is known,

▼In the old days many children were taught to learn by rote, or constant repetition of a lesson.

▲*In modern schools, audio-visual aids are widely used to make subject material easier to understand.*

however, that learning must be stimulated. A *stimulus* is a kind of signal that alerts one or more of the senses (sight, hearing, touch, taste, and smell). A person then *reacts* or *responds* to the stimulus. Most often, this response is some kind of movement. For instance, you hear a door open (stimulus), and you look up (response) to see who is entering the room. Or you hear a baby cry (stimulus), and you go to his crib (response) to find out why he is crying. In both cases, you respond because of past learning. You look up to see who is entering the room because from past experience you know that the sound of a door being opened means that someone is coming. You go to check on the baby because from past experience you know that his crying means that he needs or wants something.

REASONS AND REWARDS. People who study the nature of learning are called *educational psychologists*. They work with animals, children, and adults as the "subjects" of their studies. Although psychologists have developed many different *theories*, or ideas, about learning, most of them agree that people learn faster if they have some *motivation* (a real need or desire) to learn. You learn your lines if you want to do well in a class play. You learn to use a typewriter if you think typewritten reports will help you get better grades in school. Sometimes the satisfaction you feel as a result of learning is a

kind of motivation. A high grade or higher pay is another kind of motivation. For the student, the reward is often the knowledge that he has done a good job with a certain learning task.

Methods of Learning

Learning and teaching are so closely connected that any article about learning must also mention teaching methods. Laboratory schools try out different teaching methods, or ways of teaching, in order to find the best ways to bring about learning.

▲*Computers aid learning. A computer poses problems and asks questions. When a student gives the right answer, the computer goes on to the next question.*

PROGRAMMED LEARNING. One new teaching method is *programmed learning*. This uses one of several kinds of teaching machines which provide a stimulus (question) to the learner who then makes a response (answer). If the answer is correct, another question is given. If the answer is wrong, the information is taught again, and then the question is repeated. In this way, if the student does not learn the first time, he has another chance. The machine also leads the learner through a series of steps, each one more advanced than the one before, until he or she acquires the skill or knowledge being taught.

ALSO READ: EDUCATION, INTELLIGENCE, MEMORY, SCHOOL.

▼*Not everything is learned in school. A first step in learning how to swim is practicing with a kickboard. Wanting to learn a new skill is very important to learning.*

LEATHER The very useful material called leather is made from the skins of animals. Most of these skins come from animals bred to provide food for man, such as cows, sheep, goats, and pigs. The skin is considered to be a secondary product of the meat-packing industry. But many wild animals, such as alligators, kangaroos, and lizards, are often killed just to supply skins to make leather. For this reason, some wild animals are in danger of being killed off entirely (becoming extinct). Many people will no longer buy products made from the skins of these fast disappearing animals.

Early man probably made his first articles of clothing from animal skins with fur and hair still on them. Since then man has found ways to treat animal skins to shape them into shoes, gloves, suitcases, book bindings, furniture covering, footballs, and many other products.

The process by which an animal skin is treated is called *tanning* and takes place in factories called *tanneries*. Each skin may be treated by various tanning processes, depending on the use for which the leather is intended. The two main tanning processes are vegetable tanning and mineral, or chrome, tanning.

Before tanning, the raw skins are "cured" by being soaked in *brine* (salt water) for a few weeks. Next, the skins are soaked in pure water to remove all salt, dirt, and blood. The flesh and hair on the skins is removed by chemicals (lime and sodium sulfide) and machines. The skins are then soaked in a weak solution of acid to reduce the swelling caused by the lime. At the same time, the skins are treated with an enzyme solution to make the skin soft and flexible. Then the skins are ready to be tanned.

In *vegetable tanning*, the skins are treated with a strong solution of *tannin*, a chemical made from tree bark. This makes the leather very strong and water resistant. *Flexible* (able to stretch or bend) vegetable-tanned leathers to be used for luggage or upholstery are less heavily tanned than leather intended for shoe bottoms.

In *mineral*, or *chrome, tanning*, the skins are treated with a solution of various chemicals, usually containing chromium. Chrome-tanned leathers stretch more than vegetable-tanned leathers and can be used for handbags, shoe uppers, gloves, and clothing. Sometimes skins are chrome-tanned and then vegetable-tanned, to produce a leather having the advantages of each type.

Tanned leather is stiff, and must be oiled to soften it. Then the leather is dyed, cut, and shaped into the final product. Leather for various purposes will receive many different kinds of treatment. For example, several coats of a thick, oily varnish are needed to give patent leather its high gloss. Leather is still in wide use, but modern factories now make synthetic (man-made) materials that look and feel like leather. Artificial leathers are less expensive than real leather and are much easier to care for.

ALSO READ: MANUFACTURING, PLASTIC, SHOES.

LEBANON Beautiful Mediterranean beaches and snow-capped mountains, the ruins of ancient cities, and castles built by the Crusaders attract thousands of tourists to Lebanon each year. The republic's capital, Beirut, is a leading communications and transportation center in the Middle East. (See the map with the article on the MIDDLE EAST.)

Lebanon is divided into four geographical regions. A narrow coastal plain in the west joins the Lebanon Mountains. East of this mountain range is the narrow Bekaa valley. Another mountain range called the Anti-Lebanon rises on the eastern side of the valley, and continues into Syria. Lebanon has only two sea-

▲ *The softly tanned skins piled up here have just been removed from the large drum where they were dyed.*

LEBANON

Capital City: Beirut (700,000 people).
Area: 3,475 square miles.
Population: 2,645,000 people.
Languages: Arabic, French, and English.
Export Products: Fruits and vegetables, iron and steel items, and hides and skins.
Unit of Money: Lebanese Pound.

sons. Winters are cool and moist, and summers are warm and dry.

About half of the Lebanese earn their living in agriculture. Wheat and barley are the main crops, and livestock raising is also important. Fruits are grown along the coastal plain. Trade is a more important part of the Lebanese economy than agriculture. The country's location makes it easy to trade with other Middle Eastern nations, and with the rest of the world. Pipelines bring oil from Saudi Arabia and Iraq. The oil is loaded into tankers and shipped to other nations. The Lebanese also earn a living in tourism, banking, oil refining, food processing, and textile manufacturing.

In most Middle Eastern countries except Israel, the majority of the people are Muslims. In Lebanon, however, only half of the people follow the religion of Islam. The other half are Christians.

Ancient Lebanon was a part of the Phoenician Empire, and later a part of the Byzantine Empire. In those days it was noted for the fine cedarwood that came from its forests. In the 800s, it came under Arab control. French Crusaders occupied the land between the 1000s and 1300s. The Turks were the next rulers, and controlled the land until the end of World War I. At that time, the French took over Lebanon and administered it until 1941, when it became an independent republic.

ALSO READ: BYZANTINE EMPIRE, MIDDLE EAST, PHOENICIA.

LEE, ROBERT E. (1807–1870) January 19 is a day of celebration in some southern states. It is the birthday of Robert E. Lee, commander in chief of the Confederate army during the Civil War. He was a highly respected man, admired not only by his own soldiers, but by northerners as well.

Robert Edward Lee was born in Stratford, Virginia. His father, Henry "Light Horse Harry" Lee, had been a brilliant general in the Revolutionary War. As a young man, Robert E. Lee attended the U.S. Military Academy at West Point, and graduated with honors.

He served in Georgia, Virginia, Ohio, and New York in his early army career. While in Virginia, he married Mary Custis, great-granddaughter of George Washington's

▼*Saida, a port on the southern coast of Lebanon. It is located on the site of Sidon, once a great Phoenician trade center.*

wife, Martha. The Lees had seven children and lived in the Custis mansion in Arlington, Virginia, on a hill overlooking Washington, D.C.

Lee fought for the first time in 1846, when the Mexican War broke out. He became well known for his skill and courage, and was promoted to *brevet* (honorary) colonel. In 1852, he became superintendent of the U.S. Military Academy at West Point for three years. Then he was assigned to duty on the Texas frontier. When Texas dropped out of the Union in 1861, Lee was sent back to Washington. President Abraham Lincoln offered him the field command of the United States Army in the war against the South.

Lee had to make a difficult decision. He was not in favor of slavery, and he was not in favor of a divided nation. But he had a great love for the South and for his home state, Virginia. He felt that individual freedom—freedom for each person to live as he pleases—was the main issue in the South's position, and he was in favor of that. He decided to join the Confederate Army, and he hoped the war would not last long. At first he served as a military adviser to the Confederate president, Jefferson Davis. He was promoted to full general in May, 1861. One year later, after serving in South Carolina and western Virginia, he took command of the Confederate Army of Northern Virginia. Lee scored some important military victories in Virginia, but he lost important battles at Antietam, Maryland, and Gettysburg, Pennsylvania.

Lee was made commander in chief of all the Confederate Armies in February, 1865. At that time, the Confederate forces were already in retreat. Lee knew well that he was losing. On April 9, 1865, he surrendered to General Ulysses S. Grant, commander in chief of the Union forces, at the Appomattox Court House in Virginia.

Lee became president of Washington College in Lexington, Virginia, after the war. He quickly improved the college and started new programs, including schools of commerce and journalism. After his death, the college was renamed Washington and Lee University.

ALSO READ: CIVIL WAR; CONFEDERATE STATES OF AMERICA; DAVIS, JEFFERSON; GRANT, ULYSSES SIMPSON; LINCOLN, ABRAHAM; MEXICAN WAR; VIRGINIA.

LEGEND The word "legend" instantly brings colorful pictures to mind. The adventures of King Arthur and Robin Hood, and the tales told about Davy Crockett are legends. People have always loved to listen to marvelous stories. Over the years, countless storytellers have spun wonderful tales to fascinate their listeners. Some of the old folk tales were called *myths*, and were about gods and goddesses, and imaginary happenings. A *legend* is a story that is told as true, but cannot be proved. It may have some truth to it, and it may be about a real person or a real place. But it is usually an exaggeration of what really happened. Many folk tales were passed on by word of mouth. But legends were usually written down. The word "legend" comes from a Latin word, *legenda*. It means "things to be read."

Legends of Long Ago

Legends were carried all over the ancient world by travelers, merchants, sailors, and roaming tribes. Some of the earliest recorded legends were told in the cold, icy land of the Vikings, where storytellers made the long winters seem shorter. Another part of the world, the sun-drenched land of Greece, was the home of other legends about great heroes and fantastic voyages. From Greece came the *Iliad* and the *Odyssey*, stories of the Trojan War and the adventures of the hero

▲*Robert E. Lee, commander in chief of the Confederate armies.*

▼*The legend of King Arthur tells how the dead king was taken to the island of Avalon. An arm rose from the water and took the king's sword, Excalibur.*

▲ *A scene from the* Odyssey, *a long poem that tells of the legendary wanderings of Ulysses, who fought in the Trojan wars* (above). *Romulus and Remus, the legendary founders of Rome, being cared for by wolves* (right).

Odysseus, who was also called Ulysses. These stories were written by the Greek poet, Homer. During the Middle Ages in Europe, "legend" often meant a collection of stories about holy men called saints. A famous book of these tales, written in the 1200s, was the *Legenda Aurea*, "The Golden Legend," by Jacobus de Voragine. These stories about the saints were usually read aloud in monasteries and churches. Stories about non-religious subjects later became more popular. The English poet Geoffrey Chaucer wrote *The Legend of Good Women*, about nine ladies noted for their suffering in the name of love. The tales of King Arthur are some of the greatest adventure legends ever told. Arthur may have been a real person, a chieftain in ancient Britain. Robin Hood and his Merry Men are the subjects of many stirring tales. Another European legend, about a mysterious ghost ship, the *Flying Dutchman*, has awed listeners for centuries.

Legends in the United States

The European settlers who came to America brought their own tales with them. But as the land was explored, and the frontier moved west, new legends were created. Stories grew up around the lives of famous men and women. The first President of the United States, George Washington, is said to have cut down his father's cherry tree when he was a

boy. When asked about it, he gave the legendary answer, "I cannot tell a lie. I did it with my hatchet." The legend of Johnny Appleseed is about a man whose real name was John Chapman. He is said to have planted apple trees all along the Ohio River valley, from Ohio to Illinois. President Abraham Lincoln became the subject of many legends. His backwoods upbringing and his great physical strength have been made into many romantic stories.

Many legendary stories were told about hard-riding westerners such as Jesse James and Billy the Kid. But of all the American folk heroes about whom tales have been told, Davy Crockett stands a head above the rest. His real life was unusual enough to be a legend. He was a Tennessee backwoodsman, an Indian fighter and famed hunter of bears, a United States Congressman, and a wildly funny storyteller. Many of his best stories were about himself. Davy claimed he had such a powerful grin that one flash of it could make a raccoon fall out of a tree. He is said one day to have spied a raccoon high up on a branch. Crockett smiled his terrible smile, again and again. Nothing happened. Finally, he went to look and found that the raccoon was only a giant knothole. But Davy had grinned the bark right off the tree.

Some of the most fantastic American legends are about people who may have been imaginary. Paul Bunyan is the hero of the "tallest," most exaggerated stories ever. No one knows whether a lumberjack with amazing strength ever really lived in the great North Woods of America. Mike Fink was the legendary hero of the riverboat men, and Pecos Bill's adventures were described in tall stories told on the western range. Many writers have used legends they have heard in stories of their own. Washington Irving's *Legend of Sleepy Hollow* is a spooky story based on a Dutch tale from his own New York State.

Handed down from one generation to the next, legends have carried tradition, history, romance, adventure, and laughter along with them. Each new generation has added its own legends. Today, many of the old legends have been retold on films and television. Some day, legends will be told about our own time. Perhaps they will be told about the fantastic explorations of the astronauts, about the evil ways of men such as the dictator Adolf Hitler, or about the good deeds of men such as the German doctor Albert Schweitzer or the American civil rights leader, Dr. Martin Luther King.

ALSO READ: APPLESEED, JOHNNY; ARTHUR, KING; BUNYAN, PAUL; CROCKETT, DAVY; FOLKLORE; LINCOLN, ABRAHAM; OUTLAW; ROBIN HOOD; WASHINGTON, GEORGE.

LEGISLATURE The branch of a government which has the power to make, change, or abolish that government's laws is called a *legislature*. Most modern legislatures are made up of representatives elected by the people.

In the past, legislatures were created as a result of disputes between early European kings and their subjects. The people wanted to take part in the making of laws that would affect them. If they were taxed, they wanted to be sure it was

▲ *Hiawatha says goodbye to his people. According to legend, he founded the Iroquois Confederacy of tribes in New York State.*

a fair and necessary tax. Since the thousands of citizens in one country could not spend all their time discussing government business, they elected people to do this for them.

Most modern governments have a *bicameral* (two-house) legislature. The national legislature of the United States (Congress) has two houses. The upper house (Senate) consists of two elected senators from each state. The lower house (House of Representatives) has one representative for every 450,000 people.

Legislatures have various names, such as Congress (United States), Parliament (Great Britain), Bundestag (West Germany), Knesset (Israel), and Supreme Soviet (Soviet Union). The powers and duties of most legislatures are set up in the constitution and laws of the country. The U.S. Congress gets its powers from the Constitution of the United States. State legislatures get their powers from state constitutions. Local legislative groups, such as city councils, get power from documents known as charters, which must usually be approved by state legislatures.

Some nations and states have *unicameral* (one-house) legislatures. A few of these are New Zealand, Tanzania, Egypt, Israel, Sweden, and the state of Nebraska.

ALSO READ: CONGRESS, UNITED STATES; CONSTITUTION, UNITED STATES; LAW; PARLIAMENT.

The 500-year-old bicameral (two-house) legislature of Sweden was changed to a unicameral (one-house) body by constitutional change in 1971. Both houses had become so much alike that they could no longer work together.

LEMONADE　　Lemonade is a game that is also known as *Occupations*. Two teams stand facing each other about 25 feet apart, each behind a line on the ground. Team One walks up to the Team Two's line, saying, "Here we come." Team Two asks, "Where from?" Team One replies, "New York." Team Two asks, "What's your trade?" Team One answers, "Lemonade." Team Two shouts, "Go to work!" Team One then begins to act out an occupation—ditch-digging, painting, farming, or typing, for example. Team Two guesses what occupation Team One is acting out. As soon as Team Two makes the correct guess, Team One players run back as fast as they can to their line. Team Two chases them. If any players are tagged before they reach their line, they must join the other side. The game is over when all members of one team are tagged.

LEMUR　　The lemur is a *primate*, a relative of the monkey. Scientists think that monkeys may have descended from the lemur family millions of years ago. Lemurs look a little bit like monkeys, but they have long, bushy tails and fox-like faces. Most lemurs are about the size of a cat, but some are only as small as squirrels.

Lemurs once lived everywhere on earth. Today, they live only on the island of Madagascar (the Republic of Malagasy). The lemur is a very shy, gentle animal. It spends all of its life in the forest. It almost never comes down to the ground. During the day, most lemurs sleep in the hollow of a tree. They wake up when the sun goes down and spend the night hours looking for food with other lemurs. Lemurs eat many different things—leaves and twigs, fruit, insects, birds' eggs, and even birds.

The lemur's chief enemy is man. The people of Malagasy hunt lemurs with dogs. When the dogs trap a lemur in a tree, the hunters try to knock the lemur to the ground with stones. If the lemur falls out of the tree, it plays dead. Then, suddenly, it jumps up again and tries to escape by running up another tree.

ALSO READ: MALAGASY, MONKEY.

LENIN, NIKOLAI (1870–1924) The people of the Soviet Union honor the memory of Nikolai Lenin just as the people of the United States honor the memory of George Washington. Lenin was the father of his country. He was the leader of the revolution that overthrew the Russian government in 1917.

Lenin was born in the Russian town of Simbirsk (now Ulyanov). His real name was Vladimir Ilyich Ulyanov. When Lenin was a young student, he decided that the Russian government under the czar (king) was bad. The czar and his officials did little to improve the lives of the millions of poor people in Russia. Some groups of people were working secretly to change the government. Lenin's older brother, Alexander, belonged to one of these groups. Alexander was arrested in 1887, accused of plotting to kill the czar, and executed. Young Vladimir was deeply affected by this. He became involved in revolutionary activities and began to use the name Lenin to keep the czar's police from learning his real identity. He was arrested in 1895 and sent to prison for 14 months. After that, he was exiled to Siberia for three years.

Lenin's revolutionary ideas were greatly influenced by the writings of Karl Marx, a German Communist. Marx believed that the capitalist system, in which rich people owned the industries, was wrong. He wrote that the poor workers would revolt and take over the industries. He believed this would result in Communism, a system in which all the people would belong to the same social class. Lenin thought that Marx was right and that Russia would be better off under Communism.

▼*The ring-tailed lemur, unlike most other lemurs, is active during the day.*

Lenin returned to Russia from his exile in Siberia, but he did not stay there long. He spent most of the next 17 years in Germany and Switzerland. He met with other followers of Marx, wrote against the Russian government, and organized the Bolshevik party.

◀*Nikolai Lenin, leader of the Russian Revolution, speaking to a group of workers.*

Russia fought against Germany in World War I. The Russians suffered many losses, and the government began to lose control over the people. A group of moderate revolutionaries overthrew the czar's government in March, 1917. This group, led by Alexander Kerensky, wanted to keep Russia in the war against Germany. The Bolsheviks wanted to get out of the war. The Germans allowed Lenin to go back to Russia. When he got there, he led the Bolsheviks to power. Lenin became head of the new Communist government. He worked until his death to spread Communism to other countries.

ALSO READ: CAPITALISM; COMMUNISM; MARX, KARL; RUSSIAN HISTORY; SOVIET UNION; STALIN, JOSEPH; TROTSKY, LEON; WORLD WAR I.

LENS As you read this page, move the book close to your eyes. Can you see the words clearly? Now move the book slowly back until the words are sharp and clear. At this distance, your eyes have focused on the words. This has happened be-cause in each of your eyes there is a lens, a clear, solid material with a smoothly curved surface. The light rays reflected from the page pass through the lens of each eye and are focused on the retina on the back of each eye. If the lenses in your eyes are not curved correctly or your eyes are the wrong shape, you must wear glasses to give you proper vision. Glasses are among the many types of lenses that man has invented to make things appear clearer or larger.

A lens is a transparent object that has one or more curved surfaces. Until recent times, all lenses were made of special kinds of glass. Now, many lenses are made of hard, clear plastic. A plastic lens will not break so easily as a glass lens, but its surface is more likely to get scratched.

Light rays travel through the air in a straight line. Something happens to them when they pass through a lens. The rays are *refracted* (bent) when they pass through a lens. They may bend so that they *converge* (come together), or *diverge* (spread out). A lens with a surface curved outward is called a *convex* lens. This type of lens is thicker in the middle than at the ends, and it will converge light rays. A lens with a surface curved inward is called a *concave* lens. It is thinner in the middle than at the ends, and it will diverge light rays.

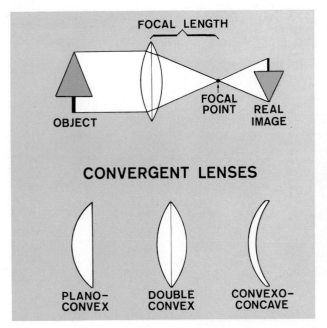

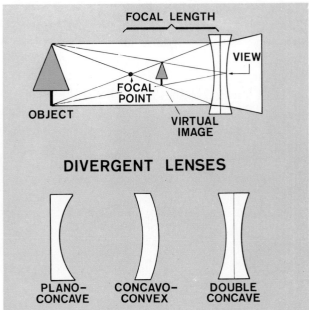

A convex lens can be used as a burning glass. It focuses the light rays from the sun to a tiny spot, which becomes very hot. Grass, paper, or twigs can be set on fire in this way. The ancient Egyptians and Babylonians probably used convex lenses as burning glasses thousands of years ago.

A convex lens can also be used to form a *real image* of a distant scene. This type of image can be projected onto a screen. But the real image formed by a lens is upside down, or inverted. The lens of the human eye is a convex lens. It forms an inverted real image on the retina. However, the brain automatically reverses this image to look right side up.

Concave lenses form *virtual images*. A virtual image is right side up, but it cannot be projected on a screen as a real image can. A concave lens cannot form a real image.

A convex lens can form either real or virtual images. You can prove this with a magnifying glass, which is a convex lens. Look at this page through a magnifying glass. You will see an enlarged image that is right side up. This is a virtual image. Now stand near a window and focus the lens on a sheet of white paper. The image is upside down. This is a real image.

One of the basic properties of a lens is its *focal length*. The focal length is the distance from the lens to the focal point where the light converges (comes together). To measure the focal length of a magnifying glass, focus the rays from the sun onto a piece of cardboard. The distance between the lens and the cardboard is the focal length of the lens. Examine several different lenses. The more strongly curved the lens the shorter its focal length.

Some lenses are flat on one side and concave or convex on the other side. These are *plano-convex* or *plano-concave* lenses. If both sides of a lens are convex, the lens is *bi-convex*, and a *bi-concave* lens has two concave sides. Some lenses have one side concave and the other convex. These are *concavo-convex* (meniscus) lenses. Most lenses for eyeglasses are actually concavo-convex lenses.

Very small lenses are used in microscopes. These are strongly curved and give great magnification. Telescopes use lenses, too. The largest telescope lens in the world is 40 inches across. Larger lenses have not been built because it is very difficult and extremely expensive to make them. Bigger telescopes all use curved mirrors.

▼ *The 40-inch refracting lens at Yerkes Observatory, the largest refractor in the world. (Reflections from other objects show in this picture.)*

Microscope and telescope lenses have extended man's vision and shown him new worlds. Lenses have enabled him to see single-celled organisms such as bacteria. Telescopes have helped man learn about the other planets of the solar system and the stars of the universe.

ALSO READ: EYE, LIGHT, MICROSCOPE, TELESCOPE.

LEONARDO DA VINCI (1452–1519)

One of the greatest artists who ever lived was also one of the world's greatest geniuses—the Italian Leonardo da Vinci. He was born in the small village of Vinci in Tuscany in that exciting time of awakening of knowledge called the Renaissance. Leonardo was interested in a wide range of subjects. He kept notebooks in which he asked many questions, answered those he could, and did sketches of his theories and his ideas for inventions. He even sketched his plan for an experimental airplane.

He would ask questions like, "How does a heart pump blood?" "What happens when you sneeze?" He wanted to know scientifically what lay underneath the skin he was painting. He did scientific drawings of legs (while studying human anatomy), showing exposed muscles and bones.

Leonardo studied painting in Florence, in the studio of Verrochio, a leading artist of the day. At the age of 30 he went to the city of Milan, where he worked for some time under the sponsorship of the Duke of Milan. Leonardo was curious about the results of using different kinds of paints. Unfortunately, some of the paint experiments failed. The paint did not last, and few of Leonardo's paintings remain today. Shown below is one of his best known works, his painting of *The Last Supper*. This great painting shows Christ at supper with his twelve apostles. He has just told them that one of the twelve will betray him. Look at their reactions. Each apostle seems to be asking Christ, "Is it I, Lord?" See if you can find Judas, the one who betrayed him. This painting is famous for its use of perspective. *The Last Supper* is in poor condition today because Leonardo used his experimental paint.

Mona Lisa by Leonardo, also shown here, is possibly the best known and most loved painting in the world. Why do you think the woman is smiling? People have been asking that question ever since Leonardo painted the picture.

Poems and songs have been written about the Mona Lisa's mysterious smile. The painting seems to glow with a mysterious light from within. Leonardo was able to get this effect by building up many layers of very thin glazes on the painting. The painting is not very large—only 30 by 21 inches. It

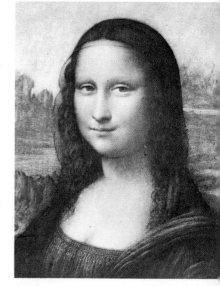

▲ Mona Lisa, *by Leonardo da Vinci.*

◄The Last Supper, *by Leonardo da Vinci.*

commands great attention at the Louvre in Paris, where it is usually exhibited. In 1962 the French loaned the painting to the United States. It was exhibited in Washington, D.C., and then in New York City. At both museums, thousands of people stood in line to be able to walk by the picture for a glimpse of the mysterious lady.

Only one of his paintings is not in a museum or collection in Europe. His portrait of Ginevra de Benci, an attractive young woman, hangs in the National Gallery in Washington.

Leonardo da Vinci was the most versatile (many-talented) genius of the Renaissance period. He left more than 7,000 pages of notebooks with scientific ideas and theories and sketches to go with them. The great value of his work was not really understood until the twentieth century. A creator in art, a discoverer in many branches of science. and an inventor in technology—Leonardo da Vinci could be called a "universal man."

ALSO READ: ART HISTORY, RENAISSANCE.

LESOTHO The Kingdom of Lesotho, formerly a British dependency known as Basutoland, is completely surrounded by the Republic of South Africa. (See the map with the article on AFRICA.) Unlike some African countries, Lesotho has no white settlers. The small numbers of white people who live in Lesotho are mainly European traders, missionaries, and foreign diplomats.

The climate is dry. Temperatures in the western lowlands range from 90 degrees in the summer months to 20 degrees in the winter. Lesotho has many mountains and plateaus. The snow-capped Drakensberg Mountains are in the eastern part of the country.

The people of Lesotho are called Basothos. They are descendants of Bantu-speaking peoples who came to southern Africa during the early 1600s. Most Basothos make a living by farming corn, wheat, and sorghum, or by raising sheep, goats, and cattle. Nearly half of the men work in the Republic of South Africa, in mines, industries, and farms. The country's exports are wool, mohair, hides, livestock, and diamonds. Lesotho depends heavily on foreign aid. Transportation is underdeveloped. There is only one railroad, which connects the capital city of Maseru with South Africa. The country has few paved roads. Lesotho has a good educational system, and most Basothos read and write.

Lesotho came under British rule in 1868. Moshesh I, the king of the country, asked the British to protect his people from the Boers (white South Africans of Dutch descent) who wanted to settle on his land. Lesotho became independent on October 4, 1966. The government

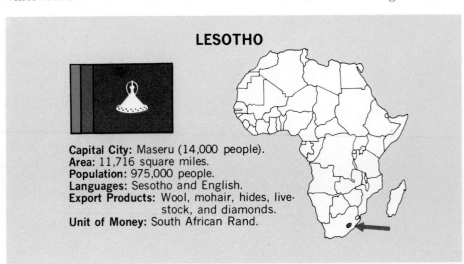

LESOTHO

Capital City: Maseru (14,000 people).
Area: 11,716 square miles.
Population: 975,000 people.
Languages: Sesotho and English.
Export Products: Wool, mohair, hides, livestock, and diamonds.
Unit of Money: South African Rand.

then consisted of a king, an elected national assembly of 60 members, a senate, a cabinet, and a prime minister. The prime minister, Chief Leabua Jonathan, seized control of the government in January, 1970. He placed the king, Moshoeshoe II, under arrest, and suspended the parliament for five years.

ALSO READ: AFRICA, SOUTH AFRICA.

LETTER WRITING A letter can "speak" for you when you are miles away from someone. A letter is a message between people. Because the person who writes the letter will not be present to explain it, a letter must be written so that it can be easily understood.

When writing to a friend, use the same words you would use if you were talking with him. Unless he knows your address very well, you should write it at the top of your letter on the right hand side. The date of your letter should be written below the address.

Here is a sample of a personal letter:

> 9910 Holmhurst Road
> Bethesda, Maryland 20034
> January 9, 1972

Dear Greg,

I looked for the belt which you thought you left at our house, but I couldn't find it. Maybe the dog buried it in the back yard!

If it turns up I will bring it with me when I visit you next weekend. Dad will drive me down on Saturday.

> Yours truly,
> Jeff

There are several rules to follow when writing a business letter. When addressing the envelope, the name of the person comes first if you are writing to someone in particular, and then his title, if he has one, such as—

> "Mr. Thomas Wilson
> Assistant Principal"

On the line after this, you write the name of the company or the building, if there is a name, such as "Sandhurst Elementary School." The street number follows on the next line. Below that go the city, state, and zip code number.

The address that is on the envelope goes on the letter, too. Here is a sample of a business letter. This one begins "Gentlemen" because no particular name is known.

> 9910 Holmhurst Road
> Bethesda, Maryland 20034
> April 17, 1972

National Wildlife Federation
1412 16th Street N.W.
Washington, D.C. 20036

Gentlemen:

I am writing a school paper on animals and birds that are becoming extinct. If you could send me a colored picture of the North American Bald Eagle, I would appreciate it very much.

> Sincerely yours,
> Jeffrey Naylor

A letter is a poor messenger if the writing is so messy that it is hard to read, if the words are misspelled, or the meaning is not clear.

ALSO READ: COMMUNICATION.

LEWIS, JOHN L. (1880–1969) John Llewellyn Lewis was a coal miner who became one of the best known labor leaders in the United States. He was born in Lucas, Iowa. His father was a Welsh coal miner who had settled in the U.S., and Lewis went to work in the Iowa mines as a young boy. His career as a labor leader began in 1906 with his first job for the United Mine Workers (UMW). In 1920, he became president of that union. The UMW was at that time a member of the American Federation of Labor (AFL), a large organization made up of many labor unions. Lewis thought

▲*A citizen of Lesotho in bright traditional costume.*

▲ *John L. Lewis, American labor leader.*

that the AFL did not fully represent the interests of industrial workers. He broke with the AFL in 1935 and persuaded several other labor union leaders to join him in forming the Committee for Industrial Organization, which later became the Congress of Industrial Organizations (CIO). He took his mine workers out of the CIO in 1942 because of disagreements with the organization's policies. The UMW rejoined the AFL for a short time, but then left to become an independent union.

Lewis was a stormy and dramatic man, with shaggy eyebrows and a fierce appearance. His efforts on behalf of the coal miners brought them much improved working conditions, increased wages, and a better way of life. Lewis was often criticized because of his demands for the coal miners. He had many battles with other union organizations and with the government. But in 1964, he was given the honored Presidential Medal of Freedom for his contributions to the welfare of mine workers.

ALSO READ: LABOR UNION.

LEWIS, SINCLAIR (1885–1951)

In 1930, Sinclair Lewis became the first American to be awarded the Nobel Prize for literature. Lewis was born in Sauk Centre, Minnesota, and was educated at Yale University. He wrote several stories for magazines, and wrote five novels which were not widely popular. He achieved his first great success in 1920, with the publication of his sixth novel, *Main Street.*

Main Street describes the kind of middle-class life Lewis considered typical of the small American towns of the 1920s—where many people were dull, ignorant, and narrow-minded, but others were anxious to improve the quality of local life. In *Babbitt,* Lewis satirizes (points out the foolishness of something by making fun of it) the life of a middle-class American business-

▼ *Sinclair Lewis, American author, with his wife, Dorothy Thompson.*

man who values only money and possessions. Lewis also wrote *Arrowsmith,* about a doctor who wants to help mankind, and struggles to keep his ideals in a profession in which many others are interested only in making money.

Lewis was one of a group of American writers in the early part of this century who tried to write realistically, rather than romantically, about American life.

ALSO READ: LITERATURE.

LEWIS AND CLARK EXPEDITION

In 1803, the United States bought 885,000 square miles of land from France. The total cost of the land was 15 million dollars, only about four cents an acre! This territory, the Louisiana Purchase, was so large that it included what are now seven entire states and parts of six others.

Very little was known about this land in the early 1800s. President Thomas Jefferson wanted to find out everything he could about it, so he organized an expedition to explore the land.

He appointed two young army officers, Meriwether Lewis and William Clark, to command the expedition. The President instructed them to find a good route to the Pacific Ocean for future settlers to travel. Lewis and Clark hired a group of 39 soldiers, three interpreters (to speak with the Indians), and a Negro slave. The slave, whose name was York, was really more of a *valet* (man's servant) for Captain Clark. Three large boats were built to carry all the men and supplies up the Missouri River. After more than a year of preparation, the expedition officially started from St. Louis, Missouri, on May 14, 1804.

The explorers covered about ten miles a day. They had several unfriendly meetings with Indians, but attacks by grizzly bears were actually more of a danger. Through the aid of the expedition's interpreters, most of the Indians they met were not only friendly, but also helpful.

In October, 1804, the expedition arrived at a Mandan Indian village, in what is now North Dakota. The men built Fort Mandan and stayed there for the winter. During the winter, Lewis hired a French-Canadian fur-trapper, Toussaint Charbonneau, and his wife, an Indian girl named Sacagawea, also called "Bird Woman," to act as guides and interpreters. The couple brought along their baby son on the journey.

The expedition started out again in April, 1805. The group continued up the Missouri River, into what is now Montana. There the big river divided into three branches. The explorers went up one branch in canoes as far as they could go. Then they left the river and bought horses from Sacagawea's tribe, the Shoshone Indians. The expedition continued overland across the Rocky Mountains to the Clearwater River in Idaho. They then paddled down the Clearwater to the Columbia River. They followed the Columbia to its mouth, and on November 15, 1805, they reached the Pacific Ocean. No other men had ever before crossed the continent north of Mexico.

The expedition spent a hard winter on the Pacific Coast, in a camp fortified against possible Indian attack. On March 23, 1806, they began their long journey home. The explorers returned to St. Louis on September 23, 1806—nearly 2½ years after they had left. Cheering crowds stood along the river to greet them. The government rewarded the members of the expedition with grants of land.

The Lewis and Clark Expedition is regarded as one of the great feats of exploration. Both Lewis and Clark kept journals during the trip, and they brought back valuable information about the geography, climate, wildlife, and Indians of the American West. The journey cov-

▲Lewis and Clark and their fellow adventurers on the Columbia River at the end of their long westward journey of exploration.

ered more than 8,500 miles. If you trace the expedition's route on the map of explorations (see the map with the article on EXPLORATION), you can understand better what a great adventure it must have been.

ALSO READ: AMERICAN HISTORY; COLUMBIA RIVER; EXPLORATION; IDAHO; INDIANS, AMERICAN; JEFFERSON, THOMAS; LOUISIANA PURCHASE; MISSOURI; MONTANA; NORTH DAKOTA; OREGON; ROCKY MOUNTAINS; WESTWARD MOVEMENT.

LIBERIA The Republic of Liberia is one of the oldest independent African nations. It has never been controlled by a European country. Liberia was founded by freed Negro slaves from the United States.

Liberia lies on the southwest tip of the West African bulge. Its neighbors are the Ivory Coast to the east, Guinea to the north, and Sierra Leone to the northwest. It has a 350-mile coastline on the Atlantic Ocean. Liberia is slightly larger than Ohio. (See the map with the article on AFRICA.) Tropical rain forest covers much of the land. The rainy season lasts for eight months, when an inch or more of rain falls almost every day. Liberia has no natural

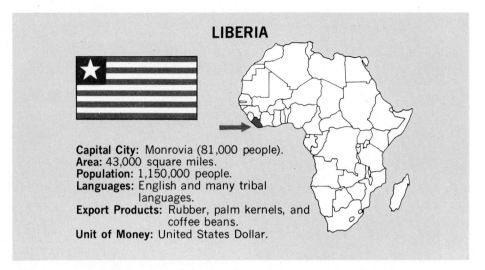

LIBERIA

Capital City: Monrovia (81,000 people).
Area: 43,000 square miles.
Population: 1,150,000 people.
Languages: English and many tribal
languages.
Export Products: Rubber, palm kernels, and
coffee beans.
Unit of Money: United States Dollar.

The first president of Liberia was Joseph Jenkins Roberts (1809–1876). He was born free in Petersburg, Virginia, and went to Liberia with his family in 1829. Liberia had been founded in 1822 as a home for free Negroes.

▼*These students are proud of being Africans as well as Liberians. They are celebrating Africa Day by parading in tribal costumes in Monrovia, Liberia's capital.*

harbor. However, it has a man-made harbor, a free port near Monrovia, the capital. This port was built between 1945 and 1948 with United States funds. The port was turned over to the Liberian government in 1964.

Although Liberia is rich in resources, it is underdeveloped. Coffee, rice, sugar cane, and cassava are grown in small amounts along the coast. Palm kernels, used for soap, and palm fibers are important forest products. The growing of rubber on plantations was once the most important industry. Iron mining is the most important one today. Other mineral resources are diamonds and gold.

Monrovia, the nation's capital, was the first settlement in Liberia. Freed Negroes settled there in 1822. Monrovia was named after the

United States President, James Monroe. The country became a republic on July 26, 1847. Its constitution is modeled on the United States Constitution. Liberia's new president, William Tolbert, was sworn into office in January, 1972. An elected senate and house of representatives help Liberia's president to govern the country.

Few Liberians are of American Negro descent. Those who are speak English, live near the coast, and work in business and government. Other Liberians, who are mostly descendants of tribesmen who came to the area in the 1400s, live inland and work as farmers. They follow tribal religions and speak their own tribal languages.
ALSO READ: AFRICA.

LIBERTY BELL A huge bell, located in Independence Hall in Philadelphia, Pennsylvania, displays these words: "Proclaim Liberty throughout all the land unto all the inhabitants thereof. . . ." Visitors touring Independence Hall can see the Liberty Bell on the ground floor. This bell rang out the news when the Declaration of Independence was proclaimed on July 8, 1776. The bell later became a symbol of U.S. independence from Great Britain.

The Liberty Bell weighs over 2,000 pounds and measures 12 feet around at the rim. The original bell was brought from England in 1752. When it arrived, the bell was tested, and it cracked. Workmen melted it down, and a new bell was made in 1753. Like the first bell, this one was defective. A third bell, made later that year, worked. It was hung in the wooden tower of the building now called Independence Hall.

▼*The Liberty Bell rings no more, but it still stands as a symbol of independence.*

During the Revolutionary War, the bell was taken down and hidden in Allentown, Pennsylvania, from 1777–1778. After the Revolution, the bell was returned to Independence Hall. It was rung to celebrate special occasions until 1835. In that year, the Liberty Bell was damaged while tolling for the funeral of John Marshall, Chief Justice of the Supreme Court. Workmen tried to fix the bell, but it cracked again when it was rung on George Washington's birthday in 1846.

ALSO READ: DECLARATION OF INDE-PENDENCE, INDEPENDENCE HALL, PENNSYLVANIA.

LIBRARY Books and pamphlets and other materials are collected and arranged in a library for reading and reference. By reading books that a library has on its shelves, it is possible to gain in knowledge and imagination and to enjoy all the cultures of the world.

Touring the Library

The hours that a public library is open are often posted near the front door. Notices of story hours, movies, and exhibits shown in the library may be listed also.

The main library desk is usually near the front of the library. The reader can apply for a library card there. He can ask for the rules about checking out books and other materials. If the library is very large, a floor plan will probably be displayed to show where the various rooms are located.

The main room of the library also contains the card catalog and various file cabinets. The card catalog is a key to the books on the shelves. It saves the reader many minutes in his search for books. The file cabinets contain pamphlets, pictures, and other materials.

The largest part of the library is taken up by the shelves containing books. The juvenile, or children's, books are usually in a separate room of the library. The tables and chairs there fit the readers who use that part of the library. The adult and the children's books are divided into several sections. One section, often a separate room, contains the reference books. The other books are divided into two categories—storybooks, also called "fiction," and factual books or "non-fiction." These books can be taken out by anyone with a library card.

▼*Most schools have libraries where students can spend their study periods usefully.*

Large libraries sometimes have other specialized rooms. Some have rooms with magazines and comfortable chairs. A room may have a collection of books on a special subject, such as the history of the state. Some libraries have rooms where clubs meet and movies are shown. The library staff has rooms for offices and for preparing the books before they are put on the shelves. But these rooms are not available for readers.

Library Skills

After touring the library to find where everything is located, it is a good idea to return to the card catalog and learn how to use it. The card catalog has at least one card for every book in the library. Many of the cards have numbers in the upper left corner. These numbers are probably arranged by the Dewey Decimal System and are mostly for the non-fiction books. The numbers shown on the card are also on the back of the book it describes, and the books are on the shelves in numerical order.

The *Dewey Decimal System* was invented by an American, Melvil Dewey, in 1876. It is used in libraries all over the world because it is based on numbers rather than letters or words. Numbers are the same in all countries and can be used with any language.

Dewey divided all knowledge into ten groups, called "classes." The ten classes are numbered from 000 to 900 this way:

000	General knowledge
100	Philosophy
200	Religion
300	Social sciences
400	Language
500	Pure science
600	Technology
700	Arts and recreation
800	Literature
900	History

Each of the ten classes is divided into ten separate sections. This is how the 000 is divided:

000	General works
010	Bibliography
020	Library science
030	General encyclopedias
040	General collections and essays
050	General periodicals
060	General organizations
070	Newspapers, journalism
080	Collected works
090	Manuscripts and rare books

Each of these sections is again divided into ten other sections. The number 030 is the Dewey Decimal number for encyclopedias. Using 030 as a sample, encyclopedias are divided in this way:

031	American encyclopedias
032	English encyclopedias
033	German encyclopedias
034	French encyclopedias
035	Italian encyclopedias
036	Spanish encyclopedias
037	Slavic encyclopedias
038	Scandinavian encyclopedias
039	Other encyclopedias

A decimal point and other numbers often follow the first three numbers. For example, the number for Portuguese encyclopedias is 036.9. You can see from the list above that 036 is the number for Spanish encyclopedias. The number .9 was added to show that Portuguese and Spanish encyclopedias are different, although the languages are similar.

The Dewey Decimal System is constantly being changed, or added to, with the discovery of new information or inventions. For example, a new number, 629.1334, was added recently for books about jet aircraft.

Both reference and circulating books are put on the shelves according to the numbers in the Dewey Decimal System. The library has signs, often clipped to the library shelves, telling where the numbers begin. In very large libraries, one of the classes may have a room to itself. For instance, a whole room may be full of history books (900). Even in smaller libraries, the books

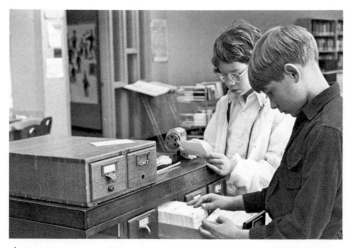

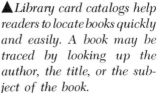

▲*Library card catalogs help readers to locate books quickly and easily. A book may be traced by looking up the author, the title, or the subject of the book.*

▼*A reader locates a book through its number in the card catalog, which is also written on the spine of the book. Signs direct him to the correct shelf.*

▲*If books do not give the current information a student needs, he may find it by using one of the available indexes to magazines (periodicals).*

▲*A student stamps the date on the card of a book which he is borrowing from the library. In many libraries, the librarians stamp the books.*

on art are sometimes separated from the others, because art books are often oversized and need special shelves.

Reference and Specialized Material
The books in the reference section are always in the library, since they cannot be taken out. Many specialized books, such as atlases and almanacs, are found in the reference section. Encyclopedias are an important part of the reference section, as are large volumes of technical data.

The library tries to provide as much up-to-date information as it can. Some of this is in the pamphlet file. It contains pamphlets, maps, and newspaper clippings that give

more recent information than is contained in the reference books. Pamphlets, clippings, and maps can usually be taken out and are used often for school work.

Some libraries have files of colored pictures that may not be found in books. These include prints of famous paintings and copies of portraits of famous people.

Libraries may have music sections containing records that may be taken out. Some libraries have small booths where people can listen to records they might wish to borrow. Large libraries have music scores, or sheet music, that can be used by music lovers in playing instruments or for following music while listening to records.

▲ *Some libraries have micro-film readers so that back copies of newspapers may be more easily stored. The librarian will be glad to make one of the machines available to you should you wish to use one.*

Magazines and newspapers are also available to readers. Many large libraries have put newspapers on photostatic tape and have rooms in which readers can view the tapes. Photostatic tape saves a great deal of storage space for the library.

Bookmobiles

The bookmobile is a large bus or truck full of books for both adults and children. It is arranged just like a library, with shelves of books and a charging desk. A bookmobile goes to certain places on a regular schedule, and a librarian checks out books and receives books returned by the readers in that area.

The bookmobile began as a way to take the library into farming and mountain areas, where people lived far away from a library. However, cities have become so large that bookmobiles are now part of city library systems. They are sent to parts of the city where there are no library branches.

Librarians

Today's libraries could not function without highly trained and skilled librarians. They are the people who order all the material found in the library. They have to know the community so they can buy what

people want to read. They also have to find out what books are needed to help readers in their school work, their hobbies, and their jobs. Librarians have usually taken special courses (called *library science*) in school to learn their jobs.

The work needed to keep a library useful requires librarians with specialized jobs. The first librarian a visitor sees is in the circulation department. This librarian issues the library cards and checks the books in and out. If a reader needs help in finding information about a certain subject, he is referred to the reference librarian. Other librarians prepare all the books for the shelves and all the pamphlets and pictures

▼ *Librarians are happy to help a reader find the information he wants. If a book is not available, the librarian will usually order it from elsewhere.*

for the files. They keep the books in order, so the reader can find the ones he wants. Librarians also prepare the cards for the catalog and keep the catalog up to date. Young people who like books and enjoy meeting and helping people sometimes study to become librarians.

Early Libraries

The earliest known libraries were collections of books written on clay tablets, or blocks, and on papyrus (a paper-like material), in ancient Babylonia and Egypt. The Greeks started a public library in Athens in

about 540 B.C. Several public libraries were also established in Rome. One of the greatest libraries in the ancient world was in Alexandria, Egypt.

When barbarians invaded Europe, monks kept many libraries safe by storing their contents in monasteries. As Christianity spread, more books were made, since Christians wanted to be able to read the Bible themselves. The development of the printing press in the 1400s also increased the number of books available for collection in libraries. Several great university libraries were established in Europe during this period. The British Museum, which contains a world-famous library, was started in the 1700s.

The first library in America was established at Henrico College in Virginia in 1621. Benjamin Franklin established the first subscription library in Philadelphia, Pennsylvania, in 1732. Members paid to join it and then paid yearly dues.

The Library of Congress, the national library of the U.S., was established in 1800. The Library of Congress uses a system that resembles the Dewey Decimal System, except that each major class, or group, of books is marked by a letter of the alphabet. Subdivisions are shown by an additional letter with numerals. Many special scholarly, college, and large libraries use the Library of Congress system.

Tax-supported public libraries were first established in New York in the 1800s. Free public libraries today are supported by private donations and by federal and state taxes.

For further information on:
History of Books and Printing, *see* EGYPT, ANCIENT; FRANKLIN, BENJAMIN; GUTENBERG, JOHANNES; MIDDLE AGES; MONASTERY; WEBSTER, NOAH.
Printed Matter, *see* BOOK, MAGAZINE, NEWSPAPER, PRINTING, PUBLISHING, TYPESETTING.
Reference Tools, *see* ALMANAC,
ATLAS, BIBLIOGRAPHY, CARD CATALOG, DICTIONARY, ENCYCLOPEDIA, GAZETTEER, INDEX, LIBRARY OF CONGRESS, MAP, RECORDING, REFERENCE BOOK.

LIBRARY OF CONGRESS One of the largest libraries in the world started with 11 trunks of books and a case of maps. This was the beginning of the Library of Congress, in Washington, D.C. In 1800, Congress had set aside 5,000 dollars for a library of books to be placed in the new Capitol building. To begin with, 740 volumes arrived from England in trunks. These first books were about law and government and were for the use of the President and members of Congress.

Many people began giving books to the new library. By 1814, the library had 3,000 books. During the War of 1812, the British army invaded Washington and burned the Capitol, destroying all the library's books. After the war, Congress bought Thomas Jefferson's collection of 6,000 books to get the library started again. The number of books in the library increased greatly over the years. In 1897, the library was moved to a beautiful new building near the Capitol.

▲*The reading room of the British Museum in London is a special library facility for people who cannot find the materials they need in an ordinary library. This library stocks one of the largest collections of rare books in the world.*

▼*The main reading room of the Library of Congress is an impressive center of learning. Students from all over the world come here to study rare books and other written materials.*

Today the Library of Congress has more than 10 million books. Some of these are very old and very valuable. It even has some ancient books written on stone tablets. The library has a collection of musical instruments which includes four Stradivarius violins. Early phonographs, photographic equipment, and moving picture cameras are also part of the library's collection. Many people from all over the United States use the Library of Congress daily for research work, but the library is still primarily for the use of the members of Congress.

One of the departments of the Library of Congress is the Copyright Office. Copyrights protect authors, composers, and artists from having their creations copied. The library receives two free copies of every book copyrighted in the U.S. It also prints library catalog cards for all copyrighted books printed in the United States.

ALSO READ: LIBRARY, PATENTS AND COPYRIGHTS.

▲*An oasis stands green and cool in the rocky desert land that covers most of Libya.*

LIBYA Libya is a republic on the northern coast of Africa. It is sandwiched between Algeria on the west and Egypt on the east. Chad and the Republic of Niger lie to the South. Libya has two capital cities—Tripoli and Benghazi. This was done to satisfy tribal loyalties in a poorly unified country. (See the map with the article on AFRICA.)

Most of the country lies in the hot and dry Sahara Desert. Summer temperatures are over 100 degrees. The climate along the Mediterranean coast is much cooler. The narrow coastal lands also receive much rainfall.

Libyans are mainly Arabs and Berbers, who follow the religion of Islam. Most of them are farmers who live along the Mediterranean coast. They raise dates, citrus fruits, olives, and almonds. However, the farmers depend mainly on livestock —cattle, sheep, and goats—for their livelihood. Some Libyans are fishermen who catch tuna and sardines from the Mediterranean Sea. More and more Libyans are moving into the cities to get jobs in the growing oil industry.

Libya was for many years one of the poorest countries in Africa, mainly because of its lack of good farmland and natural resources. But it is rapidly growing more prosperous. An American company, drilling for oil in the desert, struck water instead. They found a huge underground lake. The water has been used to irrigate a large part of the desert which is now used for farming. Oil was discovered in the country in 1959, and Libya is now one of the world's leading exporters of oil. Natural gas has also been found recently near Libya's western border. The money from oil and gas has enabled the government to build

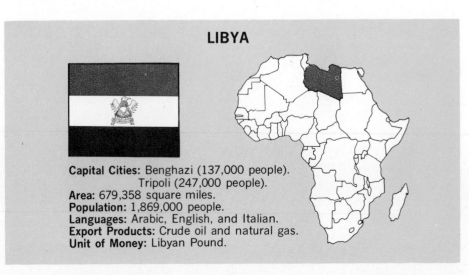

LIBYA

Capital Cities: Benghazi (137,000 people).
                 Tripoli (247,000 people).
Area: 679,358 square miles.
Population: 1,869,000 people.
Languages: Arabic, English, and Italian.
Export Products: Crude oil and natural gas.
Unit of Money: Libyan Pound.

more schools, provide free health care, and improve the lives of the people in many ways.

Phoenician traders settled the northern coast of the Libyan region about 700 B.C. Rome later ruled the region for several centuries. Arabs ruled it from the 600s to the 1500s, when Libya became part of the Turkish Ottoman Empire. Libya was a colony of Italy between 1912 and the end of World War II. The United Kingdom of Libya was proclaimed in 1952. Young Libyan army officers forced out King Idris in 1969 and formed the Libyan Arab Republic.

ALSO READ: BARBARY COAST, ISLAM.

LICE see LOUSE.

▲*The most common type of lichen grows on rocks in cold climates all over the world. It is often called reindeer moss.*

LICHEN A lichen is a plant that is made up of two kinds of other plants—an alga and a fungus—living together in a partnership. The alga makes food, some of which the fungus uses. The fungus absorbs moisture from the air, providing water the alga needs for making food.

Lichens can be found all over the world, growing on bare rocks, tree trunks, and fence posts. Lichens may be gray, blue, green, orange, yellow, or brown. There are at least 15,000 kinds of lichens. They are among the oldest plants, having first lived at least 550 million years ago.

Lichens have no roots, stems, leaves, or flowers. They consist of stalk-like parts called *thalli*. These may be shaped like leaves, shells, cups, sponges, and so on.

Lichens in general multiply by means of *fragments* that break off the plant and are carried away by wind or flowing water. When a fragment comes to rest, it may grow into a new lichen plant.

Some lichens are useful to man. The reindeer's food is *reindeer moss,* a· kind of lichen. Eskimos and other people living in the far North depend on reindeer for food and clothing. People make bread out of ground *Iceland moss,* another kind of lichen. The dye *litmus* comes from a lichen plant.

ALSO READ: PLANT, PLANT KINGDOM.

LIECHTENSTEIN Liechtenstein is the fourth smallest country in the world. Like a land in a fairy tale, it is ruled by a prince who lives in a beautiful old castle. The castle overlooks the small capital city of Vaduz. The Rhine River forms the country's western border with Switzerland. Austria lies to the east. The snowcapped peaks of the Alps rise in the east and south. (See the map with the article on EUROPE.)

Liechtensteiners are of Germanic origin. Most of them are farmers, but many are now working in factories. Farmers grow grapes, corn, wheat, and potatoes. Many also raise dairy cattle that graze in summer on pastures high in the mountains, just below the snow line. They come down to the valleys in the fall. Factory workers produce textiles, ceramics, drugs, canned food, precision instruments, and optical lenses.

Liechtenstein is a prosperous country. Many international companies make their headquarters there because the taxes are low. An important source of income for Liechtenstein comes from the sale of its

▼*A cliffside mansion nestled in the beautiful countryside surrounding Vaduz, Liechtenstein's capital.*

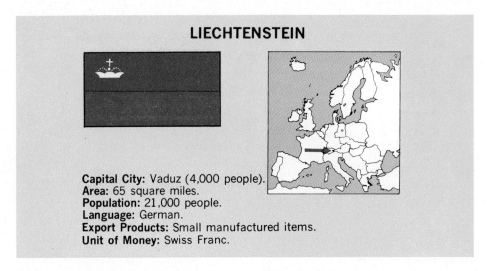

LIECHTENSTEIN

Capital City: Vaduz (4,000 people).
Area: 65 square miles.
Population: 21,000 people.
Language: German.
Export Products: Small manufactured items.
Unit of Money: Swiss Franc.

postage stamps, which are prized by stamp collectors. Tourism also brings money to Liechtenstein. Visitors love the beautiful scenery. The tiny country does not have an army. During the two world wars, while armies fought in the rest of Europe, Liechtenstein and Switzerland were at peace. The two countries are good friends. Switzerland runs the postal, telegraph, and telephone systems for Liechtenstein. Swiss diplomats also represent Liechtenstein in foreign countries. The two countries use the same money, the Swiss Franc.

Liechtenstein became a principality (a territory ruled by a prince) in 1719. Prince Franz Josef II has been the ruler since 1938. The prince appoints a prime minister and approves the laws made by the governing body, called the Diet. Members of the Diet are elected by men. Women in this country cannot vote.
ALSO READ: ALPS MOUNTAINS, RHINE RIVER, SWITZERLAND.

LIE DETECTOR Have you ever told a lie? If you have, you probably felt a little nervous or guilty about it—most people do. When a person feels nervous, certain changes take place in his breathing, pulse rate, blood pressure, perspiration, and other functions. These changes can be measured by a machine called the lie detector, or *polygraph*. Police sometimes use a lie detector when

they question a suspect, to help determine whether or not he is telling the truth. Some private businesses and government agencies, such as the FBI, also use lie detectors when they interview people applying for jobs. The lie detector helps them to decide if a person is able to handle a job that calls for great honesty.

To take a lie detector test, a person sits in a chair in front of a table on which the lie detector machine rests. The examiner—a person specially trained to ask questions and judge the results—places a thin tube around the person's chest, to measure his breathing. An arm cuff, for measuring blood pressure, goes around the arm. Another instrument, attached to the hand, measures the flow of perspiration on the palm. The chest tube, arm cuff, and palm instrument contain wires that are connected to the polygraph machine.

The examiner asks a series of questions, all of which can be answered by "yes" or "no." As the person answers, the machine makes little wavy or zigzag lines on a paper. These lines record the pulse rate and other bodily activity. The examiner usually starts with questions that the person is likely to answer truthfully, such as "Is your name John Doe? Do you live in the United States?" Then he asks questions about the crime, such as "Did you steal the jewels?" If the person lies, the lines made by the lie detector may suddenly change, showing that the person has had a nervous or emotional reaction to the question. The examiner then carefully studies the person's reactions to *all* the questions and decides which questions showed a possible false answer.

If used correctly, polygraphs can be very helpful. But they are not always reliable. The changes in a person's body reactions may not necessarily come from lying. Also, even if the person's reactions are normal, it is not definite proof that he is telling the truth. For these reasons, most courts have not allowed polygraph tests to be used as evidence in court.

ALSO READ: CRIME.

LIFE   It is not easy to explain exactly what life is. It seems easy to tell whether something is alive or not. A dog and a tree are alive, and a rock is not. But we must know what else, besides appearance, sets apart the living dog from the non-living rock.

All living things are made up of matter called *protoplasm*. Protoplasm can take in food materials and change them into more protoplasm. Protoplasm can move, grow, and rid itself of waste materials. It responds —by moving or acting in some way— to light, heat, touch, electricity, and other influences. Protoplasm can reproduce itself. It can form more protoplasm like itself.

In all living things, protoplasm is in the form of cells. A living thing grows by increasing its number of cells. Non-living things are not made up of protoplasm. They can move only when some outside force moves them. A rock moves when something pushes it. Some non-living things, such as icicles, seem to grow, but not by adding cells.

Where Did Life Come From?

All religions teach that life was created by a divine being or force.

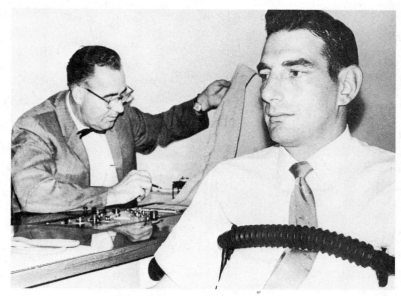

▲*A polygraph expert inspects results of a lie detector test he has just given to a candidate for political office. The candidate wanted to prove his honesty to the voters.*

The Old Testament of the Bible teaches that God created the world in six days. He created Adam and Eve, the first man and woman, and all the plants and animals.

One scientific theory says that life came to Earth from outer space in the form of spores. These seed-like living things survived the cold and dryness of space, and then began to grow when they arrived in the warmth and moisture found on Earth.

Another modern theory about the beginning of life on Earth says that life began when certain chemical compounds combined simply by chance. In the early years of the Earth's existence, the atmosphere contained large amounts of various gases that are now rare or have disappeared. The energy supplied by lightning and sunlight caused some of these gases to form large molecules that dissolved in the ocean. After many billions of years, these molecules combined, forming *proteins*, the substances found in all living matter. In about a billion years, the proteins formed protoplasm.

ALSO READ: BIOCHEMISTRY, CELL.

LIFESAVING   Next time you go to swim at a pool or public beach, look around to see who is guarding your life. That, in plain words, is what a lifeguard does. Swimming is

▲*Life jackets are important lifesaving aids. They should always be put on before boarding a boat.*

the favorite sport of millions. But there is always danger, because a drowning can happen very quickly. A swimmer hardly need worry at a pool or beach where good water safety procedures and lifesaving skills are carried out by trained lifeguards.

The American Red Cross may have trained your favorite lifeguard. Red Cross chapters sponsor lifesaving and water safety courses for thousands of people every year. You can take a Junior Lifesaving course at the age of 11 if you swim well. Senior Lifesaving courses are open to young people at age 15. Outstanding swimmers can train to become Water Safety Instructors at 18. Many lifeguards have completed this course. The Young Men's Christian Association (YMCA) also has lifesaving courses for people at various age levels.

But every person who swims or goes boating or water skiing should know a few simple lifesaving rules. If you ever see a person struggling in deep water, your first thought would be to jump in and go to him. That is actually the last thing to do—and then only if you are a very good swimmer. He may panic, try to climb up on you to get his head above water, and pull you both under. If he is close to shore, or near the edge of a pool, hold out your hand or a shirt, a long stick or pole.

If he is farther out, throw a life preserver out to him, or push a raft, plank, or any other floating object to him. Call the lifeguard or an adult right away. If you have a boat, you may be able to row out to him if he is very far out.

If you are swimming in shallow water and see someone unconscious underwater, put your hand under his chin and lift his head out of the water. Then call for help. Remember that drowning happens very quickly, so it is important to do this as fast as possible. This simple assist is taught in beginning swimming classes by the American Red Cross. Several children have saved the lives of fellow swimmers by knowing it.

A swimmer who becomes unconscious and stops breathing must be helped to start breathing again by artificial respiration. Mouth-to-mouth breathing by a trained person is often used. Most pools and supervised beaches have mechanical resuscitators.

Rules for Swimming Safety

Good swimmers say, "No one swims alone." Even in a pool or at a beach with a lifeguard, it is a good idea to go swimming with a friend. A buddy and you can keep a minute-to-minute check on each other at a crowded waterfront. If you do not swim, stay in shallow water. If you are a beginning swimmer, a good

▶*The cross-chest carry for a drowning person is demonstrated here by two members of the Junior Red Cross. Good swimmers should take courses in lifesaving.*

idea is to walk out, then swim back. That way you won't find yourself in deep water without knowing it.

Don't float out into deep water on a rubber raft or inner tube. Sometimes the air leaks out. Don't swim in dirty water, or in any place where you don't know how deep the water is. Don't swim at night in unlighted water. If you suddenly needed help, no one could see you. Be careful when swimming in rough water. You can be knocked around in the breaking waves.

Wait a half hour after eating before going into the water. This will help prevent muscle tightness, or cramps. If you get a cramp, try to stretch, or change the way you are swimming. If the cramp does not go away, float until someone can help you.

Don't swim in areas where people are surfing or riding in motorboats. If you are going out in a boat, make sure there is a life preserver for each person. If your boat turns over in deep water, or starts to fill with water, hang on to it. It will float. Last of all, learn to swim as well as you can just as young as you can. Being a good swimmer is the best kind of water safety.

ALSO READ: ARTIFICIAL RESPIRATION, BOATS AND BOATING, FIRST AID, SAFETY, SWIMMING.

LIGHT You know that when the sun shines during the day, everything is visible as far as the eye can see. You also know that after the sun has set, the night is dark. This happens because the sun is the original source of light. A burning match, a bonfire, or a lighted electric bulb are sources of light. But there would be no matches, fires, or electricity if the sun had not been shining on our planet Earth for billions of years. All the fuels used to provide light— wood, coal, and oil, for instance— were made by the heat and light of the sun. Without the sun, there would be no light on Earth. With-

◀Lifeguards keep a constant watch over swimmers in public bathing areas. They sit on very high chairs so that they can easily see and go to anyone who gets in trouble.

out the sun, there would be no life on Earth.

The sun is a star, about 93 million miles away from the Earth. Light from the sun travels this great distance faster than anything else. It moves at the tremendous speed of 186,000 miles a second. Can you imagine being able to travel at this speed? You would be able to go around the Earth more than seven times in one second!

Movement of Light

Light travels in the form of waves in much the same way that waves travel in water. Light waves are a tiny fraction of an inch in length. Light travels through air in a straight line. You can see this by looking at the straight beam of a flashlight. But you could not see the beam if it were not for the fact that light can be *reflected*. Light rays are reflected when they "bounce off" an object. You see the beam from the

▼The light from the setting sun silhouettes the buildings of a city against the sky. The colors are reflected in the water.

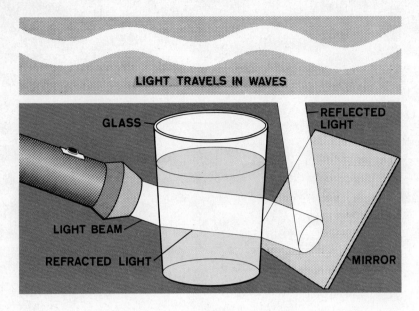

LIGHT TRAVELS IN WAVES

GLASS

REFLECTED LIGHT

LIGHT BEAM

REFRACTED LIGHT

MIRROR

flashlight because the light is reflected by particles of dust or moisture in the air. Astronauts in a space ship, traveling far above the atmosphere of the Earth, are in total darkness because there are no dust particles or droplets of moisture to reflect the rays of the sun. You see trees, houses, roads, people, and other objects because they reflect light. You see yourself in a mirror because light rays are reflected from you to the mirror and your image is reflected back from the mirror.

When light rays hit some objects, they are not only reflected, they may also pass through them. Anything that allows light to pass through it is *transparent*. Clear glass, water, and air are transparent. Anything that breaks up the light as it passes through is *translucent*. You cannot see clearly through a translucent object, such as a pane of frosted glass. Anything that does not allow light to pass through it is *opaque*. A stone wall is opaque.

When light passes through substances, including air, its speed is slowed down. When light passes from one substance to a different one, it is *refracted*. This means the light rays are bent. You can see this by looking at a glass of water that has a straw in it. The straw seems to bend at the surface of the water. The fact that light can be refracted

has led to the invention of lenses that can control the bending of light rays to suit man's purposes. The lens of a telescope can make distant objects appear near. The lens on a microscope can make tiny objects, invisible to the naked eye, appear large enough to be studied. The lens on a camera is used to *focus* images (make them appear clear and sharp) on the film in the camera. If you do not see things sharply and clearly, you need glasses to correct your vision. The lenses that are correct for you are made to bend the light rays that enter your eyes just enough to correct any errors in your eye.

Sunlight appears to be white, but when it is refracted through a wedge-shaped piece of glass called a *prism*, a rainbow-like band streams through the glass. This band of light is called a *spectrum*. It shows that light is made up of many different colors. Each color has a different wave length. Violet, at one end of the spectrum, has the shortest rays—which also bend the most. Red, at the other end of the spectrum, has the longest rays—which bend the least. Between violet and red are indigo, blue, green, yellow, and orange. The rays of each color differ both in length and amount of bend. A rainbow may appear in the sky after a rainstorm because there are still tiny drops of water in the air. These drops of water act as prisms to bend the sunlight into the colors of the spectrum. When you direct a fine spray from a garden hose in the sunlit air, you may see a rainbow in the spray.

Sources of Light
Many things that burn are a source of light. The color of the rays given off by a fire depends on the temperature and on what is being burned. A gas flame on a kitchen range has a bluish color, because the rays given off come from a very hot flame. The flame of a candle looks yellow, because the temperature is

▲*The red glass on the back of the bicycle will reflect light at night. Shiny red reflective tape helps make the bicycle visible to drivers.*

much lower than for the gas. Many of the things you see are not sources of light. They are *non-luminous*— they only reflect light. But some things that reflect light seem to be luminous. The moon is a good example of this. It only seems to shine because it reflects light from the sun. Some road signs contain many beads that seem luminous when the headlights of an automobile shine on them. But these beaded signs only reflect the light from the headlights, which are the real source of the light.

Light is measured by *candlepower*. The light given off one foot away from the flame of a candle is called "one candlepower." The light from the sun, shining on the Earth on a cloudless day, is measured at 10,000 candlepower. If you are reading this page near a window on a clear day, you are getting about 1,000 candlepower of light on the page. The bulb in a reading lamp will give you about 50 candlepower. Photographers use light meters to measure the amount of light that is reflected from the object they want to photograph. By knowing the amount of light available, the photographer can widen or narrow the shutter opening on his camera to allow more or less light to enter the

camera. He can also control the amount of time the shutter should remain open to allow the light rays that enter the camera to create a good sharp image on the film.

You may try a simple experiment to prove that light rays can be refracted. Put a quarter in an empty, deep bowl. Put the bowl on a table in front of you. Move the bowl away from you until you can no longer see the quarter over the rim of the bowl. Now, without moving your head, slowly pour water into the bowl. Suddenly, you will be able to see the quarter again. The water in the bowl has reached a point where it bends the light rays reflected from the quarter so that they are directed to your eyes.

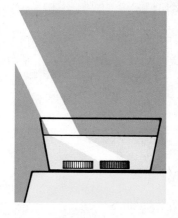

For further information on:

Characteristics of Light, *see* ATMOSPHERE, AURORA, COLOR, DAY AND NIGHT, ECLIPSE, RAINBOW, SPECTRUM, WAVE.

Scientific Studies of Light, *see* COPERNICUS, NICOLAUS; EDISON, THOMAS ALVA; EINSTEIN, ALBERT; EYE; RELATIVITY; SIGHT.

Sources of Light, *see* ASTRONOMY, CANDLE, ELECTRICITY, ELECTRIC POWER, FIRE, MOON, STAR, SUN.

Uses of Light, *see* CAMERA, GLASSES, KALEIDOSCOPE, LENS, LIGHTHOUSE, LIGHTING, MASERS AND LASERS, MATCH, MICROFILM, MICROSCOPE, MIRROR, PHOTOELECTRICITY, PHOTOSYNTHESIS, TELESCOPE, X-RAY.

▼*Beams of light from the sun shine through a darkened forest, casting a beautiful pattern of shadows. The sun's light shows as beams when it strikes dust in the air.*

▶Lighthouses are located at dangerous points along rocky coasts (right).

▶A Coast Guardsman inserts a new light bulb inside a lighthouse beacon. The mirror behind the bulb reflects and intensifies the light from the bulb. The light from the beacon can be seen 15 miles away (far right).

LIGHTHOUSE Before the days of radio and radar, ships sometimes were wrecked at night on rocky coasts. Sailors feared getting too close to land at night, because helmsmen, steering the ship, could not see dangerous rocks or sandbars. A way of warning ships was needed, so the lighthouse came into being.

The first known lighthouses were built in Egypt about 300 B.C. The great lighthouse of Pharos guided ships that were sailing near Alexandria at night. Priests kept bright fires burning at the top of the lighthouse. Sailors saw the fires and knew where the land was.

The most common lighthouse in modern times is a round building built of rock or brick. At the top of the lighthouse is a powerful lamp. Even in bad weather, the light can be seen for several miles. The light spins in a circle, slowly moving its bright beam out across the sky. Most lighthouses have shields that keep the light from shining on land. But each time the light comes around to the water side, sailors can see it.

Until the middle of the 1800s, light was provided by candles or coal oil lamps. The first lighthouse to use an electric light was South Foreland Light, England, in 1858. About the same time, lighthouses began using a lens system to make the light beam stronger.

Some lighthouses remain in operation today, even though radio and radar signals now guide ships through the night without danger of hitting land. A few lights are kept burning by nuclear power. But one day lighthouses may be only relics of the past.

ALSO READ: SHIPS AND SHIPPING.

LIGHTING With only a touch of your finger on the light switch, you can have light in a dark room at night. But not many years ago, homes did not have electric light.

Once people could work and play only in daylight, and went to bed when the sun went down. Then they learned to burn bundles of rushes to light their living places. *Archeologists*, who study ancient history, have found lamps from around 1000 B.C. The lamps were made with woven *wicks*, or strings, which absorbed oil, and drew it toward the lighted end of the wick. Roman lamps burned olive oil. The Dutch "Betty" lamp, made of iron, was brought to America by the Pilgrims. It burned whale oil.

Candles, which are wicks dipped into tallow or beeswax many times, were used through the 1700s for lighting. People still use candles today for special lighting.

In 1784, a Swiss, Aimé Argand, invented a lamp with a space for oil and a circular wick which gave more light than a string wick. Later he added a glass chimney for a brighter glow.

Americans used gas light in the early 1800s. At first just the bluish flame provided the light. Then a mantle, a small net cup which glowed in the flame, was added to give more light. Kerosene was a popular fuel for lamps after 1860. It was cheaper than whale oil.

Electric Light

Thomas A. Edison, an American inventor, wanted to make a safe electric lamp to replace gas lamps. Other men had operated electric lamps for short times before the materials burned up. Edison found that *carbon* was the material to use in a light. It could be heated to give off light, but would not burn to an ash. Edison ran an electric lamp for 40 hours in 1879 and proved that electric lighting was possible.

Edison's first bulb used a filament made of sewing thread covered with carbon. He tried to use paper, hair, wood, cardboard, and grasses in making the carbon thread. One day he tried a splinter from a bamboo fan he was holding. The bulb burned for 400 hours.

Bulbs by themselves would have been of little use, but Edison invented electric generators to send

current around the cities. In 1882 the generators he designed were in use in New York at the first city power station. Ten city blocks could be lighted. The public saw electric lighting at the Chicago World's Fair of 1893. By 1900 many homes had made the change from gas lighting to electricity.

Edison kept improving and changing electric lighting. Tungsten filaments replaced carbon in 1907. Then gases were sealed into the bulbs to brighten the light. In 1926 the bulbs were frosted inside to lessen the glare. Indirect lighting was introduced in 1934, and then three-strength bulbs.

▲*Spotlights in the ceiling of this room help to illuminate the pictures on the wall.*

◀*An indirect lighting fixture in the ceiling makes every part of this kitchen bright (far left).*

◀*A lovely crystal chandelier furnishes the main lighting for this dining room (left). The spotlights on the wall shine on the side tables.*

►*A beautiful living room gets its light from a chandelier with shaded bulbs and from properly placed table lamps. The mirrored fireplace wall reflects the light and makes it more effective.*

Fluorescent and Neon

Fluorescent lights have no filaments. The glass tubes are coated on the inside with shiny substances called *phosphors*. Then the tube is sealed and filled with mercury vapor. Electricity passes through the vapor and makes the phosphors glow with strong, steady light. This form of lighting became popular after 1938, in stores, offices and schools. It gives more light for less electricity and looks almost like daylight.

Sir William Ramsey discovered a new gas in 1898. He called it neon. Tubes filled with neon glow very brightly when a current of electricity goes through them. They make the brilliant red lights used in advertising signs. Other gases make the blue and green ones. Lamps filled with sodium make a bright orange light and are used on busy highways and at dangerous intersections.

Look around the room when you and your family are reading or writing. See if each person has enough light. If you are right-handed, you should have light coming over your left shoulder. If you are left-handed, you need light over your right shoulder. Be sure the bulb is strong enough to give a good light.

ALSO READ: CANDLE; EDISON, THOMAS ALVA; ELECTRIC APPLIANCE; INTERIOR DECORATION; LIGHT.

LIGHTNING AND THUNDER

A flash of bright light spears its way across the sky. Then a crackling, rumbling sound occurs. The flash is lightning, a giant spark. The sound is thunder, caused by the lightning. The large electric spark which is lightning is electricity moving very rapidly between a cloud and the Earth, between two clouds, or between two parts of the same cloud. Clouds in which lightning forms are called *thunderclouds*. Vast numbers of positive charges collect at the bottom of the cloud. Negative charges collect at the top of the cloud. Negative and positive electric charges *attract* (pull toward) each other. Therefore, the positive charges in the cloud and the negative charges in another cloud, in the top of the same cloud, or on Earth, attract each other.

When a very large number of positive charges collect at the bottom of the cloud, they become strong enough to force their way through the air. They jump to a negative charge, making a huge spark, called a lightning bolt.

Lightning has several forms. *Forked*, or *chain*, lightning is the crooked lightning you see zigzagging across the sky in any thunderstorm. *Ball* lightning looks like balloons of fire that drop from the sky and explode when they hit the ground. Ball lightning sometimes rolls along the ground until it crashes into a tree or wall. *Sheet* lightning lights up the whole sky. It has no special shape. Sheet lightning is actually the light from a chain lightning flash that occurs very far away.

A flash of lightning heats the air around it. The heated air *expands* (spreads out), forming an air wave or sound wave. The lightning bolt is a zigzag. Each part of the zigzag bolt causes an air wave in a slightly different direction. The air waves pass you one after another, so you hear thunder as a series of rumbles. If you are caught outdoors in a thunderstorm, stay away from trees because they attract lightning. Do not use an umbrella, because the metal part of the umbrella also attracts lightning. It is certainly better to be wet than dead.

ALSO READ: CLOUD, ELECTRICITY, SOUND.

LILIUOKALANI, LYDIA KAME-KEHA (1838-1917) The song "Aloha Oe" ("Farewell to Thee") was written by Liliuokalani, the last ruler of the kingdom of Hawaii. She was born in Honolulu and attended the Royal School. Liliuokalani married an American, John Dominis. Her brother, King David Kalakaua, died in 1891. Liliuokalani became queen. She tried to defend her power against American plantation owners in Hawaii who wanted to control the islands. But in January, 1893, the leaders of this group rebelled and took over the government. United States Marines landed to prevent any fighting, and the rebels made Liliuokalani give up her throne. The following year, Hawaii became a republic.

Liliuokalani asked United States President Grover Cleveland to help her regain her throne. But the plantation owners who governed Hawaii decided that the islands should become a part of the United States. They knew this would give them a good market for their crops. The United States annexed (took control of) Hawaii in 1898. Liliuokalani lived the rest of her life in Honolulu. ALSO READ: HAWAII.

LIMERICK A limerick is a short poem, usually humorous. It always has five lines. The first two lines rhyme. The third and fourth lines are usually shorter than the others and rhyme with each other. And the fifth line rhymes with the first two. Each limerick tells a little story. Here is a limerick about a tiger:

There was a young man from the city,
Who met what he thought was a kitty.
He gave it a pat,
And said, "Nice little cat."
They buried his clothes, out of pity.

No one knows for sure where the limerick began or how it got its name. Some sources say that even in ancient Greece, people made up limerick-like verses. Limericks are found in Shakespeare's plays and in the operettas of Gilbert and Sullivan. Many people throughout the centuries wrote limericks. Oliver Wendell Holmes, Lewis Carroll (author of *Alice in Wonderland*), Mark Twain, Ogden Nash, U.S. President Woodrow Wilson, and Robert Louis Stevenson are a few of them. Here is a limerick by Lewis Carroll (a hod is a tray):

There was a young man of Oporta
Who daily got shorter and shorter.
The reason, he said,
Was the hod on his head,
Which was filled with the heaviest mortar.

This is one by President Woodrow Wilson:

As a beauty I'm not a great star,
There are others more handsome by far,
But my face, I don't mind it,

▲ *Forked lightning creates a dazzling pattern in a dark, stormy sky.*

▼ *Queen Liliuokalani of Hawaii.*

Because I'm behind it,
'Tis the folks in the front that I jar.

The name "limerick" probably came from Ireland, where a county and seaport are both named Limerick. One story says that a band of soldiers, the Irish Brigade, used to sing limericks at their gatherings. Each verse would end with a chorus which went, in part, "Won't you . . . Come all the way up to Limerick?" The soldiers may have brought the limerick from France. But limericks have become more popular in England than in any other country.

Edward Lear, a British poet who wrote and illustrated nonsense rhymes, made the limerick so popular that his name is almost always associated with it. This is one of Edward Lear's limericks:

There was a young lady of Greenwich,
Whose garments were bordered with spinach,
But a large spotty calf
Bit her shawl quite in half,
Which alarmed that young lady of Greenwich.

Around the beginning of the 1900s, many newspapers in England ran contests for the best examples of limericks. Try making up a funny limerick yourself!

ALSO READ: LEAR, EDWARD; POETRY.

LIMPET see SNAILS AND SLUGS.

LINCOLN, ABRAHAM (1809-1865) Few men have had greater influence on American history than Abraham Lincoln. He served as President during the Civil War, and took the firm steps necessary to prevent the North and South from becoming two separate nations. His kindness, wit, and ability to express great truths in words that everyone could understand have made "Honest Abe" one of the United States' most beloved leaders.

Early Life
Lincoln was the sixteenth President, and the first one who did not start life in one of the 13 original states. He was born in a log cabin near what is now Hodgenville, Kentucky. He moved with his parents and an older sister, Sarah, to the backwoods of Indiana when he was seven. His mother, Nancy, died two years later. His father, Tom, was a carpenter and farmer, and was very poor. Conditions improved for the Lincoln children after Tom married his second wife, Sarah Bush Johnson, who took a special interest in young Abe. She encouraged him to educate himself, even though he had less than a year's schooling. She could neither read nor write, but she owned several books which Abe began to study. Abe helped support the family by splitting logs for fence rails and working at other odd jobs

---

SIXTEENTH PRESIDENT   MARCH 4, 1861—APRIL 15, 1865

ABRAHAM LINCOLN

Born: February 12, 1809, near Hodgenville, Kentucky
Parents: Thomas (Tom) and Nancy Hanks Lincoln
Education: Self-educated
Religion: No special denomination. Attended Presbyterian Church during his Presidency.
Occupation: Lawyer
Political Party: Republican
State Represented: Illinois
Married: 1842 to Mary Todd Lincoln (1818–1882)
Children: 4 sons (2 died in childhood, another at age 18)
Died: April 15, 1865, Washington, D.C.
Buried: Oak Ridge Cemetery, Springfield, Illinois

during the 14 years that the Lincolns lived in Indiana. The family left Indiana for Illinois when Abe was 21, and he helped his father set up a new farm there.

Lincoln then set out on his own. He lived for six years (1831–1837) in the village of New Salem. He clerked in a store for a while, was appointed postmaster, served in the Black Hawk War (1832), and studied law in his spare time. An old legend, revived in books and poems, tells that Abe fell in love with a New Salem girl named Ann Rutledge during this time. She and Lincoln were good friends, and he was filled with sorrow when she died in 1835, but the story of their romance is probably a myth.

The awkward, rather homely young Lincoln, who was well over six feet tall, was a skillful wrestler and liked to tell funny stories. He made friends easily, and was elected to the Illinois legislature in 1834. Three years later, he received his license to practice law, and moved to Springfield, where he became a successful lawyer and one of the town's leading citizens. He married an ambitious young woman, Mary Todd, who boasted to her friends that she intended to help her husband become President of the United States.

Political Career

Lincoln was elected to the United States Congress in 1847. His two years in Washington were a disappointment, however. Because he had spoken out against the government's policy in going to war against Mexico, he was not popular in his home district. He did not run for a second term in Congress, but returned to his law practice in Springfield. He seemed to lose interest in politics until Congress passed the Kansas-Nebraska Act in 1854.

This new law made it possible for people to own slaves in the new western territory being opened to

◀Abraham Lincoln was a deeply religious man. Here, he is reading the Bible to his son Thomas (nicknamed "Tad").

settlers. Slavery was then legal in the southern states, but Lincoln felt that territory which was still free must be kept that way. In 1856, he joined the new Republican Party, which had been formed to fight the spread of slavery. The Republicans in Illinois nominated him for the U.S. Senate in 1858. That summer he and Stephen A. Douglas, the nominee of the Democratic Party, held debates in seven different Illinois towns.

Douglas defended the Kansas-Nebraska Act. Lincoln opposed it. In one debate he summed up what he thought slavery meant. One race of men, he said, had no right to make slaves of another race and "live by the fruits of their labor."

"Honest Abe" won his nickname in New Salem. He and a man named William Berry bought a store there. When Berry died and the business failed, Lincoln worked for several years to pay back the store's debts of 1,100 dollars.

▼President Lincoln entering Richmond, the Confederate capital, a few days before Lee surrendered to Grant.

▲ *President Lincoln meeting with General Sherman, General Grant, and Admiral Porter in March, 1865, to discuss the peace terms to be offered to the South.*

▼*A shocked nation read of the death of the President in newspapers throughout the land.*

Lincoln lost the election for the Senate, but his speeches during the Lincoln-Douglas debates helped make him nationally known. He was nicknamed the "Railsplitter," because of his days spent splitting logs for fence rails. The Republican Party nominated him for President in 1860, and he won the election easily. Many Southerners were afraid to live under a President who was so firmly against slavery. Several southern states had seceded by the time Lincoln was inaugurated. They left the Union and formed a new nation, which they called the Confederate States of America.

The President thought that no state had the legal right to break up the Union. He believed that people in a democracy must be willing to obey the laws and live under the officials that most of the voters want. His main purpose in fighting the Civil War that followed (1861–65) was to keep all of the states together as one country.

Lincoln issued the Emancipation Proclamation on January 1, 1863, while war was still raging. This document stated that the slaves in states or parts of states then in rebellion against the U.S. government should be "thenceforward and forever free." He defined democracy later that year in his famous Gettysburg Address. He said it should be

"government of the people, by the people, for the people." The war was being fought, he said, to test whether a nation founded on democratic principles "can long endure."

Victory was in sight by the time Lincoln began his second term as President in March, 1865. In his Second Inaugural Address, he said that America's next task was "to bind up the nation's wounds . . . and to do all which may achieve a just and lasting peace. . . ." He wanted to make it easy for the states that had seceded to take their places again in the Union, but he did not live to carry out his plans. He attended a play at Ford's Theatre in Washington, D.C., on the evening of April 14, 1865. There, he was shot by John Wilkes Booth, an actor half mad with disappointment because the South had lost.

Abraham Lincoln died the following morning. "Now he belongs to the ages," said Secretary of War Edwin M. Stanton. A special train took Abe Lincoln's body back to Illinois for burial. Mourners lined the tracks in the states along the way to honor the martyred President. Lin-

▼*A majestic statue of President Lincoln can be seen inside the Lincoln Memorial in Washington, D.C.*

coln's memory is still revered today. Every year thousands of people climb the marble steps of the Lincoln Memorial in Washington, D.C. They look up at the gigantic statue of the seated Lincoln, his face lined and sad. They read the words inscribed on one of the marble walls:

In this temple
as in the hearts of the people
for whom he saved the Union
the memory of Abraham Lincoln
is enshrined forever.

ALSO READ: CIVIL WAR; CONFEDERATE STATES OF AMERICA; DOUGLAS, STEPHEN A.; EMANCIPATION PROCLAMATION; GETTYSBURG ADDRESS; ILLINOIS; PRESIDENCY.

LINDBERGH, CHARLES A. (born 1902) Years ago, a small, single-engine airplane named *Spirit of St. Louis* took off from Roosevelt Field on Long Island, New York, and headed out over the Atlantic Ocean. Just 33 hours and 39 minutes later, the little plane landed at Le Bourget Airport near Paris, France. It had flown 3,600 miles. The date was May 21, 1927. The news spread rapidly around the world. Charles Lindbergh had become the first person to fly alone across the Atlantic without stopping. Fliers had crossed the Atlantic before—but never alone.

Lindbergh decided to make the flight when a wealthy New Yorker offered a 25,000 dollar prize to the first person to make a solo, nonstop flight from New York to Paris. A group of businessmen from St. Louis, Missouri, gave Lindbergh money to build a plane. Lindbergh flew the *Spirit of St. Louis* on a practice run from San Diego, California, to New York City on May 10, 1927. This trip took 21 hours and 45 minutes. It set a new record for *transcontinental flight* (flight across the continent).

Charles Lindbergh was born in Detroit, Michigan, on February 4, 1902. He grew up in the small town

▲*Charles A. Lindbergh standing beside the airplane in which he made the first solo nonstop flight across the Atlantic Ocean.*

of Little Falls, Minnesota. He liked working on engines. At the age of nine, he could take an engine apart, fix it, and put it back together. Lindbergh worked as an airplane mechanic and stunt man at air shows and earned enough money to buy his own airplane at age 19. In school he did especially well in mechanics. When he became an Army flying cadet, he was first in his class.

Lindbergh was only 25 years old when he made his historic nonstop flight from New York to Paris. Overnight, he became a world hero, and was awarded the Congressional Medal of Honor. Later the same year he made a good-will flight from Washington, D.C., to Mexico City, Mexico. The next year he flew to Central America, carrying the first air mail. He and his wife, the author Anne Morrow Lindbergh, flew to the Orient in 1931. Their eldest son was kidnaped and killed the next year, a great sorrow to the hero and his family.

In World War II Lindbergh went to the Pacific as a civilian adviser, and flew several military combat missions. After the war, Lindbergh worked as an aviation adviser for several airline companies.

ALSO READ: AIRLINE, AIRPLANE, AIRPORT, ATLANTIC OCEAN, AVIATION, WORLD WAR II.

▲*Carolus Linnaeus, Swedish botanist.*

LINNAEUS, CAROLUS (1707-1778) This is the Latin form of the name of Karl von Linné. He devised the *binomial* (two name) system of scientific names for plants and animals. In this system, every living thing is given a name in Latin or Greek. Each name has two parts. The first part names the *genus*, or group that an animal or plant belongs to. The second part names the exact *species*, the exact kind of plant or animal within the genus. For example, the wolf's scientific name is *Canis lupus. Canis* means "dog." This tells us that a wolf belongs to the dog group. *Lupus* means "wolf," and tells the species of dog.

Karl von Linné was born in Rashult, Sweden, and attended medical school. While a student, he ran a small botanical garden. He took careful notes describing the plants in this garden. His notes became the basis for his system of names.

In 1732, von Linné was given some money by the Swedish Royal Society of Science. He used it to take a walking trip through Lapland, collecting plants. Afterwards he went to the Netherlands, where he finished his medical studies. When he returned to Sweden, he was made professor of botany and natural science at Uppsala University and became physician to the king. In his lifetime, he wrote 180 books. He wrote them in Latin, using the name Carolus Linnaeus.

ALSO READ: ANIMAL KINGDOM, BIOLOGY, BOTANY, PLANT KINGDOM.

LION The lion has long been known as the "king of the beasts" because of its dignified appearance, its strength, and its size. The lion is the largest member of the cat family, except for tigers. A full-grown male lion is about 3 feet high at the shoulder, about 7 feet long, and may weigh up to 500 pounds. It has a long tail that is tipped with a tuft of dark hair. Many lions may reach a length of more than 10 feet from the tip of the nose to the end of the tail. Female lions, called *lionesses*, are slightly smaller than the males.

The adult male lion has a long, shaggy growth of hair, called a *mane*, around its head, neck, and shoulders. Young males, or *lionets*, begin to grow manes at about three years of age. The color of the mane usually matches the lion's coat, which is all one color, varying from silvery-gray to dark brown.

A lioness produces from two to six cubs in a litter. A cub is about the size of a house cat and has similar streaks and spots. The cubs are very playful, behaving like kittens. They often wrestle with each other. The lion family lives together in a den, which is usually a cave-like hole hollowed out of a thick growth of bushes. The family will stay together, the adults bringing the cubs food and teaching them to hunt, until the cubs are about two years old. Then the cubs go off to find their own mates. They are completely mature at the age of 4 or 5, and will live for 15 to 20 years.

Lions will kill only when they are attacked or hungry. They are equipped to be excellent hunters. They have extremely powerful muscles. They can break another animal's neck with one blow of a paw or tear the throat of a victim with their sharp, hooked claws or their sharp fangs.

Lions are *carnivorous*, or meat eaters. They feed on zebras, antelope, pigs, buffalo, and sometimes young elephants. Lions usually hunt together, at night, in small groups called *prides*. When the prey is seen, the males and females will often work together. The males will roar ferociously, scaring the victim toward the females, who are lying in wait. Sometimes a lion will quietly creep up to its victim until it is close enough to attack. Then it will make a swift, running leap onto the victim's back. Lions will eat as much meat as they can hold at a sitting,

▲Two lionesses and a lion at rest in Kenya, Africa (left). You might like to have this lion cub (above) for a pet, but it is big enough to be dangerous.

leaving the rest of the killed animal for hyenas and vultures. When it is finished eating, a lion washes its face and paws with its tongue. It will not kill again until it is hungry.

Man has always admired the king of the beasts for its strength and courage. Unfortunately, this admiration has led men to hunt lions as a demonstration of their own strength and courage. Once lions roamed over many parts of the Earth, including Europe. But today they are mostly found in central and eastern Africa and western India. Lions live in open, grassy plains, although they have sometimes been called the "king of the jungle." When not hunting, the peaceful lion will lie around in the tall grass. A lion will only attack a human being if it is attacked first or if it is old or wounded and cannot hunt larger or faster animals. Today, most wild lions live on game preserves, protected from hunters.

ALSO READ: CARNIVORE; CAT, WILD.

LIQUID   Everything in the world is a form of matter. Some matter is solid, such as the book you are holding. Some matter is gas, such as the air you are breathing. Some matter is liquid, such as water. All matter is made up of tiny particles called molecules.

In solids, the molecules are packed close together and fixed firmly in place. In liquids, the mole-culcs are also packed close together, but they are not fixed firmly in place. They can move about freely. The molecules in gases are packed very loosely, and they can move about even more freely. The free movement of the molecules makes liquids and gases *fluids*, which means they flow.

Because a solid is not fluid, it keeps its shape. If you put a stone into a pitcher, the stone keeps its shape. If you pour water into the pitcher, the water spreads out and takes the shape of the pitcher. If you spill water on any surface such as a floor it spreads out flat. Gas also takes the shape of the container. The gas in a balloon has the shape of the balloon.

Liquid differs from gases in one important way. The molecules in liquids tend to stay close together. This is called *cohesion*. But the molecules in gases tend to move away from each other. You can understand this fact by half-filling a bottle with water. The water takes on the shape of the bottle but it does not expand to fill the bottle. Any gas put into a container will expand to fill the container.

The molecules in a liquid are attracted to other substances. This is called *adhesion*. You get wet when you are in water because of adhesion. The molecules in the water are attracted to your skin.

The molecules of a liquid attract each other strongly enough to give its surface some strength. This attraction is called *surface tension*. You can show how surface tension works. Place a needle across the tines of a fork. Slowly and gently lower the fork into a glass of water. The needle is made of steel, which is much heavier than water, so the needle should sink. But it floats, because the surface tension of the water holds it up.

A substance is called a liquid when it is a liquid at ordinary temperatures. Liquids become gases if they are heated to higher temperatures. Water heated to 212 degrees becomes steam, a gas. Liquids cooled to lower temperatures become solids. Water cooled below 32 degrees becomes ice, a solid.

ALSO READ: CHEMISTRY, ELEMENT, GAS, MATTER, SOLID.

LISTER, JOSEPH (1827–1912)

Until the middle of the nineteenth century, almost half of the people who had open wounds or underwent surgery died of infection. An English surgeon, Joseph Lister, revolutionized surgical practice by introducing modern *antiseptic surgery*, or surgery without the risk of infection.

Joseph Lister was born at Upton, in Essex County, England. He was educated at University College, London, and at the University of Edinburgh (Scotland). He later became a professor of surgery.

Lister knew of the work of the French biochemist Louis Pasteur, who had shown that infections are caused by the action of live bacteria. The English surgeon experimented with various chemicals to find a way to kill bacteria. He got his first successful results, in 1868, with a solution of carbolic acid.

Lister used this *antiseptic* (germ-killing) solution to clean wounds and *surgical incisions* (cuts made by a surgeon). He also used it to scrub his hands and arms thoroughly before operating. He even had the oper-

▲*Joseph Lister, British surgeon.*

▼*Franz Liszt, Hungarian composer and pianist.*

ating room sprayed with the carbolic acid solution. Surgical instruments were made bacteria-free by being heated at high temperatures.

Lister made other contributions to modern surgery, devising new operations and inventing several surgical instruments. He also introduced the use of *catgut*—strong thread made from sheep's intestines—for sewing surgical incisions.

ALSO READ: ANTIBIOTIC; MEDICINE; PASTEUR, LOUIS; SURGERY.

LISZT, FRANZ (1811–1886)

Hungarian musician Franz Liszt is remembered today as a composer of music for the piano and orchestra. During his lifetime, he was best known as a pianist. His showmanship and dazzling playing ability made him a musical sensation in Europe.

Liszt was born in Raiding, Hungary. His parents recognized his musical talent when he was still a child. They took him to Vienna, Austria, when he was ten, for piano lessons. As a young man, he went on a nine-year concert tour of Europe and became internationally famous. After the tour, he devoted most of his time to teaching, composing, and conducting. He helped the great German composer, Richard Wagner, in his early career. Wagner later became Liszt's son-in-law.

Much of Liszt's music is as brilliant and passionate as his piano playing must have been. In his *Hungarian Rhapsodies* for piano, he used the lilting and fiery music of the Hungarian gypsies. Liszt also wrote several popular symphonic tone poems—works for orchestra which tell a story or paint a picture with music. One of his most famous works of this kind is *Les Preludes*.

When he was 55, Liszt became a Roman Catholic abbé, but he continued his musical work. He died in Bayreuth, Germany.

ALSO READ: MUSIC, PIANO, ORCHESTRAS AND BANDS.

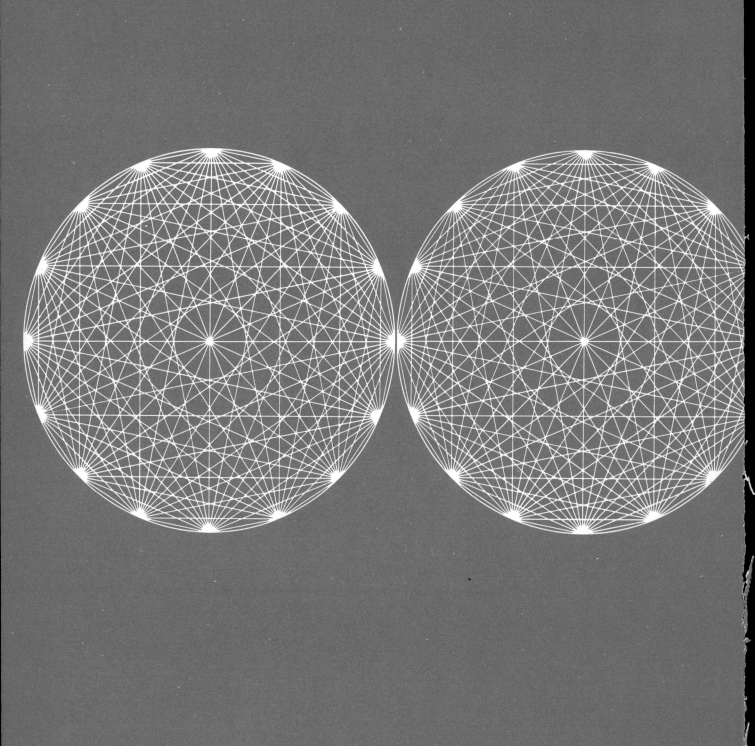